THE HOME BUSINESS BIBLE

THE HOME BUSINESS BIBLE

EVERYTHING YOU NEED TO KNOW TO START AND RUN YOUR SUCCESSFUL HOME-BASED BUSINESS

David R. Eyler

John Wiley & Sons, Inc.
New York • Chichester • Brisbane • Toronto • Singapore

Library of Congress Cataloging-in-Publication Data

Eyler, David R.
    The home business bible : everything you need to know to start and run your successful home-based business / by David R. Eyler.
        p.   cm.
    Includes bibliographical references.
    ISBN 0-471-59578-0 (cloth/disk–acid-free paper). —ISBN 0-471-59577-2 (paper–acid-free paper)
    1. Home-based businesses—Management.   2. New business enterprises.   I. Title.
    HD62.38.E95   1994
    658'.041—dc20   94-4925

Printed in the United States of America

10 9 8 7 6 5 4 3 2 1

To Rosemary and Max,
the farm and the fish.

Preface

A cartoon in a national trade magazine shows a street vendor selling books from behind a makeshift display, balancing a notebook computer on his knee, and offering to do an electronic search for a title he doesn't have in stock. It says a lot about the narrowing gap between heavily capitalized traditional businesses and entrepreneurs with limited resources who are rising to challenge them—on their own terms, *with* the technology and services their customers expect.

Users of this book almost certainly have comfortable roofs over their heads (and their businesses), but they are still Davids in a world of Goliaths. Today's small businesses aren't limited to second-tier operations or constrained to local markets. Low costs, mass-marketed communications, and information processing technology let them enter the business arena as formidable players in any market.

Popularly priced technology is to the modern small business what the Colt .45 revolver was to the American frontier—the great equalizer. Starting and operating a one-person, home-based enterprise today requires knowing the language of that technology and the business culture it serves. For you to succeed as a home-based small business operator, you need to know the meaning of the current terminology. If you have already worked in the business world, you are no stranger to the telephones, computers, faxes, and overnight delivery services that knit commerce together; if you have had no business-world experience, you may find these aids and their capabilities bewildering.

Even the best informed small business persons have fragmented knowledge. They are unable to "know it all" in a fast-paced environment that constantly spawns new approaches, devices, and terminology. Large companies have departments staffed with specialists. As an entrepreneur, you lack that luxury—and can be successful without it. Broad knowledge that reveals the possibilities and helps you to chart a profitable course is more relevant for you than in-depth knowledge in each business specialty. You need the wide spectrum of a modern business vocabulary, but just enough depth to know what is going on—what the terms mean, what the concepts are, where to go for help or to learn more, or how to determine whether a topic is worth pursuing.

The Home Business Bible is designed to meet those needs. It places at your fingertips a convenient, alphabetically arranged explanation of almost any topic you might encounter in the course of establishing and operating a small business. Every item is defined in the commonsense language of the small business person—not in the terms that attorneys, accountants, economists, or business school professors use when they speak to each other. The book's goal is to give you the instant literacy needed to understand and consult with business specialists without having to become one. Every topic is cross-referenced. By scanning the list of **Related topics** each time you explore a specific aspect of your business, you can informally audit other things you might otherwise be neglecting.

The format is friendly, simple, and consistent. If you already know what a topic means and just want to identify a source where you can buy a service or get more information, skip the **What you need to know** and **Why you need to know it** sections and go directly to **Where to learn more**. While you're there, scan the **Related topics** to see whether there is something you've overlooked. If there is, you can immediately turn to that topic. You'll find the same familiar format, complete with all the information you need but sparing you the necessity of reading through material that you already know or don't care about.

Part One orients you to the home-based business world and the people working there. It introduces you to the possibilities and excitement of the small business movement, which mushroomed in the 1980s and shows no sign of letting up in the years ahead. There are also suggestions for selecting the small business specialty that is right for you and making the transition from employee to independent business person.

Part Two tells you how to make the most of the reference core of the book. It explains the arrangement, content, and interactive nature of the 150 key small business topics that are discussed and extensively cross-referenced.

Part Three, "An A-to-Z Reference of Essential Microbusiness Topics," offers the uniformly formatted statements of **What you need to know, Why you need to know it, Where to learn more,** and **Related topics**. Each cross-referenced topic appears elsewhere in the book, in alphabetical order and in the same format.

Appendixes A through D provide the latest in business forms technology (not just samples of forms); addresses and telephone numbers of organizations to contact for various kinds of small business assistance; a list of publishers and suppliers of microbusiness books, goods, and services; and a directory of computer and software company user-assistance telephone numbers.

Appendix E reproduces IRS Publication 587, "Business Use of Your Home," the latest information on how the government expects your home-based business to comply with the tax codes.

The Bibliography supplements the **Where to learn more** sections and might suggest the nucleus for your personal bookshelf of publications in this field.

The Home Business Bible is a necessary tool as you plan and operate your company. Its presentation provides the straightforward answers you need to conceive, plan, refine, implement, and run a successful microbusiness in the 1990s and on into the next century.

DAVID R. EYLER

Arlington, Virginia

Contents

Introduction

When you attend a sports competition for the first time, you can't tell the players without a program. When you begin to assemble and operate a successful small business, you must know what your accountant, attorney, local zoning department, IRS district office, advertising agency, and other "voices" you'll encounter along the way are saying when they speak with you. Information is everything, but you learn quickly that you cannot snag from the daily flood the information you should study in depth or expect to retain. On occasions when you need to know something, you need a primer where you can find easily what you need to know—and *only as much* as you want to know at the time. Growing your business keeps you busy enough without having to wade through folksy, home-based small business-as-cult books in the hope of finding the gem of information you need *now*.

The Home Business Bible is your authority on the language of microbusiness operations. Your morning paper mentions "business incubators," and you find the term intriguing but alien. Your accountant suggests that it might be time to ask your attorney to revise your legal form of "business organization." A TV business reporter quotes an expert on the importance of "ergonomics." You are paying your accountant, attorney, and other service professionals to explain and advise on topics that belong on your list of business priorities. You expect them to implement the nitty-gritty of forming your organization and fitting it into your way of doing business. But you *should not* need them to spell out for you every general microbusiness concept. Your own independent general knowledge of such topics will make you an intelligent consumer of professional services.

The same is true when it comes to making good use of technology. What is a BBS, and how can it improve your business? What are the pluses and minuses of telephone call routing devices versus additional telephone lines? Where can you buy such a device, and what will it cost? How easily can files from an IBM-compatible notebook computer be converted to your Apple Macintosh desktop unit? How could getting bonded or establishing an escrow account make it easier to sell your services to clients who don't know you well enough to entrust you with advance payments? You've heard hundreds of things mentioned in the course of doing business, but, with your present knowledge, you aren't comfortable enough to discuss them or make business decisions that involve them. *The Home Business Bible* will help you answer questions and solve problems like these.

The book begins by imparting a healthy respect for your status as a home-based microbusiness person. Your self-image could be trailing reality and limiting the confidence it takes to forge ahead. Companies run by people just like you—whether from their homes, from time-share offices, or from other nontraditional settings— have become a substantial and increasingly respected force in the economy. Part One, "Working at Home," helps you put yourself in a justifiably favorable context. As you purchase equipment, buy services, and contend with regulatory bodies whose view of the microbusiness person may be far removed from today's realities, it helps to know the scope of the movement of which you are a part. You should be aware of its growing purchasing power and political clout as you function in the microbusiness world.

Part One also gives you an opportunity to examine the working-from-home lifestyle. It discusses the advantages of a low-cost, low-risk home office start-up and tells you, step by step, how to evaluate your situation and select a specialty.

In predicting the fate of your enterprise, practical business knowledge and the efficient use of your time are second only to having adequate financial resources. Even the curse of limited funds is eased by knowing what you're doing and concentrating on the bottom line. You can't afford the time or the expense of seeking out expert assistance every time you need to know something about a suddenly important microbusiness topic. You need to be able to learn just enough to judge its importance to your business. And this book makes that possible.

Part Two, "How to Use *The Home Business Bible*," is your key to gaining essential knowledge quickly and easily. Once you grasp the straightforward arrangement of Part Three, "An A-to-Z Reference of Essential Microbusiness Topics," you will need only minimal time to find what you need to know. Each topic is uniformly formatted to address your information needs specifically and directly:

- **What you need to know** explains the topic in the context of a small business. If you already know the topic to your satisfaction, this entry can be easily scanned or skipped entirely.

- **Why you need to know it** goes beyond the definition and elaborates on why the topic is especially important to you as a microbusiness person.

- **Where to learn more** points the way if the topic needs in-depth treatment. It tells you where to look or whom to consult for a more elaborate explanation. A telephone number (often toll-free) is included wherever possible, if you want to discuss the topic or purchase the product or service.

- **Related topics** creates valuable linkages among the topics cataloged in this book. Some connections are direct; others are more obscure. You must judge what warrants pursuing. By scanning the list of related terms, you can painlessly jog your thinking and recognize topics you may not have been taking into account. After you become familiar with the topics in Part Three, you will have less need to look up the cross-references or consider them further. When you do consult them, there is the convenience of a uniform format that comfortably and efficiently leads you to the next line of inquiry for solving your problem.

In a few instances, the individual topics of the reference core are not expansive enough to form a reasonable linkage. For these topics, the appendixes offer exhaustive lists of examples, names, telephone numbers, and other information that supplements guidance given elsewhere in the book.

The Home Business Bible is exactly what its name implies—a reference to be consulted when needed rather than a book to be read from cover to cover. After reading this introductory material, give yourself the benefit of Part One's overview of the working-from-home movement. Examine the useful approaches suggested in Part Two and become comfortable with how to use the book.

Then let *The Home Business Bible* start working alongside you in the day-to-day practice of successfully growing your microbusiness.

Part One

Working
from
Home

You could not have picked a better time to start a microbusiness from your home. Only in recent years have the modern tools of the trade become available at popular prices. A smart, ambitious person with a service or product to sell and a surplus of personal energy can succeed as a home-based microbusiness person, thanks principally to two developments unique to our times:

1. Technical and mass marketing breakthroughs in communications and information processing. You can play in the big leagues with an unassailably professional image, from the relatively low-expense, low-profile base of a home office, completely in touch from wherever you choose to be to wherever your clients are.

2. A services-oriented economy that welcomes your participation. You can compete as an equal with established, traditional businesses, as long as you are competent, knowledgeable in your field, and respectful of common business protocols, and can deliver what is wanted, when it is wanted, at a competitive price.

In today's business environment, you have both the markets to serve and the means to reach them from a home office. Regardless of the specialty you choose to pursue, the new, off-the-shelf technology that is becoming available daily can make the home-based character of your operation irrelevant. Computers, modems, on-line information and communication services, copiers, high-quality printers, mobile telephones, and fax machines allow you to equip your office with total technology for only a few thousand dollars.

The Growing Home Office Movement

The opportunities presented by our changing technological times have been recognized by millions of people who might never have become independent were it not for the home office approach. The numbers are dramatic: 5.7 million people working at home in 1980[1] became 41.1 million by 1993.[2] The 1993 total translates into roughly one in three members of the total U.S. work force working at home either full- or part-time. About 40 percent are self-employed and working full-time, almost as many are self-employed and working part-time, and around 20 percent work at home for others as "telecommuters." By 1995, there are expected to be 42.5 million home workers[3] in an overall American labor market of about 125 million employees.[4]

Whether you are working for someone else from your own home or running your own company, as a home worker you are part of a growing segment of the larger economy. Flexibility, avoidance of traffic congestion and of inner-city air pollution, and accommodation to changed life-styles are among the many reasons why the movement is popular. The average commuter spends 157,600 hours traveling to and from work in a lifetime.[5] People have become less willing to do that or to subordinate their families and personal satisfaction to careers in large organizations that offer a less secure future with each passing year. When an option to work from home presents itself, many people are saying yes.

Profile of the Home Worker

The home worker is a typical middle-income employee, demographically. A 1993 survey[6] by *Home Office Computing* magazine revealed these averages on its readers who were working from home:

Age: 43

Gender: 58 percent men/42 percent women

Marital status: 78 percent married

Family: Two children

Home workers are pleased with their lot. Of those surveyed, only 6 percent plan a return to the corporate world. More than 95 percent are happier running their own businesses than working for someone else, would recommend working from home to others, and plan to be running a business in five years. The biggest challenges they face are: (1) getting new business, (2) promoting their businesses, (3) growing their businesses, and (4) managing their time. Distant secondary concerns include tax planning and preparation, being a smart business person, money management, retirement planning, legal issues, and office design. The most popular home-based enterprises are business support services (28 percent), consulting (11 percent), computer programming and services (9 percent), communications (8 percent), and secretarial and word processing services (7 percent). Financial support services, graphic and fine arts, marketing and advertising, medical services, and real estate are about equal: each is in the 4 to 5 percent range. What home workers miss most about the corporate world is company-paid health insurance and retirement plans.

Illustrating the upscale trend of the home-based business movement, *The Washington Post* noted that the highly educated and affluent suburbs of the capital are a hotbed for technology-enabled home businesses.[7] As an example, the newspaper described Nick Davis, a graphic artist who adapted successfully to recessionary pressures in his traditional business by laying off nine employees and moving into the basement of his Fairfax County residence. He now comfortably runs a scaled-down version of his business and has more time with his family. Davis has installed two Macintosh computers, a laser printer, a copier, a facsimile machine, a drafting table, and a high-resolution image printer—equipment that only a major company could have afforded not many years ago. Similarly, Janice Caldwell moved her law practice from an office politics-laden Washington firm to a spare bedroom at home. With a fax, telephone, and computer, she happily serves clients as far away as Brazil.

Home Office Purchasing Power

Major company advertisements set in home office situations are indicative of the growing economic importance of the home office microbusiness consumer. Market surveys show that home workers spend over $25 billion a year on equipment and services. Annual increases of approximately 18 percent are expected. Technology has made today's working-from-home revolution possible, and technology is what home workers purchase: 17 percent of their dollars go for computers, 20 percent for printers, and 19 percent for telephone products. Home office purchases alone were expected to account for a 25 percent rise in the sales of personal computers and for fully half of the fax machines sold in 1992.[8]

A whole support industry is growing up around the home office phenomenon. Mail-order catalogs target the home-based worker, and professional associations and insurance products recognize the segment as a viable market. Credit card companies welcome the home microbusiness person with travel and other incentives that rival their corporate card benefits.

The Home-Based Microbusiness Advantage

Going into business is not as complicated as it used to be. There was a time when planning a business meant calculating the cost of renting an office, furnishing it in the traditional way, and staffing it with at least a receptionist. These were the benchmark minimums for a professional business start-up. No more. You can begin this way:

- Select the part of the country from which you wish to offer your services;
- Make that decision totally independent of the existence of a job opening in someone else's company;
- Transition your way to successful self-employment without the costs, complications, and risks of a traditional "cold turkey" business start-up;
- Invest in modern business and communications technology that will make your business easily transportable to your ultimate geographic location;
- Live a combination work–leisure life-style of your own design.

This more flexible, less capital-intensive, and less risk-laden approach to starting a business is the direct outgrowth of the home office option.

The contemporary economy is driven more by the services of skilled people than by the brawn of workers toiling in smokestack industries. There is burgeoning opportunity for people who have experienced the traditional workplace, understand how it functions, are literate in its terminology and technology, and yet are perceptive enough to identify needs that can be met independently.

The future belongs to the work force's more flexible members. People with the insight and independently valued skills to do so are stepping outside of organizations. Often, they turn around and serve the needs of the large businesses they left, but they do it with more creativity, profitability, and satisfaction as home-based microbusiness people.

Today, your prospects for starting a successful, professional-level business at home are better than ever. You have the advantage of easing your way into a career change by defining a transitional path that suits your circumstances and goals. It can begin from the comfort of your own home office on a part-time basis—with your existing position and support systems intact. When your business proves itself commercially, it can grow into a prosperous full-time home microbusiness. At that point, you will have three pleasant choices:

1. Stay put and enjoy what you have created, free from the burdens of a commercial office and employees;

2. Assuming that your clients can be served from anywhere with the support of modern technology, relocate to where you would really like to be—efficiently moving your office and home together, and hardly missing a beat with your existing client base;

3. Go on to become a traditional microbusiness, transitioning from the security of an established home-based enterprise—at your present location or in another part of the country.

With a home-based microbusiness, you don't have to limit yourself to these choices: a structured job in another person's company, the struggle of establishing a traditional business start-up, or employment far removed from the valuable skills nurtured during your organizational career.

Starting Your Home-Based Business

Many people have discovered that their skills can be applied independently and profitably without the support of a large organization—or its staff and facilities. If you see yourself among these people, start as a home-based business person and focus your energy and resources on establishing a solid demand for your services instead of straining to emulate a traditional company. Here are the first three steps you should take:

1. Possess (or acquire) the ability to offer a valued service that lends itself to efficient delivery with the support of modern business technology;

2. Define a market for this service and exploit it independently;

3. Designate your home as your place of business—whether you are currently buying, renting, or relocating—to define a comfortable combination of personal life-style and economic reality.

With these things done, you have something to sell, the means to reach your market, and a place from which to live and do business.

Going into business with an unproved idea and constraints on your time and resources calls for efficiency. You have a home and there is a good chance that you already have the personal computer, telephone, and other actual necessities of your trade. Forget about office rent, furniture leases, nonessential support staff, and all the unnecessary overhead of the traditional business start-up. Clients are more interested in your competence, reliability, and price (in that order) than your office's location or ambience.

Dress casually, except when you go calling on clients in their environment or when they come to see you—if ever. More and more, business is initiated, developed, and consummated by telephone, fax, and overnight delivery services. The world can literally be your marketplace, and your opportunity to prosper in it is limited only by your ability to define and cultivate a growing set of users for what you have to offer.

As a home based microbusiness person, you can choose whatever personal life style suits you. Using marketing that is sensitive to time zones, you are free to be a morning person—or the opposite, if you prefer. The only remnants of business formality that need be a part of your day are the protocols and terminology used in the markets you have identified.

Selecting Your Specialty

The starting point in your search for a specialty should be your present field. The advantages include a thorough knowledge of the industry and its practices, and familiarity with the directories and publications that serve as the basis for your business contacts.

If you would find it awkward to work for yourself while still engaged in (or after just recently leaving) your present occupation, consider reaching beyond your immediate geographical bounds and plying your trade in another region of the country. Remember, you can probably do business at any location where there is long-distance telephone service. You might be able to select a narrow specialty within your overall industry that would complement rather than conflict with your traditional career.

You may find it either necessary or desirable to enter an entirely new field. If so, choose something that interests you and something that you can do well. Ask yourself what you might choose to do if you had your career to start over again.

In providing any service to an industry, you do not have to be an all-around expert in that industry. You do, however, need to have a broad sense of how the business operates, its needs, and the jargon with which its members communicate.

Whether you elect to stay with your present field or venture into a new one that you must investigate thoroughly, these are some tests to apply to your selection:

1. Do potential clients with this industry currently purchase the types of services you plan to provide? To gather this information, make some calls, send letters, and conduct a survey.

2. Are there sufficient trade directories and publications to help you develop a customer list? You will find it easier to grow a business in an area that is already defined by directories and trade publications. National on-line and CD-ROM business directories can be helpful, but a directory for the specific trade or profession of your choice is invaluable. This is such an important factor that you might even approach your selection by first determining what industries offer strong support in the way of directories and trade organizations, and then choosing one of them. Whether your business plan calls for direct mail or targeted telephone contact, you will have a distinct advantage if you can identify and reach your potential customers readily.

3. Do you now have, or can you develop, a grasp of the terminology used in the specialty? You need to become comfortable with accepted business practices for your chosen field. What terms are used? What performance criteria are mentioned and what do they mean? What professional certifications (CPA,

PE, CPC, etc.) are highly regarded? You can develop this knowledge base for almost any specialty you select. You must decide whether to do this or to operate from your existing knowledge.

4. Is this an occupation and/or industry that truly interests you? The choice is yours; select something that will capture your imagination and make your work enjoyable. If you always thought you might have made a good (name the profession), perhaps that's an excellent choice for your field of business specialization.

Can you be a generalist and go after business anywhere you find it? That is not an effective approach. As a home-based worker, you will have limited time and resources and you will need to become profitable as quickly as you can. Specialization lets you to target your time and energy for the most efficient use of the hours you have available.

Regardless of the business service you provide, you will probably do much of your work on speculation or on a contingency fee basis. At times, you may invest many hours only to have a competitor walk away with the job and the fee. If you are working within a narrow specialty, your efforts are not in vain. You can use what you learned—and the contacts you made—in subsequent projects.

As a specialist, you become an expert in your particular aspect of the business. In time, you learn a great deal about who occupies key positions throughout your industry. More importantly, you come to know many of them well—if not as friends, as respected, periodic, professional contacts. All business thrives on a core of knowledge and contacts, and you can master your business essentials better as a specialist. Whether you provide merchandise or services, you become a valued part of the business community when you learn things that other people need to know. You accumulate this knowledge in the general course of communicating with your contacts, and it is apt to be more powerful and useful if you specialize.

Jump-Start Your Business

One way to get your business going quickly is the immersion method. Identify a highly regarded training workshop or seminar in your new field and attend it. National associations in various fields can guide you to such educational experiences. You will return home motivated and already in touch with a network of people who can help you solve future problems. Another fast-start technique is to contract for a day or more of one-on-one training and consultation with a person already highly regarded in your field.

Other ways of making a rapid entry into a specialized business include buying a respected franchise or going to work for a franchisee temporarily. It would be wise to anticipate the "noncompete" agreements you might have to sign. They often pose no problem if you relocate beyond the prohibited range (e.g., don't operate a similar business within 50 miles of their outlets) after learning the tricks of the trade. One more possibility is to buy an existing business from someone who is successful but wants out. Make a hard-nosed evaluation of how transportable his or her success actually is before putting your money down. Many small businesses *are* their owners, and you may be left with little more than their counsel after they're gone. If that is what you really are buying, pay accordingly, and expect to pick the owner's brain even as you are making a major effort to succeed independently.

Regardless of how you decide to launch your new enterprise, the home office approach can improve your chances of surviving, learning the unexpected lessons, and finding success within the risk, dislocation, and cost parameters you find comfortable.

Acquire a Successful Small Business Vocabulary

As the chief cook and bottle washer of your own microbusiness, you had better know what the players in your world are talking about. Knowledge of your own specialty is one thing; it is presumed that you have that. But familiarity with the jargon of everyone trying to help you establish and grow your business—the people selling you office technology, your accountant, insurance broker, loan officer, attorney, and a host of others—is something else entirely. You don't have to be an expert at everything, but you had better be able to understand communications from these people.

This book is devoted to providing that kind of knowledge in a reference format that lets you quickly enter the knowledge curve at whatever point you find yourself. You can follow the curve as far as you must to serve your own vital business interests of the moment. If what you need is a quick explanation of a term, it's there for you. If you want to know why it makes any difference to you, a separate section addresses that concern. When you need to know more or want to make contact with those who do, a list of resources tells you where to go for information. Finally, if you need to flesh out the concept by relating it to other terms, that option is waiting for you. From this point on, *The Home Business Bible* is a tool with which to work, not a tome to digest. Let it inform you as your needs for information arise. Part Two suggests useful ways of doing so.

ENDNOTES

1. Jo Ann Tooly, "Leaving the Office Nest," *U.S. News & World Report*, December 26, 1988–January 2, 1989, p. 120.
2. Peter Pae, "In Area Homes, Businesses Are Booming," *The Washington Post*, October 24, 1993, p. B6. [Quoting LINK Resources Corporation research]
3. Hugh Roome, "The Bright Spot," *Home Office Computing*, September 1992, p. 2.
4. Ronald E. Kutscher, "New BLS Projections: Findings and Implications," *Outlook 1990–2005*, BLS Bulletin 2402, May 1992, p. 5. Washington; DC: U.S. Department of Labor, Bureau of Labor Statistics.
5. Jeff Davidson, *Breathing Space*. New York: Mastermedia, Ltd., 1992.
6. "1993 Reader Survey," *Home Office Computing*, September 1993, p. 40.
7. Pae, "In Area Homes," pp. B1 and B6.
8. Roome, "The Bright Spot," p. 2.

Part Two

How to Use
*The Home
Business Bible*

The Introduction and Part One have covered the general aspects of the home-based microbusiness movement. What remains is the essential reference core of *The Home Business Bible*. The following 150 topics are defined, discussed, and cross-referenced. Referrals are made for pursuing them in detail when necessary.

Alphabetical List of the Microbusiness Topics

accountant
accounting
advertising
agents and brokers
answering machines and voice mail
associations
attitude
attorney
banking services
bankruptcy
bartering
Better Business Bureau (BBB)
bidding
billing
bonding
bookkeeping
budgeting
Bulletin Board System (BBS)
business address and location
business associates
business basics
business cards
business ideas
business image
business incubator
business name
business organization
business plan
business travel
business use of car
business use of home
buying a business
camera-ready copy
cash flow
Chamber of Commerce
checking accounts

competition
computer equipment
computer on-line services
computer software
computer use
concerns about working from home
conferences, seminars, shows, and
    workshops
consulting
continuing education
contracts
copiers
copyright, patent, trademark and
    service mark
credit cards
credit unions
customer relations
debt collection and creditworthiness
desktop publishing
direct mail and mailing lists
direct selling and multilevel marketing
disabilities
disaster planning
diversification
electronic banking
employees
environmental considerations
equipment and furniture
ergonomics
escrow
ethics
evaluating your business
expense sharing and joint ventures
expert witness
family
fax

fees and pricing
financial formulas
financial planning
foreign markets and languages
forms
franchises
getting organized and managing
    information
goal setting
government customers
homeowners' associations
independent contractor status
information sources and research
insurance
investing
labor laws
leasing
legal liability
legal/illegal business operation
license
lighting
loans, credit, and venture capital
mail and overnight delivery
    services
mail order
managing growth
marketing and market research
media relations
merchandise buying services
money management
moonlighting
motivation
multimedia
negotiating
networking
newsletters
noise
office planning and decorating
overhead expenses
paper
payroll
personnel policies

presentations
printing
professional help
profit
projections
promoting your business
proposals
proprietary information
psychological factors
public relations
records
reducing expenses
regulations
retirement
role
sales representatives
security
separating business and personal
Service Corps of Retired Executives
    (SCORE)
Small Business Administration (SBA)
start-up
stress and overworking
success and failure
supplies
syndication
tax checklist
telecommuting
telephone equipment
telephone services
telephone use
temporary help
time management
time-share offices
training
transitioning
undercapitalization
vacation, work styles, and schedules
values
women's programs
zoning

How to Use the Alphabetical List of Microbusiness Topics

- **The list is an index.** Use it to easily find the term most nearly representing the topic you want to investigate, then find the term in Part Three, "A-to-Z Reference of Essential Microbusiness Topics," as you would in a dictionary.

- **The list is a tool for prompting your best thinking on any microbusiness subject.** Among the 150 topics are ideas and linkages to new avenues of inquiry on almost any aspect of small business planning or operations. If you are wondering where to go next for an idea or a constructive way to address a concern, spend a moment letting this master list stimulate your thinking. Use it as a one-person brainstorming session or engage a colleague in sharing and scanning half of the list. The end product of the exercise will be whole new avenues to explore, and all the information needed for developing them will be located conveniently at your fingertips.

An Example of a Listing

① ▶ **Bulletin Board System (BBS)**

② ▶ **What you need to know**   Bulletin board systems are electronic information exchanges on which subscribers post and respond to messages. There are about 40,000 public and over 100,000 private bulletin boards that focus on everything from home-based business operators to special-interest medical and economic groups. Some bulletin boards are run by government agencies such as the Small Business Administration (SBA); others are add-ons to commercial networks like CompuServe. Each BBS has a "sysop" (system operator) who runs the system. The sysop provides the computer database and communications products that make the system available. The sysop sets standards, establishes and collects fees, and maintains discipline on the system—determining what users are allowed to do and say, prohibiting illegal software exchanges, and so on. Users have their own unique electronic "addresses" on the service so others can respond directly to them. BBSs are a popular source of legitimate free or low-cost user-supported software known as shareware or freeware. A hazard of downloading applications from BBSs is computer viruses, but the problem can be controlled by computer programs that screen for them. In addition to being an information source, like 900 telephone number services, BBSs represent a home business opportunity for those who can define an information service that people will pay to use. It is a crowded market, but one to consider if you have the right idea and want to add another profit center to your business.

③ ▶

④ ▶ **Why you need to know it**   The BBSs are vital communications links for many home business people. You can use them for the companionship of interacting with others in your circumstances, thereby breaking the isolation of working alone, or you can approach them as strictly a means to do business—networking with people you can profit from knowing, and getting answers from those who can help you run your business and
⑤ ▶   meet the needs of your clients. Some BBSs amount to a form of advertising: you can reach a target audience with your commercial or professional message. Publishers use BBSs to let authors interact with their readers. Interacting on a BBS is like having a written conversation on a computer screen. An added advantage is the ability to use either interactive or time-delayed postings that can be acted on by either party at his or her convenience.

⑥ ▶ **Where to learn more**

- On-line services like CompuServe, GEnie, Prodigy, American Online, and the like have lists of BBSs they support (see COMPUTER ON-LINE SERVICES).

- Computer magazines and local users' groups are good sources of information on BBSs.

- Government agencies' information numbers can guide you to specialized BBSs they support. You can find the agency numbers in Matthew Lasko's *Information U.S.A.* or in Washington (DC) telephone books, which are available in many libraries. An example is SBA Online, a free 24-hour-a-day source of small business information that you can reach at 800-859-4636 (2400bps) or 800-697-4636 (9600bps). Set your parameters to N (no parity), eight data bits, and one stop bit.

- To set up a BBS of your own, read John Hedtke's *Using Computer Bulletin Boards* (MIS Press; 800-628-9658 or 212-886-9210) or *Boardwatch* magazine, 7586 West Jewell Avenue, Suite 200, Lakewood, CO 80232; 800-933-6038 or 307-973-6068.

⑦ ▶ **Related topics**

Advertising	Customer relations
Associations	**Information sources and research**
Bartering	Mail order
Business address and location	Marketing and market research
Business ideas	Merchandise buying services
Competition	**Networking**
Computer equipment	Newsletters
Computer on-line services	Promoting your business
Computer software	Psychological factors
Computer use	

How to Use the Individual Listings

Using the numbered annotations in this example of a typical listing, you learn the kinds of information that are provided on each of the 150 microbusiness topics. Every topic appears in this uniform format, so you can go to the part of the listing that interests you most. Here is the information you can expect to find when you turn to any topic:

① The name of the topic as it is listed in the Alphabetical List of the Microbusiness Topics (pages 13–14) and in the list of related topics at the end of each entry.

② **What you need to know** is the heading that signals the definition of the term and explains the topic in language relevant to the home-based microbusiness person.

③ In the body of the **What you need to know** section are the buzz words commonly associated with the topic and a commonsense statement of what they mean. When relevant and available, just enough statistical data are provided to give you a feel for the scope of the topic. If the term discussed lends itself to becoming a microbusiness profit center, that is mentioned.

④ **Why you need to know it** is the heading that cues you to a section of information telling you precisely why the topic might matter to you as a home-based microbusiness person. If you already know what the topic means, scan **What you need to know** quickly, and spend your time on **Why you need to know it**, if that is your primary concern. In either case, the topics are clearly separated for your efficient review.

⑤ Many times, a quick example is the best way to convey a topic's usefulness. When that is the case, one or more examples are inserted into the closing sentences of the **Why you need to know it** section.

⑥ **Where to learn more** is your individual consultant's report on how to proceed if the topic really interests you. The content of this section varies depending on the nature of the topic. In many cases, you will be given suggestions and details for acquiring the service or item—such as agency or company names, addresses, and telephone numbers. Or, you may be guided to more detailed sources of information, such as books or reports on the subject. If an on-line computer service or software is available, that resource will be identified. For general topics, where exact referrals might be less useful, you are told how to approach the topic locally via your library, telephone book, or a particular kind of resource person.

⑦ **Related topics** is an abbreviated version of the Alphabetical List of the Microbusiness Topics especially refined to complement the individual topic. Use it the same way you use the complete list:

  • As an index;

  • As a tool for prompting your best thinking on *this particular* microbusiness subject.

The **Related topics** list has another important use. Give extra consideration to the terms printed in **bold** type. They relate more directly to the topic you are exploring and might warrant immediate scanning or reading. The topics in regular type are primarily for audit and brainstorming purposes—to be sure you haven't overlooked something, and to stimulate the kind of relational thinking that might lead you to creative and profitable alternatives. Each topic listed has the features of the example just described and will lead you through an ever-expanding inquiry, to the extent that it is useful for the problem you are addressing.

Appendixes

The Home Business Bible concludes with a series of five appendixes to provide you with additional information in these special interest areas:

Appendix A. Computer-Based Business Forms

Business forms were once necessarily bought, preprinted, in large quantities; stored for long-term use; laboriously printed on a "tractor fed" contact printer (to make carbon impressions); discarded when revisions were needed; and mailed to and from customers. A computer software revolution has compressed the whole process. You now have options that let you keep as much or as little of the old "hard copy" way of doing business as you like. As a home-based microbusiness person with limited space/clerical support/time to do things the traditional way, you owe it to yourself to become aware of electronic business forms creation, completion, filing, distribution, reports generation, and printing. You can find this information in Appendix A. Several vendors are identified, and information for requesting demonstration disks is included.

Appendix B. Information Resources

There are places where you can find the answers you need to a variety of small business questions. You need only call, fax, or write to the right organization. Appendix B, a cross-section of these resources, gives the information necessary to contact them directly. Often, these organizations either are nonprofit or do not operate in a heavily commercial mode.

Appendix C. Supplies and Software, Books and Other Printed Materials

Certain kinds of small business information correctly have to be purchased from commercial vendors. Appendix C is your guide to suppliers of a variety of products that may be useful in building and running your business. No endorsement is implied, but, to the best of the author's knowledge and personal experience, these are reputable sources. You are, however, encouraged to exercise the same prudence you would in making any significant purchase. Should you have unsatisfactory experiences with any product or company listed, please advise me via the publisher. Your input will be taken into account in future editions.

Appendix D. Computer and Software Companies' User-Assistance Telephone Numbers

When you have a question about the potential applications, system requirements, or proper use of a computer or software product, your best friend is the technical assistance representative for the company selling the product. Appendix D is a directory of user-assistance numbers for many popular computer and software companies, listed alphabetically.

Appendix E. Business Use of Your Home, IRS Publication 587

When you become an operator of a home-based business, the challenge of dealing with the IRS ranks second only to the successful execution of a sound business idea. Publication 587 is the IRS's rulebook for determining home-based business tax deductions.

Appendix F. Getting Started and Installing IN THE BLACK*

If you are considering using a computer to assist you in operating your business or if you are contemplating a full-featured small business accounting system with some useful add-ons, Appendix F introduces you to Microrim's *In The Black* accounting and client contact manager software that can help you run your business more efficiently. Appendix F tells you exactly what you'll find in this software developed specifically to fill the microbusiness niche.

---

*Note that this Appendix applies to the cloth edition of this book which contains diskettes.

Part Three

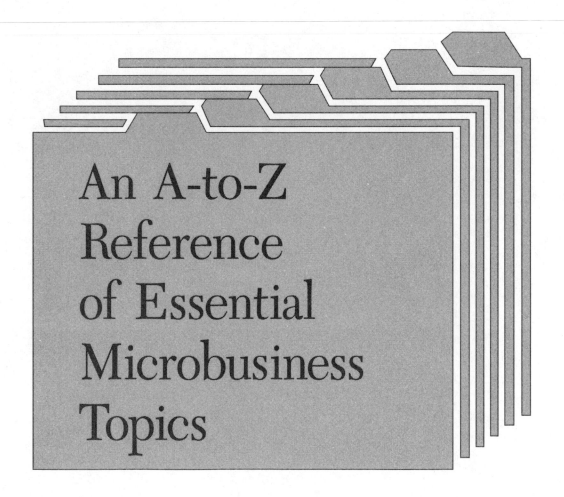

An A-to-Z
Reference
of Essential
Microbusiness
Topics

ACCOUNTANT

What you need to know   An accountant records and interprets the financial transactions of businesses. A certified public accountant is a fully qualified professional who has passed a rigorous examination prepared by the American Institute of Certified Public Accountants (AICPA), is authorized to use the designation CPA, and operates under the license of the state in which he or she practices. CPAs in good standing with the AICPA complete a college accounting degree, pass the Uniform CPA Examination, meet postgraduate-study or job-experience requirements, take continuing education courses, and adhere to a strict code of professional ethics. Depending on where you do business, other persons who are not authorized to represent themselves as CPAs may be allowed to operate as accountants. Their common titles include Public Accountant, Tax Consultant, and Bookkeeper. Some of these related practitioners complement the work of CPAs by performing everyday tasks such as maintaining records and filing routine reports; others have specialized expertise that rivals that of most CPAs.

Why you need to know it   You need an accountant to help you choose the best form of organization and to guide you in satisfying your tax obligations at the lowest cost. Your accountant is an important professional reference who enhances your image in the business and financial communities. He or she is a necessary part of your network, and can provide leads regarding everything from financing to sales. If a tax audit occurs, a CPA can act on your behalf, keep a desirable distance between you and the IRS, and leave you free to run your business while the audit unfolds. A professional accountant is more adept than you are at providing auditors with only what is required and no more. Self-represented taxpayers can inadvertently open new avenues of inquiry. As your business either grows or experiences difficulties, the periodic statements prepared by your CPA provide the strongest position from which to negotiate with financial institutions and other businesses. Books, articles, and financial software can help you, but there is no substitute for the judgment of the full-time professional who stays on top of the constantly changing regulations affecting your business.

Where to learn more

▶ State or local chapters of the AICPA can provide information and assist you in choosing an accountant.

▶ Bankers, attorneys, and business associates recommend accountants.

▶ The American Institute of Certified Public Accountants, 1211 Avenue of the Americas, New York, NY 10036; 212-575-3655, is the national professional association representing 75 percent of the CPAs in the United States. It verifies membership, provides free publications, and makes referrals.

▶ The Wharton School of the University of Pennsylvania sells a complete video seminar on finance and accounting for nonfinancial managers through Kantola Productions, 55 Sunnyside Avenue, Mill Valley, CA 94941; 800-989-8272. Under $200.

Related topics

Accounting	**Financial planning**
Bankruptcy	Forms
Bookkeeping	Investing
Budgeting	Leasing
Business associates	**Loans, credit, and venture capital**
Business basics	**Managing growth**
Business organization	**Money management**
Business plan	Networking
Business travel	Professional help
Business use of car	**Profit**
Business use of home	**Projections**
Buying a business	Records
Cash flow	**Regulations**
Computer software	Retirement
Ethics	Separating business and personal
Evaluating your business	**Tax checklist**
Financial formulas	Undercapitalization

ACCOUNTING

What you need to know   Accounting is a standardized and disciplined set of procedures for tracking what your business does financially—a formal record of its transactions. Depending on the size and complexity of your company, you will operate on either a cash basis or an accrual basis and will use either single-entry or double-entry bookkeeping. These terms are explained under BOOKKEEPING. Accounting involves recording financial transactions and interpreting the results to show business performance. An accounting system accomplishes a variety of things with the information it gathers. Budgeting uses past transactions to help plan the company's financial future. Cost accounting collects information on producing a certain product or service, allocates costs to individual items, and compares those costs with others produced at different times, under different conditions, or by other firms. Auditing determines the accuracy, completeness, and reliability of a company's financial records. The balance sheet and statement of operations show the condition and creditworthiness of a business.

Why you need to know it   You are never in business alone. Although you may not have partners or stockholders, you interact with customers, suppliers, government agencies, and financial institutions that want to know the condition of your business. Their expectations grow with the size and complexity of your business, but even a one-person start-up is required to have a simple accounting and financial reporting system. Income tax reporting alone requires formal financial record keeping. You also need to know whether your business is profitable; too often, small businesses fail because they are ignorant of their own profitability. With proper—and not necessarily complicated—accounting procedures, you can tell whether you are making or losing money before it becomes painfully obvious through tax penalties, bankruptcy, or other negative consequences. Accounting is the control panel of your home-based business. It provides the gauges you monitor to keep your business functioning and developing in the right direction.

Where to learn more

‣ Review a basic book on accounting in the business section of your library or find one in a bookstore. Learn the terminology.

‣ Audit (enroll for no credit or grade) an applied accounting course at a community college, or visit the college bookstore and purchase the text, if all you want is an overview.

‣ Select an accountant, discuss your needs, and take his or her advice on how to approach your financial record keeping.

‣ Select computer software that is appropriate to your needs, and read the manuals that come with it. Computerized business accounting is the recommended solution for small businesses because modern software greatly simplifies the task. Review software catalogs and computer magazines until you find something that appeals to you. Consult your accountant on whether compatibility with his or her software is desirable. *Quicken* and related products by Intuit are excellent applied accounting software products. (See your software reseller or the catalogs in Appendix C.) Microrim's *In The Black* is a highly usable double-entry accounting system.

Related topics

Accountant
Billing
Bookkeeping
Budgeting
Business basics
Cash flow
Computer software
Debt collection and creditworthiness
Disaster planning
Evaluating your business
Financial planning

Loans, credit, and venture capital
Money management
Payroll
Professional help
Profit
Projections
Records
Regulations
Separating business and personal
Tax checklist

ADVERTISING

What you need to know   Advertising is the measures you employ to develop new business. It can be in the form of print communications that reach your potential customers in a circulating publication (a newspaper, magazine, or trade journal), or a handout or mailing piece ranging from a matchbook to an announcement of professional services. Advertising can be electronic, reaching listeners or viewers via radio, television, or an on-line computer service. Some advertising is free: you might appear on a community-interest cable channel or agree to be interviewed on a commercial channel. Computer disks and video tapes that demonstrate what you do and how it can help those who patronize you is also advertising. Advertising can lead your audience to voice mail systems that deliver more detailed information. Unsolicited fax advertising is illegal in many jurisdictions, but legitimate fax response can be an excellent way to provide requested information. The measure of advertising's success is whether it immediately increases sales or makes your product sufficiently better known and aids future sales. Keys to successful use of advertising include: analyzing your customers and matching their characteristics (demographics) with the advertising medium; researching the cost of ad preparation and space to reach your audience economically; verifying market penetration claims before investing; testing the ad before committing heavily; and tracking and analyzing the results.

Why you need to know it   A home-based business is relatively isolated, especially until it is well established and becomes a known source for what it provides. A major advertising campaign isn't necessary, but constant exposure of new clients and customers to your products or services is essential. Advertising is how you let people know you are ready to serve them. The IRS recognizes advertising as a legitimate pretax business expense. You need to be prudent about advertising and keep its cost in proportion to your overall operating budget, but don't ignore it as an essential cost of doing business.

Where to learn more

▶ Look at how your successful competitors advertise, and follow their lead.

▶ Call the advertising sales representatives of media that interest you, and ask for a rate sheet. It provides cost, format, and mechanical requirements (how your advertising copy has to be prepared) as well as circulation and demographic information.

▶ The mastheads of national magazines and newspapers list advertising sales representatives by geographic region.

▶ Libraries contain business references like the *Standard Rate and Data Service* directories that are updated regularly.

▶ The telephone book yellow pages list advertising agencies; inquire about their fees and interest in handling small accounts.

⏺ Network with other home-based businesses locally or nationally via computer
bulletin boards to reach an advertising specialist who appreciates your circumstances. Advertising is a popular home-based business, and you may find someone
with real empathy for your needs.

⏺ Interstate Enterprises Advertising Agency, P. O. Drawer 19689-L, Houston, TX
77224, sells advertising in four income opportunity publications. It is an example
of specialized publications that serve many kinds of markets. Explore the commercial literature of your own field until you find similar publications.

Related topics

Answering machines and voice mail

Bulletin Board System (BBS)

Business address and location

Business cards

Business image

Camera-ready copy

Computer on-line services

Conferences, seminars, shows, and
    workshops

Copyright, patent, trademark, and
    service mark

Desktop publishing

Direct mail and mailing lists

Ethics

Fax

Franchises

Marketing and market research

Media relations

Newsletters

Presentations

Printing

Professional help

Promoting your business

Regulations

Sales representatives

Telephone equipment

Telephone services

Telephone use

Zoning

AGENTS AND BROKERS

What you need to know   Agents and brokers are the professional go-
betweens of the business world. Their functions can be as ordinary as the
broker who finds the best business insurance or as exciting as the agent who
represents top fashion models internationally. Every industry has its agents and
brokers acting as the deal makers; they are the middlemen. The agent or broker is an informed, connected person who puts the buyer and seller together
for a piece of the action—his or her commission. Usually, an agent or broker is
strictly the arranger for a transaction and rarely handles the goods or services
he or she represents. Agency law defines the rights and obligations assumed in
such relationships. When you choose to do business through an agent or broker, you are giving that person a limited right to act in your behalf on the business interests you agree to share. An advantage of having an agent or broker is
relief to pursue your primary business activity without devoting time to the
details of arranging deals, negotiating contracts, and collecting fees. A literary
agent's fee is generally 15 percent of royalties; an art gallery might charge
two or three times that much. Determine the going rate for your business by

contacting competing agents or brokers and the clients they represent. Fees decline as their basis increases—an agent or broker takes a smaller percentage of a million-dollar deal than one worth $10,000.

Why you need to know it   A key person in your network of business associates, your agent or broker helps you make connections with people who buy your services. He or she also links you with peers with whom you might collaborate or form joint ventures. The good offices of an established agent or broker can arbitrate situations that might otherwise cost you business or cause legal problems. In the relative isolation of the home-based business, an effective agent or broker is a vital link to your industry and a personal counselor who can help you calibrate your judgments with commercial realities. Agents and brokers can be essential gateways to markets that support your business. As a small business person, you rely on third-party services for many business necessities. Agents and brokers oversee the category of things best left to others while you concentrate on growing your business and make the most of your special talents. A good agent or broker provides you with reality checks for your ideas and serves as an invaluable source of competitive market information: What is in demand? What can you charge for it? What kind of competition do you have? Is your sense of the market accurate?

Where to learn more

▶ Most fields have directories that list agents and brokers. Examples include *LMP* (*Literary Marketplace*) and *Writer's Market* (for authors).

▶ You find active agents and brokers by reading the trade publications of your business; for example, in *Publishers Weekly,* writers will find those who are cutting the deals featured in articles.

▶ You locate highly regarded agents or brokers by inquiring among the firms where you will be represented. Do they do business with a certain individual? Whom would they recommend for someone in your circumstances?

▶ The business reference section of your library contains directories of companies in your line of business. If agent and broker directories are not available, use the generic lists and call potential clients to ask for the names of representatives they respect.

Related topics

Bidding
Business associates
Contracts
Ethics
Expense sharing and joint ventures
Fees and pricing
Information sources and research

Marketing and market research
Negotiating
Networking
Presentations
Professional help
Sales representatives

ANSWERING MACHINES AND VOICE MAIL

What you need to know   Answering machines and voice mail have become overlapping services, with many features of the latter now incorporated in the former. At discount retailers, for $50 or less, you can buy an inexpensive telephone answering machine that will respond to callers, take a message, and tell you when they called. For a few dollars more, you can buy the same services integrated into a one- or two-line telephone. The telephone company will save you the trouble of buying, installing, and maintaining the equipment if you subscribe to its services. That can be an advantage if space is a problem or you don't want to bother with your own system. If your area is prone to lightning strikes that destroy sensitive circuits, you may want to avoid in-home equipment. The sophisticated voice mail equipment and services now available come close to providing a receptionist in a box. A few years ago, such systems required a dedicated computer and cost thousands of dollars. Today, for between $300 and $500, you can buy programmable devices that will answer your phone; let the caller speak; switch over to musical hold until you respond, or channel the call to an answering machine; present a series of information options; or allow access to your fax. Paging and call forwarding are other answering machine/voice mail related services that help small business persons function fully and professionally. Be alert to business image problems lurking in poorly managed systems. Properly designed and maintained equipment or services can do the job economically and well.

Why you need to know it   Efficiency and a businesslike image are essential for the home-based business. The right kind of answering device or service can provide both. It doesn't make sense for home businesses to employ a receptionist or spend the principal's time acting like one. An alternative is the intelligent use of technology. There is a myth that machines drive customers away. Call almost any business or government agency, and you will encounter digitized menus. They exist because a properly used answering device is better received and more efficient than indifferent human answering services. Unless you can employ and continually motivate a first-rate receptionist, buy a machine and use it wisely. You will capture more business than you will lose. The bottom line for callers is reaching you in time to deal with their problem. The best equipment now lets you screen calls without crudely picking up in the middle of the greeting. If you are not available, the caller will be satisfied if you respond promptly, whether in the office or reacting to paging or a forwarded call. Avoid having business callers reach a residential message. Acquire a business line and protect your professional image.

Where to learn more

▶ Office and electronic discount stores and catalogs carry a variety of answering devices. A catalog that does a particularly good job of explaining and comparing features is circulated by Crutchfield (Charlottesville, VA; 800-446-1640).

▶ The business office of your telephone company can explain its services. Before calling, look at the advertising in the front of your telephone book.

▶ Three suppliers of voice mail systems suitable for home offices are: (1) Bogen Communications, 50 Spring Street, P. O. Box 575, Ramsey, NJ 07446 (201-934-8500); (2) ImageVox Communications, 13610 N. Scottsdale Road, Suite 10, Scottsdale, AZ 85254 (800-578-8424 or 602-585-6208); and (3) Venture Communications, Inc., 808 W. Vermont Avenue, 2nd Floor, Anaheim, CA 92805 (714-635-2000; Fax 714-635-1197).

Related topics

Advertising	Leasing
Business image	Mail order
Computer equipment	Promoting your business
Computer software	Reducing expenses
Computer use	Separating business and personal
Customer relations	**Telephone equipment**
Direct selling and multilevel	**Telephone services**
marketing	**Telephone use**
Fax	Time-share offices

ASSOCIATIONS

What you need to know   There are associations of people with common interests for nearly anything you can name. In the Washington (DC) telephone yellow pages, approximately 1,400 associations are listed, ranging from the A Tree for Me Society to Zero Population Growth, Inc. In between is everything from The Door and Hardware Institute to the World Travel and Tourism Council—literally, something for everyone. Associations give focus, provide an identity, supply a political voice, and disseminate information to their members. Most associations host national meetings that provide excellent networking opportunities. Many groups sponsor specialized continuing education programs for members, offer professional publishing opportunities, and maintain specialized libraries and formatted documents like legal contracts. Because associations' lifeblood is membership dues, many offer member services like group insurance and practical advice for those engaged in the business. Some associations lobby the government to advance and protect the special interests of their members; others only monitor government and distill regulatory information for their members. Belonging to certain trade associations is almost a form of licensure and valued evidence of a member's good standing in the profession.

Why you need to know it   Trade and professional associations are part of your home-based business network. Belonging to them and being active in their affairs can bring you business and provide endorsements or references. Even taking a less active position helps your business image and keeps you informed about the professional or trade news you need in order to be conversant in the business of your clients. When pricing health and specialized liability insurance, don't overlook the mass buying power of a small business or professional association. The small business lobby is a powerful advocate for you in tax, zoning, wage-and-hour, and other legislation that affects your business. Home business people tend to be individualists, and many shun organizations and political activities. In your own interest, you should find and support a group whose causes you consider to be reasonable. You need combined representation to remain competitive with those who would restrict your activities and raise your cost of doing business. Your association interests will probably fall into two categories: (1) professional or trade, catering to your specialty, and (2) small business, representing the tax and legislative interests of businesses like yours.

Where to learn more

▶ Gale's *Directory of Associations,* the basic reference, can be found in the business reference section of your local library.

▶ Ask colleagues and clients what associations they find useful, and investigate them. Ask to see copies of their publications and details of the member services that interest you—group health insurance and professional liability plans, for example.

▶ Read the professional and small business literature and support associations that take positions you identify with and respect.

▶ Appendix B lists several organizations that serve small business interests.

Related topics

Business associates
Business image
Conferences, seminars, shows, and workshops
Consulting
Continuing education
Contracts
Credit unions
Direct mail and mailing lists
Ethics
Expense sharing and joint ventures
Expert witness
Fees and pricing

Homeowners' associations
Information sources and research
Insurance
Marketing and market research
Media relations
Networking
Newsletters
Professional help
Promoting your business
Public relations
Regulations
Training
Women's programs

ATTITUDE

What you need to know   A well-executed, sound business concept is the starting point for any successful business, but attitude and expectations significantly affect outcomes too. More than simple positive thinking is involved, although it is an essential quality. When home-based business persons go into the marketplace, their attitude must convey the message that there is nothing second-rate about their operation. Small businesses run from homes have a common image problem among some potential customers. Owners dispel this perceived shortcoming by the personal bearing and attitude they display while conducting business. Think like a professional, and do the things you'd do if you were part of a national company with offices on Madison Avenue. You can't think your way into a successful business, but you can improve your prospects by maintaining a realistically positive attitude. The relative isolation of working from home can make it more difficult to escape the negative moments everyone encounters in operating a business. Stay connected to people who can listen to your concerns and help you make the necessary adjustments. Use motivational tapes and business books-on-tape to expand your horizons and balance your thinking with positive images. Although they are sometimes simplistic, they package inspiration into a readily available, private form that can help reverse negative thinking when it strikes.

Why you need to know it   A small business *is* its owner—people learn this when they try to sell their businesses. Business contacts, public confidence, and image are inseparable from the owner. Lenders don't attach much value to goodwill on small business financial statements because they know it belongs to the owner and cannot be foreclosed or liquidated. Until your business becomes sufficiently established to have a trained staff and a foolproof operating system that reliably produces profits without you, you *are* your business. The attitude you display every day is the spirit of your business. You literally cannot afford to be negative or lack confidence because your attitude devalues your business and your prospects for success.

Where to learn more

‣ Motivational tapes and books are available in bookstores, libraries, and catalogs.

‣ SMI International, 5000 Lakewood Drive, Waco, TX 76710, offers a catalog of tapes.

‣ Nightingale Conant (800-323-5552) is another source of tapes.

‣ *Successories* is a catalog of quality motivational art in the form of posters, cards, desk accessories, clothing, and books. Call 800-362-5500 to obtain it from High Street Emporium. Executive Gallery (800-848-2618) offers similar products.

‣ Anthony Robbins' "Mastery University" (800-445-8183) conducts a series of three seminars at resort locations over the course of a year, and features speakers like General Norman Schwarzkopf and Sir John Templeton.

‣ Seminars addressed by the likes of Mario Cuomo, Joe Gibbs (former NFL coach), Larry King, Debbi Fields (Mrs. Fields' Cookies), and motivational speakers Zig Ziglar and Peter Lowe are held in Washington and other major cities. Call 800-444-9159 for details.

Related topics

Business associates

Business image

Competition

Concerns about working from home

Consulting

Customer relations

Disabilities

Legal/illegal business operation

Media relations

Moonlighting

Motivation

Negotiating

Networking

Promoting your business

Psychological factors

Public relations

Stress and overworking

Success and failure

Transitioning

Vacation, work styles, and schedules

ATTORNEY

What you need to know   Attorneys are trained in the formal rules by which the worlds of commerce and government operate. With their knowledge and experience, attorneys can alert you to problematic aspects of business transactions that you might not notice. Books and computer software offer legal-looking documents, but the professional judgment of a competent attorney is usually needed to give them value. Draft your contracts and legal papers if you like, but use them as a starting point for discussions with the attorney who will finalize them. Base your selection of an attorney on referrals from people you trust—another attorney, your accountant or banker, or a respected business person. State and local bar associations can be helpful in identifying attorneys by their specialties. As a home business person, you want an attorney who is familiar with small business concerns. Depending on your business, you may need a legal specialist. Establish a relationship with an attorney *before* you have a problem. A consultation to choose the legal form of your business is a good place to start if you are incorporating or forming a partnership. You probably do not need to formally retain an attorney; instead, discuss fees for services, and get more specifics when you need them. Depending on the circumstances, you will be billed: (1) what you agreed to pay for a particular service (fixed rate), (2) a percentage of the recovery (contingency), (3) what the law allows (statutory), or (4) an hourly rate. Most small business legal work is billed on an hourly basis, usually in increments of tenths of an hour, sometimes with minimums. Disputes over fees are generally settled by arbitration.

Why you need to know it   There is usually too much at stake to form a business without an attorney. Your initial needs may be as simple as a single consultation to review your plans, make certain you are not overlooking anything significant, and note milestones for possible future discussions. If you are doing more than forming a sole proprietorship, definitely have an attorney assist you. Quickie self-incorporation kits can leave you with an unrealistic view of what your corporation means, even if they technically meet your registration requirements. Have the basic contracts and forms you will be using in your business reviewed by your attorney. Do the same for any significant agreements you sign—especially leases and franchise agreements. You can encounter unexpected challenges as a small business owner; when they come, you want your legal affairs to be in order. It isn't the time to discover that your corporation is flawed or your spouse shouldn't have cosigned all those notes to the franchise company. You look more businesslike and perform more competently if your basic professional relationships are in place, and your attorney forms the hub of those arrangements. In the life of your growing business will come times when you are expected to have professional help (e.g., an important client says, "Let me have my attorney call your attorney, and we're all set!"). An attorney who knows you and your business is invaluable.

Where to learn more

▶ Ask the advice of your banker, accountant, or respected business acquaintances when selecting an attorney.

▶ Contact the local or state bar association to find a small business attorney or, if necessary, a certain legal specialist.

▶ Check the *Martindale Hubbell Law Directory* in your library. It provides basic information about individual lawyers, including their rates, areas of legal expertise, and ethical standards.

▶ HALT, 1319 F Street, NW, Suite 300, Washington, DC 20004 (202-347-9600), is a 100,000-member public-interest group whose mission is making the legal system work fairly. HALT publishes a legal consumer's guide called *Using a Lawyer, and What To Do If Things Go Wrong,* by Kay Ostberg. It is available as a part of the membership fee or can be purchased separately.

Related topics

Bankruptcy

Business associates

Business basics

Business name

Business organization

Business plan

Contracts

Copyright, patent, trademark, and
  service mark

Debt collection and creditworthiness

Escrow

Ethics

Franchises

Labor laws

Legal liability

Legal/illegal business operation

Loans, credit, and venture capital

Negotiating

Professional help

Proprietary information

Regulations

Start-up

Syndication

Tax checklist

Zoning

BANKING SERVICES

What you need to know   Like an attorney or accountant, a professional banker is an essential part of your business credibility. Your banker is a required reference for suppliers and clients; he or she might provide referrals to venture capital sources, for example. Your banker is a conservative voice in your business planning. If you hear from several bankers that they won't lend you money because you are undercapitalized, pay attention; it might be true. Local banks have disappeared in much of the country, but consider using one if it is available. It may show greater interest in a local business than a larger bank will. Whether you end up dealing with a local or a regional bank, try to personalize the relationship by having an officer know who you are and what your business does. Make it clear that you plan to use him or her as your banking reference. Ask about "relationship banking" that lets you link private and commercial accounts to meet balance minimums. The actual financial services you'll want are much the same wherever you find them—a business checking account, a business credit card or other line of credit, and, depending on the nature of your business, perhaps a "sweep" account that moves deposits immediately into short-term investments. Beyond those services, what you look for most in a bank is a safe place for your money and somewhere to establish a track record of responsible financial dealing. It is important to distinguish among the services of different kinds of financial organizations. Commercial banks, savings banks (formerly S&Ls), and credit unions vary widely in their ability to deliver business services. Commercial banks are more apt to offer merchant credit card services and commercial lines of credit.

Why you need to know it   Being taken seriously as a business requires having the appearance of one. Unless you are in a situation where your clients don't care about your image, or your business image is an entirely personal one, you want business checking and other services for the same reasons you want a business telephone—exclusive use and image projection. Technically, there is nothing wrong with running a business from your personal account. Computer programs like *Quicken* make it easy to assign transactions to separate accounts and categories. In addition to basic financial services, you need the financially conservative counsel of a banker among your business associates. Although you might successfully operate beyond the level of risk your banker recommends, factor his or her judgment into your decisions, and be sure you have sound business reasons for departing from conventional financial wisdom.

Where to learn more

▶ The customer service desk of a bank will describe and price its business services for you in person or by telephone. A personal visit will tell you more about the kind of support you can expect to receive.

◗ Ask members of your small business network where they have found good banking services.

◗ The American Bankers Association, 1120 Connecticut Avenue NW, Washington, DC 20036 (202-663-5000), can assist you in understanding the role of banking and how you might best use its members' services.

Related topics

Business image	Foreign markets and languages
Buying a business	Investing
Cash flow	**Loans, credit, and venture capital**
Checking accounts	Managing growth
Credit cards	**Money management**
Credit unions	Professional help
Debt collection and creditworthiness	Records
Electronic banking	Separating business and personal
Escrow	Start-up
Evaluating your business	Tax checklist
Financial formulas	Telephone services
Financial planning	Undercapitalization

BANKRUPTCY

What you need to know   Forming a corporation is not apt to protect a small business person from bankruptcy. A properly drawn and executed incorporation offers some protection, but the general rule is that creditors will "pierce the corporate veil" and go after personal assets regardless of how your business is organized. Most small business obligations are secured personally by the husband and wife as well as the business. As you form your company, get an attorney to do what is legally possible to protect you should it fail. If you find yourself in a hopeless debt situation, consult an attorney experienced in bankruptcy cases. He or she can help you determine your options and negotiate with your creditors. Bankruptcy actions are filed in federal courts, although the rules determining the disposition of property vary by state. Not all debts are "discharged" (cleared) by bankruptcy. Among those not discharged are taxes, fines and penalties, recent student loans, child and spouse support, and judgments for drunk driving. Fraudulently incurred debts are not dischargeable, and neither are those related to illegal activity. Your attorney can help you select the most beneficial form of bankruptcy, if it becomes necessary. The choices range from Chapter 7, the simplest and most straightforward bankruptcy (it protects very little, but discharges most obligations), to Chapter 11, which helps businesses and high-asset individuals reorganize and repay their creditors without discharging their debts or losing their property, or Chapter 13, which is used by individuals and couples to protect their property while repaying their creditors (it doesn't discharge debt like Chapter 7). Chapter 12 is for farmers.

Why you need to know it   Four out of five small businesses fail. You have
to understand the odds but not be overwhelmed by them. Many of those failures were ill-conceived—a bad idea, undercapitalized, the wrong place and
time, and so on. You improve your odds enormously by planning and managing
your business well, but it is only prudent to know the consequences of failure.
Although you should never be preoccupied by the prospect of failure, intelligent planning can protect you should the worst happen. Bankruptcy is a complicated legal undertaking with long-term consequences. Never seriously
contemplate filing a do-it-yourself bankruptcy action.

Where to learn more

▶ Libraries and bookstores have books on bankruptcy. A good one is Lawrence R.
Reich and James P. Duffy, *You Can Go Bankrupt without Going Broke* (Pharos
Books, 1992).

▶ Consult your attorney and verify his or her competence in small business bankruptcy cases. If you have a need for a specialist, ask the bar association for a
recommendation.

Related topics

Accountant	Financial planning
Attorney	Legal liability
Bonding	Legal/illegal business operation
Budgeting	**Loans, credit, and venture capital**
Business image	Managing growth
Business organization	**Money management**
Business plan	**Negotiating**
Cash flow	Professional help
Concerns about working from home	**Profit**
Credit cards	Public relations
Customer relations	**Regulations**
Debt collection and creditworthiness	Separating business and personal
Escrow	Success and failure
Evaluating your business	Tax checklist
Fees and pricing	**Undercapitalization**

BARTERING

What you need to know   Barter is a huge way of doing business: nearly a
quarter of a million companies exchanged almost $6 billion worth of goods and
services in 1991. Much of the bartering was done by major companies cutting
big deals, but a substantial number of participants were small professional
services providers, some of them home-based businesses. You can trade goods
and services on the personal level by making your receptiveness to doing so

known within your circle of clients and suppliers or by joining an organization that brokers bartered goods and services for a fee. In the typical arrangement, you pay a monthly cash fee, possibly supplemented by some barter value, and split a transaction fee with your exchange partner when a deal is struck. You must enter barter transactions into your bookkeeping system as debits and credits that represent fair market value. A well-conceived barter transaction ends up having no tax consequences if the fair market values balance, but you are required to have the records to prove it. A barter company must issue you an IRS Form 1099-B at year's end. Barter can no longer be thought of as an underground economy, although many informal transactions undoubtedly occur.

Why you need to know it   Bartering is another means to network your home-based business. Through barter arrangements and listings with brokers of bartered goods and services, you can acquire business and bill hours you might not have on a traditional cash basis. Until your time is fully obligated with cash clients, barter can be a worthwhile extension of your business. You must be aware of the potential pitfalls of barter to avoid losing "credits" in the failure of an unsound barter company or becoming disillusioned with the slowness of the process. Finally, to avoid problems with the IRS, you need to appreciate the tax and record-keeping consequences of bartering.

Where to learn more

▶ Look under "Barter & Trade Exchanges" in the telephone yellow pages.

▶ For information on barter companies, send a self-addressed stamped envelope to International Reciprocal Trade Association, 9513 Beach Mill Road, Great Falls, VA 22066. The Association represents 122 barter companies nationally.

Related topics

Advertising
Agents and brokers
Buying a business
Contracts
**Debt collection and
  creditworthiness**
Direct mail and mailing lists
Ethics
Expense sharing and joint ventures
Fees and pricing

Negotiating
Networking
Office planning and decorating
Professional help
Promoting your business
Reducing expenses
Supplies
Tax checklist
Training

BETTER BUSINESS BUREAU (BBB)

What you need to know   The Better Business Bureau is a national federation of 168 independent, nonprofit, local chapters that serve as clearinghouses for information on the ethical conduct of businesses in their regions. Unlike

Chambers of Commerce, BBBs are not associated with economic development or branches of government, and have no lobbying function. They are supported by the dues of the approximately 300,000 small to medium size companies that comprise their membership core. There is no national BBB, but local chapters can refer you to other BBBs in parts of the country where you have interests. BBBs respond to inquiries about the reputations and practices of companies doing business in their areas. Endorsement is not a BBB function, and companies cannot use BBB membership in their advertising, although a window decal or small plaque may indicate membership. The typical BBB response to an inquiry is that the BBB is aware of a company's existence and that it either does or does not have a history of complaints. As a properly licensed business, you may either join a local BBB or ask to be listed as a registered nonmember. In either status, you must provide information on your company in case the BBB receives inquiries about it.

Why you need to know it   Customers and clients often want to verify the reputation of a small business when they begin doing business with it. This is especially true if you are advertising widely to the general public and cannot rely on professional references within your industry. The BBB provides a useful reference service for businesses, but you have to be alert to registering yourself properly. By responding that it has no record of your existence, the BBB can have a negative impact on your business when you have done nothing wrong. Preempt that possibility by contacting your local chapter and asking for a registration packet. With it, you can become a part of the BBB database. The BBB will acknowledge your status as a registered, licensed business, and will contact you if it receives complaints. Judge whether your firm might ever be the subject of a BBB inquiry; if not, registration is unnecessary. For many companies, however, it is worth the effort.

Where to learn more

▶ Council of Better Business Bureaus, Inc., National Headquarters, 4200 Wilson Boulevard, Suite 800, Arlington, VA 22203; 703-276-0100. Ask for information on the chapter in your area.

▶ Check your telephone book for a local chapter listing.

▶ Businesses that are members of the BBB can furnish contact information for the local chapter.

▶ If the BBB receives inquiries about your business (not necessarily negative), it may initiate contact with you.

Related topics

Advertising	Chamber of Commerce
Associations	Competition
Business image	**Customer relations**
Business name	Debt collection and
Buying a business	creditworthiness

Direct mail and mailing lists
Direct selling and multilevel
    marketing
Ethics
Franchises
Information sources and research

License
Mail order
Marketing and market research
Networking
Promoting your business
Public relations

BIDDING

What you need to know   Bidding is pricing goods or services to secure business in specific situations. It tells the buyer what he or she must pay for what you provide. Services are sold by the hour or project; products are sold by the unit. Most business is acquired by competitive bidding. The relative worth of your goods or services is decided in the marketplace, where the buyer selects the best value. You might charge more than a competitor but be seen as offering more value. The objective is to profit from the effort, not just to get business. That means your bid must represent competitive value for the buyer and enough profit for you to pay your expenses and grow your business. Although bidding is somewhat intuitive, you must calculate what to charge in order to pay yourself what you could earn working as someone's employee. Add the overhead needed to offset employee benefits and the cost of doing business. Then calculate a profit for the business above wages and overhead. With these expenses established, bid for business and you will learn whether your operation is viable. Government solicitations are usually advertised and involve sealed bids that remain secret until they are opened, evaluated, and made available in a public abstract. Responding to a solicitation carries a legal obligation to perform at the price you bid. Common bidding terminology includes "RFP" which means "request for proposal"—an invitation to bid.

Why you need to know it   Small business start-ups sometimes bid unrealistically low and go broke doing a relatively high volume of business. Succeeding in business is more than activity; it has to culminate in a profit, and that requires translating skilled pricing into intelligent bidding. Walking away from unprofitable projects is more important to survival than keeping busy. Bidding low to break into a market is acceptable, but do it in a calculated way and recognize that you won't be able to compete at that level. In bidding, you craft a miniature business plan that applies to a particular project. It contains (1) plausible estimates of costs and (2) returns that net a profit.

Where to learn more

▶ Barbara Brabec's *Homemade Money* is a good source of pricing techniques for cottage industry manufacturing and services. As obvious as most of it appears, the book does the math for those who need help identifying what to add up to determine costs, and shows how to factor-in a percentage for overhead and profit and decide whether you're making money.

‣ Government agencies offer guidance for bidders. Contact the targeted agency's purchasing department. Points of contact are listed in the *Commerce Business Daily*—the federal government's solicitation publication. Find it at your library or subscribe via the Superintendent of Documents, Government Printing Office, Washington, DC 20402-9371; 202-783-3238. *Commerce Business Daily* can also be accessed by an on-line service called CBD ONLINE.

‣ Advertised bidding is common in state and local governments. Solicitations are published in newspapers or posted publicly.

‣ Herman Holtz's consulting books discuss preparing bids. (See the Bibliography.)

Related topics

Agents and brokers	Government customers
Budgeting	Independent contractor status
Cash flow	Information sources and research
Competition	**Negotiating**
Consulting	**Presentations**
Contracts	Profit
Expense sharing and joint ventures	**Proposals**
Fees and pricing	Reducing expenses
Financial formulas	Regulations
Financial planning	Time management
Foreign markets and languages	

BILLING

What you need to know   Billing is the practice of informing customers of what you have provided them with and what it cost. Bills cover a set period of time and convey the terms of payment. Your bill should be sufficiently detailed to make clear the basis for the charges, including materials or services provided. The cost should be broken down into units of material or time. Your bill typically states that payment is expected by a certain date and informs the recipient of the consequences of not receiving payment on time—additional finance charges, and so on. The basis for billing is a plausible record of your efforts on the client's behalf. Computer software and various manual systems can help you allocate billable effort to individual projects. There are also collection notices that escalate your demands as billing periods pass without payment. Collection agencies will take over if your efforts fail, but the agencies charge a significant percentage of the recovered amount.

Why you need to know it   Collecting money should be no more difficult for a home-based business person than for anyone else, but you may have less time to devote to the task. You are not apt to have a clerk tracking hours, billing regularly, and following up when payments aren't forthcoming. That means you need to establish a billing routine that can be reliably followed with minimal disruption to your professional productivity. The most important approach to billing is having a system and being persistent. You can bill manually with forms and letters or with a computerized system. Just as it does you little good to be very busy at an unprofitable activity, you can't operate successfully without collecting for your services. If you fall behind in billing and collecting, consider the services of a part-time bookkeeper or buy computer software designed to help. An example of the latter is *Timeslips,* a flexible organizational time-billing program that tracks time, generates invoices, rebills overdue accounts, and supports your accounting software.

Where to learn more

▶ Timeslips Corporation, 239 Western Avenue, Essex, MA 01929 (508-768-6100), will supply information on its *Timeslips* computerized billing software.

▶ Invoicing software: *My Advanced Invoices* (MySoftware Company, 415-473-3600) for PCs; *OnAccount* (White Crow Software, 802-658-1270 or 800-424-0310) for Macintosh.

▶ Microrim's *In The Black* accounting package includes an accounts receivable component that is a complete system for billing customers (Appendix F).

▶ The Drawing Board, P. O. Box 2944, Hartford, CT 06104-2944 (800-527-9530), has a selection of printed invoices and collection notices.

▶ EZ Legal Books, 384 South Military Trail, Deerfield Beach, FL 33442 (305-480-8933), sells *Credit Manager,* "A complete credit and collection system of over 150 letters, agreements, notices, memos and other documents to help get you paid every time!"

Related topics

Accounting
Bookkeeping
Budgeting
Business image
Cash flow
Computer software
Contracts
Credit cards
Customer relations
**Debt collection and
   creditworthiness**

Fees and pricing
Legal/illegal business operation
Mail and overnight delivery
   services
Marketing and market research
Money management
Negotiating
Profit
Promoting your business

BONDING

What you need to know   Bonding is a form of insurance. It guarantees that what you promise will be done, within the limits of the bond agreement. A third party known as the surety bondsman looks at your situation, judges the risk, and charges a fee commensurate with the risk to guarantee your performance to your customers or clients. By offering a performance bond, you guarantee that you will do what you agreed to do. If you default, the performance bond will complete the contract or pay damages up to its value. A similar arrangement, known as a surety bond, offers essentially the same guarantee. Another kind of bonding is the fidelity bond, which insures an employer against loss caused by a dishonest employee. As an example, the owner of an armored truck service might require drivers to be bonded, to insure against liability if they drive off with a load of money. A common form of bonding is provided by a bail bondsman, who puts up money to assure a court that a person awaiting trial will appear. In every case, the bond gives assurance to someone that someone else will do what he or she has promised to do or the bondsman will pay the agreed amount. Bonds are generally secured through an insurance agency.

Why you need to know it   As a small business person, you may find yourself engaging in activities that require your customers or clients to trust you with money before you deliver goods or services. If you are an advertiser preparing a circular for printing and distribution, it is reasonable and necessary to collect the fees for the space sold before producing and distributing the circular. As a small business, possibly home-based and with no established reputation, your business development efforts will be easier if you guarantee customers that the money they advance you *will* produce the publication you promise. A formal surety bond is far more convincing than a good-faith promise. Businesses are sometimes required to post bond as part of the business licensing process. An employment agency, for example, may have to arrange for a bond because it collects fees from clients. Bonding is the state's way of protecting clients when businesses fail and fees are held for services not yet delivered. Being bonded is a sign of stability for a small business, a measure of reassurance to clients that the business person can be trusted to deliver.

Where to learn more

▶ The telephone yellow pages list "Bonds—Surety and Fidelity" and similar titles. Judge from the listing which companies offer *business* bonding and ask about your situation.

▶ The sources for business surety bonds are independent insurance agencies or specialized bonding services. If the company you approach doesn't provide the service you need, be persistent and ask a principal in the firm to refer you to an appropriate source for the bonding you seek.

Related topics

Advertising	**Escrow**
Bidding	Expense sharing and joint ventures
Business image	Insurance
Competition	Legal liability
Contracts	**Proposals**
Customer relations	Sales representatives

BOOKKEEPING

What you need to know   Bookkeeping is the procedure by which the financial records of businesses are maintained. The timing of bookkeeping entries is done in one of two ways: (1) cash basis—activities are recorded as they occur, that is, when revenues are actually received or obligations are paid; or (2) accrual basis—accounts are charged or credited during the period in which revenues are *earned* or obligations are *incurred*—not necessarily when they are received or paid. Cash basis, the simpler method, is favored by individuals and small businesses that are unconcerned about temporarily misleading portrayals of earnings resulting from revenues and expenses that are not balanced at the time of each transaction. An end-of-year transaction for a cash-basis operation might show an unrealistic profit resulting from December sales, without revealing the January bills for the merchandise sold and the charges for delivering the goods to customers. Accrual bookkeeping would reflect the pending obligations and counter the appearance of a large profit before the bills arrive. There are two methods of keeping accounts: (1) single entry, which records each transaction once, and (2) double entry, where entries are made twice, once as a debit and again as a credit so accuracy can be tested at any time, using a "trial balance" in which debits and credits are self-canceling. Like cash basis, single-entry bookkeeping is adequate only for individuals and small businesses where a more sophisticated system is unnecessary.

Why you need to know it   Your bookkeeping methods need to be appropriately matched to your business. Everything from tax obligations to credit applications depends on your ability to show your financial activity in a businesslike, authoritative way. Good bookkeeping practices allow you to monitor your business's profitability and make timely responses to changes in the business environment that affect your survival. Starting a small business requires little more than honesty, thoroughness, and timeliness for acceptable bookkeeping, but as the business grows, the advice and assistance of an accounting professional become necessary. The transition from shoebox to professional bookkeeping often coincides with rapid growth in the business. Anticipate this predictable growth stage, and get the help you need. Don't rely entirely on computer software for your bookkeeping; it can be an invaluable aid, but it is no substitute for professional judgment. Coordinate and balance your use of bookkeeping technology and the services of an accountant.

Where to learn more

♦ Articles and books explain the principles of bookkeeping and alert you to the desirability of getting professional help as things get complicated. CPA Bernard Kamoroff's *Small-Time Operator: How to Start Your Own Small Business, Keep Your Books, Pay Your Taxes, and Stay Out of Trouble* (Bell Springs Publishing, Laytonville, CA 95454; 707-984-6746) is recommended.

♦ Stationery, business supply, and discount stores carry simple small business book-keeping systems that include instructions for their use. An example is the Ideal system, a thorough and convenient product customized to different kinds of businesses. Another good series of small business accounting products, available at K Mart, is from Dome Publishing Company, Inc., Warwick, RI 02886. Each Dome publication contains practical, easily understood explanations for the accounting and tax principles involved.

♦ Software reviews in computer magazines and catalogs describe what computer-based bookkeeping systems are available.

♦ Computer software designed to do small business bookkeeping is accompanied by documentation that explains the procedural aspects of bookkeeping. The user manual that accompanies Intuit's *Quicken* and Microrim's *In The Black* does an excellent job of explaining bookkeeping principles.

♦ An accountant's professional advice is in order when judgment must be added to the mechanical tasks of bookkeeping.

♦ IRS Publication 334, "Tax Guide for Small Business" and Publication 583, "Taxpayers Starting a Business" contain practical explanations of basic bookkeeping requirements. They are available at IRS offices or by calling 800-829-FORM.

Related topics

Accountant	Financial planning
Accounting	Forms
Billing	Loans, credit, and venture capital
Budgeting	**Money management**
Cash flow	**Records**
Checking accounts	Regulations
Computer software	Separating business and personal
Debt collection and creditworthiness	Tax checklist

BUDGETING

What you need to know   Your business plan includes a budget, which is a formal financial projection that balances revenues and expenditures over a defined period of time, usually one year. The purpose of budgeting is to impose planning, order, and discipline on your spending. A budget sets priorities, placing essential expenditures ahead of luxuries that might otherwise absorb revenues needed to keep the business sound. A budget lists anticipated expenses and income and provides a road map for negotiating the planning period financially. Cash flow problems become apparent in a well-drawn budget, and reserves or lines of credit can be arranged to bridge the gaps. The terms balanced, surplus and deficit, apply to the relative status of revenue and expenditures. Balanced budgets have enough revenues to cover expenses, surplus budgets have excess revenue and are considered balanced, and deficit budgets denote spending that is greater than income.

Why you need to know it   You need a budget to plan your business and convince others of its viability. Each element of your budget has to be reasonable. A plausible budget gives to those with whom you interact financially the grounds for believing that you will meet your obligations. Your budget demonstrates that you know what obligations you face and you plan to raise the revenues necessary to meet them. It is the game plan for your future business activities and the instrument for determining, before you implement your plans, whether your efforts will likely result in a profit or a loss.

Where to learn more

▶ A small business textbook will explain the basics of budgeting.

▶ Many small business accounting or bookkeeping software packages contain budgeting features and manuals that explain them. An example is Palo Alto Software's *Business Budgeting Toolkit,* which lets you develop budgets, track milestone dates, and see actual-to-budget variances. Price: about $75; call 800-800-2222. Microrim's comprehensive *In The Black* has a complete budgeting component.

▶ Stationery, business supply, and discount stores sell bookkeeping and budgeting systems that include instructions.

▶ The Small Business Administration's *Directory of Business Development Publications* is available from: SBA Publications, P. O. Box 1000, Fort Worth, TX 76119. The Washington (DC) number is 202-653-7794.

Related topics

Accountant	Investing
Accounting	Loans, credit, and venture capital
Bookkeeping	**Managing growth**
Business basics	**Money management**
Business plan	Payroll
Cash flow	Profit
Computer software	**Projections**
Debt collection and	Separating business and personal
creditworthiness	Tax checklist
Financial planning	Undercapitalization

BULLETIN BOARD SYSTEM (BBS)

What you need to know   Bulletin board systems are electronic information exchanges on which subscribers post and respond to messages. There are about 40,000 public and over 100,000 private bulletin boards that focus on everything from home-based business operators to special-interest medical and economic groups. Some bulletin boards are run by government agencies such as the Small Business Administration (SBA); others are add-ons to commercial networks like CompuServe. Each BBS has a "sysop" (system operator) who runs the system. The sysop provides the computer database and communications products that make the system available. The sysop sets standards, establishes and collects fees, and maintains discipline on the system—determining what users are allowed to do and say, prohibiting illegal software exchanges, and so on. Users have their own unique electronic "addresses" on the service so others can respond directly to them. BBSs are a popular source of legitimate free or low-cost user-supported software known as shareware or freeware. A hazard of downloading applications from BBSs is computer viruses, but the problem can be controlled by computer programs that screen for them. In addition to being an information source, like 900 telephone number services, BBSs represent a home business opportunity for those who can define an information service that people will pay to use. It is a crowded market, but one to consider if you have the right idea and want to add another profit center to your business.

Why you need to know it   The BBSs are vital communications links for many home business people. You can use them for the companionship of interacting with others in your circumstances, thereby breaking the isolation of working alone, or you can approach them as strictly a means to do business—networking with people you can profit from knowing, and getting answers from those who can help you run your business and meet the needs of your clients. Some BBSs amount to a form of advertising: you can reach a target audience with your commercial or professional message. Publishers use BBSs to let authors interact with their readers. Interacting on a BBS is like having a written conversation on a computer screen. An added advantage is the ability to use either interactive or time-delayed postings that can be acted on by either party at his or her convenience.

Where to learn more

- On-line services like CompuServe, GEnie, Prodigy, American Online, and the like have lists of BBSs they support.

- Computer magazines and local users' groups are good sources of information on BBSs.

- Government agencies' information numbers can guide you to specialized BBSs they support. You can find the agency numbers in Matthew Lasko's *Information USA* or in Washington (DC) telephone books, which are available in many libraries. An example is SBA Online, a free 24-hour-a-day source of small business information that you can reach at 800-859-4636 (2400 bps) or 800-697-4636 (9600 bps). Set your parameters to N (no parity), eight data bits, and one stop bit.

- To set up a BBS of your own, read John Hedtke's *Using Computer Bulletin Boards* (New York: MIS Press; 800-628-9658 or 212-886-9210) or *Boardwatch* magazine, 7586 West Jewell Avenue, Suite 200, Lakewood, CO 80232; 800-933-6038 or 307-973-6068.

Related topics

Advertising

Associations

Bartering

Business address and location

Business ideas

Competition

Computer equipment

Computer on-line services

Computer software

Computer use

Customer relations

Information sources and research

Mail order

Marketing and market research

Merchandise buying services

Networking

Newsletters

Promoting your business

Psychological factors

BUSINESS ADDRESS AND LOCATION

What you need to know   Your business address represents you to the world. As a small or home-based business person, consider the various messages that address can send. When you want privacy and a tangible business address is unimportant, a post office box is an option, but it may give an impression that you have a fly-by-night operation. Whether a post office box will meet your needs depends on the kind of business you operate, how well-established you are, and your alternatives. Many well-known companies use a post office box in conjunction with a conventional street address, and so can you. In some areas, the street address can be left general enough (no house number) to protect your privacy, when used with a box number for receiving mail. Another option is to subscribe to a commercial mailbox service that lets you use a sophisticated sounding business address, if that is important and your clients wouldn't know the difference. A step up from a service is a time-share office where you pay modest rent and get in return the central services of a bona fide business address shared by a number of part-time occupants. A time-honored technique is to substitute "Suite" for "Apartment" and harmlessly add a business tone to your home business. The amount of walk-in traffic your business generates will be a factor, as will zoning laws where your office is located. It is increasingly common for a business to have an electronic address so clients and customers can communicate via computer on-line services.

Why you need to know it   You need to strike a practical balance between image and function as you craft your business address. If you are home-based or have an office in a marginal business location, and you do not receive clients at that address, it makes sense to use the techniques described above to make the most of your business card, letterhead, and advertising address. On the other hand, the practical reasons for a tangible street address range from shipping and receiving (UPS, Federal Express, and similar carriers will deliver only to a street address) to letting new business find you. Be aware that some franchises require you to keep regular business hours in a conventional business setting.

Where to learn more

▶ Verify the address requirements of your suppliers and regular delivery services, and be sure to satisfy them.

▶ Check your zoning requirements to avoid raising the profile on a prohibited use by advertising it.

▶ If you plan to use a nonstandard address, consult your local postmaster to be sure your address is satisfactory—*before* having printing done.

▶ Look at the samples in business printing catalogs for ideas on effective business address formats.

Related topics

Advertising	Legal/illegal business operation
Bulletin Board System (BBS)	License
Business cards	**Mail and overnight delivery**
Business image	**services**
Business use of home	Promoting your business
Buying a business	Psychological factors
Checking accounts	Separating business and personal
Computer on-line services	Telecommuting
Direct mail and mailing lists	Time-share offices
Franchises	Vacation, work styles, and schedules
Homeowners' associations	**Zoning**

BUSINESS ASSOCIATES

What you need to know   Small businesses rarely operate well in isolation. You need to form relationships with people who become your business associates—people with whom you exchange professional information, leads, and advice. Involve them as you grow your business, and reach beyond the essential minimums that include your attorney and accountant. Most business associates have different talents and client bases and will encounter opportunities that don't suit them. For these opportunities, they make referrals within their circle of acquaintances. The cross-fertilization helps everyone to get assignments and make new contacts. Association with other professionals who exchange referrals enhances the professional image and elevates the status of all the members of the group.

Why you need to know it   It can be a mistake to operate your home-based business as a one-person entity. Entrepreneurs generally come from backgrounds where they have worked in teams, and they rely on the interplay more than they may realize. Stimulating interaction doesn't have to be lost in operating your own small company. Business associates sustain the link between your individual endeavors and the broader business community. By affiliating, business associates fill in the blanks created by concentrating on their individual specialties. Well-chosen associates enable sole practitioners to function as multifaceted providers capable of covering more than a single aspect of their business. In addition to offering more competitive services, business associates benefit from being part of a new business marketing network of loosely coordinated colleagues who, together, reach a broader market than any of them could contact if operating alone. The result is more business for everyone.

Where to learn more

▶ Attend professional meetings, and network with colleagues.

▶ Keep lists of potential associates whose work you encounter on assignments. Contact them, compliment them on their work, and suggest an informal business associate relationship that might help you both in the future.

▶ Ask clients who they use for certain kinds of assignments that are complementary to your own work. If necessary, mention that you are building noncompeting business relationships with people who have those capabilities.

Related topics

Accountant
Agents and brokers
Attorney
Banking services
Bulletin Board System (BBS)
Chamber of Commerce
Competition
Conferences, seminars, shows,
   and workshops

Consulting
Continuing education
Expense sharing and joint
   ventures
Networking
Promoting your business
Sales representatives

BUSINESS BASICS

What you need to know   Being in business requires a different perspective than working as an employee in someone else's organization. You have to have an immediate and ongoing concern with profit and loss, sales, and government regulations. Three business basics you cannot ignore are: (1) profitability—an owner has to monitor business performance and make the necessary adjustments to ensure that revenues exceed expenditures; (2) sales—an owner engages in a continuous process of developing new business in order to move enough goods or services to generate profitable levels of income; and (3) regulations—government agencies impose taxation and operating rules that a business owner must satisfy in order to remain in business. The specific aspects of these broad categories require planning and management. The periodic services of an accountant and an attorney are needed to keep most small businesses on track. Small business owners need a second-nature awareness of these business basics, to provide sensitive oversight to the business's survival and growth while concentrating primarily on their specialty.

Why you need to know it   Being the profit center of a company *and* its manager demands a unique balance of specialized professional and business management performance. Small business people risk placing undue emphasis on either side of this equation. They focus on the mechanics of day-to-day operations and ignore the specialty that is the heart of their business, or they get lost in their "art" and don't mind the store. Small business success demands attention to the product for or service that is the profit center, while not losing sight of the business basics that let the company survive.

Where to learn more

▶ Take a small business course through the adult education division of your school system or at a community college.

▶ Small Business Administration (SBA) publications offer practical basic business checklists and information.

▶ Service Corps of Retired Executives (SCORE) consultants are excellent sources of review and assistance on business basics.

▶ Get an applied small business management book from a library or bookstore, and review the basics.

▶ Work part-time in the kind of business you plan to operate, before you take your independent plunge. Observe the tricks of the trade and the headaches you never imagined existed for the owner.

Related topics

Accountant
Advertising
Attorney
Banking services
Bookkeeping
Budgeting
Business organization
Business plan
Business use of home
Cash flow
Computer equipment
Computer software
Computer use
Contracts

Employees
Insurance
License
Loans, credit, and venture capital
Marketing and market research
Money management
Profit
Start-up
Tax checklist
Telephone equipment
Telephone services
Telephone use
Undercapitalization

BUSINESS CARDS

What you need to know   Your business card is your introduction to clients and associates alike. Because it makes a lasting impression, your card needs to fit your image. A graphic designer or office decorator will have more license for expression on a business card than an attorney will. Your task is to determine which image sells best in your particular circumstances. Is your service best promoted by the black-and-white formality of a law firm business card, the colorful creativity of a design specialist, or something in between? You have to be comfortable with the image the card creates, and so do your clients and associates. When in doubt, go with the standard of your industry. What style card is used by successful people you respect in the business? Experiment. The advent of the word processor and small batch printing gives you great flexibility. Walk through the business district of most cities and you will see signs in the windows of copy shops and small printers offering economic overnight delivery of small quantities of business cards. Specialized paper products let you produce your own business cards on your office printer at little expense. It is increasingly common to include an electronic address on business cards so clients and customers can reach you via the Internet or other on-line services. Foreign language business cards are useful if you are doing business internationally. They are often printed in English on one side and in a second language on the reverse.

Why you need to know it   As you pass through your business day, you will meet a number of people who are clients, potential clients, or people who might refer them. You need to give them an easy way to remember who you are and how to reach you. After the pleasantries are over and you've gone your separate ways, your business card lingers as a reminder of someone they've met. People like to help. They enhance their own status by making recommendations and serving as a source of information and connections. Your business card is the medium of exchange in this valuable process.

Where to learn more

▶ Check the business printers in your neighborhood. Most offer prompt, inexpensive business card service.

▶ Mail-order business supply houses like The Drawing Board, P. O. Box 2944, Hartford, CT 06104-2944 (800-527-9530), offer a wide selection of business cards. Their catalogs let you compare design options.

▶ Vending-machine printers for business cards and address labels can be found in many locations. An example is CardXpress, based in Edison, NJ (908-225-1151).

▶ For specialized paper products catalogs that show business card stock for your laser printer, contact: Paper Direct, Lyndhurst, NJ (800-A-PAPERS), or Power Up!, San Mateo, CA (800-851-2917).

▶ *Cards Now* of Madison, WI (800-233-9767), offers IBM-compatible business card software and paper stock for about $40.

Related topics

Advertising
Bulletin Board System (BBS)
Business address and location
Business image

Business name
Camera-ready copy
Conferences, seminars, shows,
    and workshops

Customer relations
Desktop publishing
Marketing and market research
Paper
Printing

Promoting your business
Separating business and personal
Start-up
Zoning

BUSINESS IDEAS

What you need to know   Choose your business by determining a genuine demand for something you do well. Then thoroughly test your idea. If possible, begin without making a total commitment—operate part-time before you burden your start-up with the demands of making your living from it. Even well-conceived ideas stand a better chance of becoming successful businesses if they can be established without having to support the owner immediately. If you examine a franchise or advertised business opportunity, start with a healthy dose of skepticism. Franchising is a regulated industry and many of the opportunities are worthy of your investment, but evaluate them thoroughly. Ask for negative references. Talk with franchise failures as well as successes. If the franchisor won't provide contacts, ask active franchise holders to put you in touch with people they knew who didn't make it. Advertised business opportunities call for even more scrutiny. Determine that they aren't avoiding the franchise label just to avoid the regulations that go with it. Don't pay for business ideas you can initiate on your own with readily available computer equipment and software, self-help books, and a few consulting fees paid to successful people who are already in the business. Beware of oversold ideas like computer-based scholarship information opportunities. Perform commonsense tests in your local market to see whether there is actually demand for scholarship searches, cost reduction consultants, lease examination services, or other ads that promise plentiful business. That information isn't hard to find *before* you invest. Consider working for the kind of business you are thinking of starting. Even a part-time experience can tell you a lot about the realities of the business before you make the career and financial commitment. None of these cautionary notes is intended to discourage prudent risk taking, but be rational in the selection of your business and in how you make the transition from salaried or dependably commissioned employee to self-employed entrepreneur.

Why you need to know it   Starting a small business enterprise can be an emotional experience full of potential for both good and bad things to happen. Don't commit to the selection of a business idea naively. Otherwise sophisticated professionals who have been successful employees can do dumb things when they start their own businesses. Be positive, persist, and find a way to implement what you determine to be a good idea, but give yourself the luxury of adequate, realistic preparations that raise your chances of success. Small business ideas lend themselves to part-time testing—an excellent way to validate your business idea while still in an environment where lessons can be learned and necessary adjustments can be made without disrupting your established life-style.

Where to learn more

▶ Libraries, bookstores, and magazines are full of small business ideas. Survey them for ideas that interest you and are within your financial and professional capabilities.

▶ Specialized magazines like *Home Office Computing* and *Entrepreneur* run regular features on people who are operating successful small businesses. Subscribe and follow the trends; look at past issues.

▶ Business plans are available for many kinds of businesses for less than $100. One source is Entrepreneur, 2392 Morse Avenue, Irvine, CA 92714; 800-421-2300. This purchase is an inexpensive way to take a relatively objective look at a business idea.

▶ Attend a franchise fair in a major city. Check with the Chamber of Commerce, major hotel convention centers, or the International Franchise Association, 1350 New York Avenue, NW, Suite 900, Washington, DC 20005; 202-628-8000.

▶ My earlier book, *Starting and Operating a Home-Based Business*, advises on selecting and initiating a small business idea. (See the Bibliography.)

Related topics

Agents and brokers
Business image
Business plan
Business use of car
Business use of home
Computer equipment
Computer software
Computer use
Conferences, seminars, shows, and workshops
Consulting

Continuing education
Copyright, patent, trademark, and service mark
Franchises
Information sources
Networking
Telephone equipment
Telephone services
Time-share offices
Women's programs
Zoning

BUSINESS IMAGE

What you need to know   Say the name of a common acquaintance, and a colleague visualizes someone; do the same with a business, and the reaction is the same. Your business needs an image—a favorable image. Your first task as a small business is to establish an image by doing business in an ever-broadening circle of clients. The quality of that image will be tempered by how you present your business—over the phone, on your business card, in your correspondence and advertising, among professional associates, through customer relations, and in the community. You and your small business are inseparable; the image of one colors the other. Aside from the obvious external images conveyed by the material aspects of your business, cultivate the subjective ones: trust, reliability, honesty, fairness, caring, dedication, professionalism. All of these qualities converge with your basic competency to shape the image of your business.

Why you need to know it   A small business, particularly one operating from a residence, must be image-conscious. A home-based business has a dual image to maintain: (1) a professional image that says you are a serious business person accessible to your customers; and (2) a good neighbor image that ensures no disruption of the predominant nonbusiness life-style of the residential area. Balancing the two is entirely possible, but it takes awareness and effort. A home-based business has to rely on its outreach activities to establish a business image. You must be available to clients in their places of business or perhaps in a time-share office or conference facility, if your business justifies it, rather than in your home. There are many exceptions. It is possible for certain kinds of businesses to have a distinctive home office in an impressive residential setting that is more inviting than a corner suite on the top floor of a commercial building. If your image includes private, discreet meetings held outside the commercial mainstream, the right home office setting could be image-enhancing. For many other home-based businesses that have little or no client contact in the office, the question is moot.

Where to learn more

▶ Because business image is an extension of the owner, be yourself but seek professional help in those areas where you might need assistance—design and layout for your business card, stationery, publications, and advertising; a professional voice for your answering machine or voice mail; designer assistance with decorating your home office. Selectively, get the help you need.

▶ Look to your competition and your former place of employment, if you are continuing in your same line of work. The image you convey may be different but must be on a par with what your clients expect in commercial settings.

▶ If periodic use of commercial space is essential (you occasionally hold meetings or need space for a presentation), check with a commercial real estate broker about time-share space. Another possibility is use of a meeting room at your bank. Private clubs are sometimes available, as are meeting rooms in hotels and other commercial buildings.

Related topics

Advertising

**Answering machines and
  voice mail**

Associations

Bonding

Bulletin Board System (BBS)

Business address and location

Business associates

Business cards

Business name

Business use of home
Camera-ready copy
Copiers
Customer relations
Desktop publishing
Direct mail and mailing lists
Direct selling and multilevel
  marketing
Employees
Environmental considerations
Equipment and furniture
Ethics
Fax

Fees and pricing
Franchises
Marketing and market research
Media relations
Newsletters
Noise
Office planning and decorating
Paper
Printing
Promoting your business
Public relations
Separating business and personal
Women's programs

BUSINESS INCUBATOR

What you need to know   Business incubators are organizations formed to cultivate the establishment of new businesses. Nationally, about 500 of them belong to the National Business Incubator Association; others operate with no such affiliation. Of those in the NBIA, 14 percent are entrepreneurial themselves and operate for profit, and 10 percent are associated with universities, many of them with a high-technology orientation. The rest are hybrids, part public/part private, with funding and support coming from the business community and private sector. Some of the incubators have a social mission, like helping the poor start a small business in an inner city, but most are mainstream, selective in choosing their clients, and quite serious about helping people succeed in business. Assistance is given as needed with everything from the business plan and financing to ongoing consultation about managing and growing the business. Some businesses rent space from the incubator during their start-up phase and receive assistance on-site; others are helped on an off-site basis. A number of computer-related success stories have come from the incubator industry. One incubator specializes in business spin-offs from the National Institutes of Health. Incubators often can provide clients access to high-technology equipment in industry and universities. Some incubator operators are experts in linking entrepreneurs with venture capital. Many deal broadly with traditional small business start-ups. Funding varies for business incubators; public and industry grants combine with rent and fees from the participants. Some for-profit incubators may take a financial position in their participating companies. Length of stay in the incubators varies from months to years, depending on the nature of the business and its progress.

Why you need to know it   If you are at the early stages of forming your business, you should determine whether an incubator is operating in your part of the country. Does it serve your kind of enterprise or represent a more narrow specialty? If you are near an incubator that matches your interests, you may have an excellent opportunity to gain an instant support system that includes vital links to venture capital and to technical, management, and marketing assistance. Another angle of the business incubator concept is the entrepreneurial one. Depending on your situation and background, you might find it lucrative to organize an incubator. It could be an entirely commercial venture in which you rent space and sell advice and services to business start-ups, or a brokered arrangement in which you are paid to manage a combination of business, university, and government interests.

Where to learn more

▶ National Business Incubation Association, One President Street, Athens, OH 45701; 614-593-4331. This association represents the interests of the incubator industry at centers that help small businesses begin and survive the start-up phase. Publications and advice are available, and a national meeting is held annually.

▶ Ask members of your local economic development council or Chamber of Commerce whether they are aware of small business support organizations in your area. These organizations will not necessarily bear the business incubator name.

Related topics

Accounting
Advertising
Associations
Attitude
Bookkeeping
Business address and location
Business associates
Business basics
Business organization
Business plan
Cash flow
Continuing education
Customer relations
Evaluating your business

Expense sharing and joint ventures
Financial planning
Franchises
Getting organized and managing information
License
Marketing and market research
Money management
Motivation
Overhead expenses
Reducing expenses
Start-up
Zoning

BUSINESS NAME

What you need to know   You have two choices in naming your business: (1) use your own full name, or (2) use any other name and file a fictitious name statement to make your association with the business name a matter of official record. Professional businesses sometimes lend themselves to the use of their owner's full name; most others do not. Having your first or last name as part of the company name (Smith Computer Consultants, Inc.) won't do it. Each city, county, or municipality has a business license agency, and it will assist you in registering your business name for a modest fee. Sometimes you see notices with the term DBA—doing business as. The object of the registration requirement is to identify the responsible business owner and collect a small tax.

Other aspects of your business name relate to its business image and advertising value. You want your name to be exclusively yours and not be confused with others. You can do that by reviewing the telephone book—and, if necessary, the local tax records—for similar listings. Local conflicts would be caught when you register the name. State conflicts might be caught at the time you incorporate. It is possible to protect your business name with a trademark or service mark if you are doing business in interstate commerce or internationally. The advertising value of your business name consists of making it obvious what you do for your clients or customers. Excessively cute names are a bad idea for most serious businesses. Your business name should command respect in the business community as well as among your clients.

Why you need to know it   Your business has to be legally established, and part of the process is registering its name, unless it is the same as your own. There is potential commercial value in the name of your business when you become successful. If your enterprise is one that someone else could run successfully, it might be sold as a going concern—including the name. Should that happen, you might wish you had given your business a name other than your own. Clarity of business purpose is necessary to attract customers—a business name must pass this test. The image value of a well-chosen business name can be substantial for a home-based business. Stay with traditional business nomenclature protocols, and avoid standing out as a uniquely amateur operation.

Where to learn more

▶ Look in the local government section of your telephone book for the business license agency. It will be able to direct you through the entire cycle of name registration and any other necessary steps.

Related topics

Advertising	Customer relations
Business address and location	Franchises
Business cards	License
Business image	Marketing and market research
Business organization	**Promoting your business**
Buying a business	Public relations
Copyright, patent, trademark, and service mark	Separating business and personal
	Zoning

BUSINESS ORGANIZATION

What you need to know   There are three ways to organize a business: (1) sole proprietorship, (2) partnership, and (3) corporation. They are listed in the order of their complexity, from the simplest to the most involved. (1) As a sole proprietor, you have the least costly start-up, the greatest freedom from regulation, direct control, a minimal capital requirement, the tax advantages of business ownership, and the right to keep all the profits. On the negative side, you have unlimited personal liability for the debts of the business (which ends with your death) and a difficult time raising capital or getting long-term financing. (2) A partnership has most of the characteristics of the sole proprietorship, although it is a little more complex to establish and operate. Partnerships have a broader management base than sole proprietorships and are more flexible than corporations; they can raise capital by adding limited partners. Disadvantages include unlimited liability, the instability of changing partners, shared control, the inability to issue stock, and the difficulty of selling one's share of ownership. A single partner can obligate all partners, and partners are not eligible for pension and other tax benefits of corporations. (3) A properly formed and operated corporation can limit your liability, raise capital more easily, allow for the efficient transfer of ownership, and exist indefinitely as an independent legal entity that survives individual owners. Centralized management, the ability to enter into contracts and agreements, and retirement and other tax benefits are additional advantages. On the other hand, corporations can be more costly to form, are taxed separately, are subject to more regulations and record-keeping requirements, and can require separate permissions when operating across state lines. A hybrid form of the corporation, the Subchapter S corporation, eliminates the double-taxation factor and otherwise personalizes and simplifies incorporation. A new form of liability protection organization, the limited-liability company (LLC), is growing in popularity because of its relative simplicity.

Why you need to know it   Unless you plan to incorporate for the sake of calling your business Jones Advertising, Inc., do not use a self-incorporation book or service. A properly formed and operated corporation is essential if you hope to benefit from the tax and liability advantages of incorporation. You need the ongoing advice of an attorney and accountant. Most small businesses can operate quite effectively as sole proprietorships or partnerships without the cost and time-consuming overhead of incorporation. The liability benefit is exaggerated for most small business owners, who have to secure all obligations personally regardless of the legal form of their business. In the event of a suit, you would be sued personally anyway. When your business matures, reaches substantial worth, or is ready to be sold or left to survivors, it may be worth incorporating. Get the advice of professionals. Your particular circumstances may warrant incorporation now.

Where to learn more

▶ The IRS has useful information on the forms of business organization. Request copies of Publication 334, "Tax Guide for Small Business," or Publication 583, "Taxpayers Starting a Business," from the number listed in your local telephone book or in Appendix B.

▶ Books and services for forming your own corporation are advertised in small business magazines—as is computer software on the subject. Ted Nicholas's *How to Form Your Own Corporation without a Lawyer for Under $50* is a legendary book in the field. Others include Michael Diamond and Julie Williams's *How to Incorporate,* and Judith H. McQuown's popular *Inc. Yourself.*

▶ Consult your accountant and attorney before making any serious effort to incorporate.

Related topics

Accountant	**Business plan**
Advertising	Getting organized and managing
Attitude	information
Attorney	**Legal liability**
Bankruptcy	License
Bookkeeping	**Regulations**
Business cards	Separating business and personal
Business image	**Tax checklist**
Business name	

BUSINESS PLAN

What you need to know   A business plan is necessary for you to test your idea on paper and work out obvious flaws before they cost you money. It is a road map for conceiving and operating your company, and it is a sales tool for convincing others to back your venture. A well-prepared business plan is dynamic. It changes as your venture unfolds; at the same time, it provides a baseline from which to chart your direction. The business plan addresses the legal form of organization, gives a general profile of the company, tells about its products or services, describes the projected marketing, and indicates how the business will be organized, managed, capitalized, and financially structured. It includes a financial plan that projects revenues and expenses. Appendixes might include resumes of the principals, information on competitors, sales projections, and expected profitability.

Why you need to know it   The sophistication of your business plan will vary widely with the type of venture you are launching. If you plan a closely held business that doesn't involve outside financing or commitments from others, your plan can be less involved than one prepared for venture capitalists. Even a small, personal business deserves careful planning, however, and the traditional planning process is an excellent way to make the process thorough and objective. You should know where you expect to be at different stages of your business's development, regardless of its size and complexity. Business planning is a worthwhile exercise: adjustments and realizations achieved at the planning stage are less costly than those discovered operationally. A good business plan is also an invaluable stepping stone for the next stage of growing your business, often encountered when you are too busy to give it the calm consideration it deserves.

Where to learn more

▶ *Home Office Computing* magazine sells a 90-minute business planning video for about $20. Call 800-325-6149.

▶ Palo Alto Software sells a *Business Plan Toolkit* that takes you through the steps of creating a business plan on your personal computer. Another choice is Jian's *BizPlanBuilder*. Each costs about $75, and they are available in both Macintosh and PC versions. Spinnaker's *PFS: Business Plan* is a similar product. These and others are available from local software resellers or can be ordered from PC or MacConnection. (See Appendix C.)

▶ Libraries and bookstores have numerous business plan books. A good one is Eric Siegel et al., *The Ernst & Young Business Plan Guide.* (See the Bibliography.)

▶ Robert Gehorsam's "Start-Up Diary," in the September 1993 issue of *Home Office Computing* magazine, is an excellent, realistic account of what you can expect to encounter in starting a serious business. Check your library or contact: Reprint Manager, *Home Office Computing*, 730 Broadway, New York, NY 10003; 212-505-3580.

Related topics

Accountant	Expense sharing and joint ventures
Attorney	**Financial planning**
Budgeting	Franchises
Business name	Goal setting
Business organization	License
Cash flow	**Loans, credit, and venture capital**
Competition	**Marketing and market research**
Copyright, patent, trademark, and service mark	Overhead expenses
	Profit
Diversification	**Projections**
Employees	Promoting your business
Environmental considerations	Start-up
Equipment and furniture	Tax checklist
Evaluating your business	

BUSINESS TRAVEL

What you need to know   Claiming the cost of business travel as an expense that is deductible before taxes is of the utmost importance. The first consideration in determining the treatment of business travel for tax purposes is whether the travel is performed as an employee. Depending on the form of organization, a business person can be considered an employee of his or her own company. If you incur business expenses as an individual and are reimbursed by your company or employer, you pass the business expenses to the company and deal with any shortfall under unreimbursed employee business expenses on your personal Schedule A (Form 1040). If you are a sole proprietor, your travel costs get resolved directly as expenses to the business. Traveling away from home, you can deduct ordinary and necessary expenses for transportation, baggage and shipping, car, lodging, meals, cleaning, telephone, tips, and other items that are logically a part of doing business. You can't deduct the costs of a general search for, or preliminary investigation of, a new business. If a trip includes pleasure and business expenses, they must be separated and prorated. Deductible local business travel expenses cannot include commuting, but the cost of visiting clients is allowed. Ordinary and necessary business entertainment expenses are 50 percent deductible. You must have records to verify all business expenses. The rules are complex. You need to review them in the IRS publications on the subject, discuss them with your accountant, and adopt a record-keeping strategy that would satisfy an IRS auditor.

Why you need to know it   In addition to the obvious benefits of doing business with clients away from home, business travel is an opportunity to network and to stimulate new ideas. It is also tiring and detracts from the day-to-day management of your enterprise. Second only to the actual business purpose, however, travel is an expense that you want to charge off before paying taxes. Doing so is a complicated procedure that requires awareness. As a small business person, you have to develop a mentality that constantly recognizes legitimate opportunities for savings by fully claiming allowable expenses. Business travel is an area ripe with opportunities to save—and to get into trouble.

Where to learn more

▶ Request copies of IRS Publication 334, "Tax Guide for Small Business," and Publication 463, "Travel, Entertainment, and Gift Expenses," from the IRS 800 number listed in your local telephone book, or call 800-829-FORM.

▶ Keep current by reading small business publications and consulting with your accountant.

Related topics

Accounting
Bookkeeping
Business image
Business use of car
Computer on-line services
Conferences, seminars, shows,
    and workshops
Ethics
Expense sharing and joint
    ventures

Foreign markets and languages
Insurance
Marketing and market research
Personnel policies
Promoting your business
Records
Reducing expenses
Separating business and personal
Tax checklist
Vacation, work styles, and schedules

BUSINESS USE OF CAR

What you need to know   If you use your car in the course of doing business, the expenses are deductible. This is as true for a home-based business person as anyone else, as long as the use is legitimate and you can prove it. The IRS watches vehicle business expenses closely, but does not actually require that you record each trip as it is taken. Its recommendation is that such records be compiled weekly. You can also reconstruct proof of business use by linking checks, receipts, appointment logs, and similar records to mileage claimed, but the IRS is more skeptical of such claims. Something approaching a log of actual use is your best bet. You can claim 28 cents a mile (always verify the current rate) for all justifiable business mileage, or deduct the actual cost of owning and operating the vehicle. Actual expenses might include depreciation, garage rent, gas, insurance, lease fees, licenses, oil, parking fees, rental fees, repairs, and tolls. Whether you claim standard mileage or actual expenses, you have to prorate business and personal use, and have the records to substantiate it. Buying and leasing are now considered a wash for tax purposes. You have the burden of proving the expenses and use in either situation. There are all kinds of fine points that you must examine in the IRS publications or with your accountant. If you begin using the mileage basis, you must be careful about switching to actual expenses. If you depreciate the vehicle, you have to account for the salvage value when you sell it. There is a luxury car limit on how much you can deduct, and it varies by year of purchase. (It isn't very high, so check it out unless you are dealing with a real economy car.) Vehicles are eligible for a deduction (up to $10,000) in the year of purchase, under Internal Revenue Code Section 179. You may prefer to take the deduction all at once if you have sufficient income to balance it. These are matters to consider with the help of your accountant.

Why you need to know it   The IRS is very alert to the possible abuse of claims for the business use of vehicles. However, you should not join the legions of small business owners who are so intimidated by the threat of IRS scrutiny that they fail to claim deductions to which they are legitimately entitled. Contrary to sensational accounts, it is not necessary to jot down every detail of vehicle business use as it occurs. It is even prudent to make a reasonable claim for car expenses related to your business and keep no special records. If what you claim is modest enough to fit the pattern of business you are obviously doing, you will have no trouble justifying it. Use common sense: figure a round trip to the post office five or six days a week, and several trips weekly to places you obviously have to go in order to conduct your business. Throw in longer trips matched to readily verifiable out-of-town business meetings, and you have the makings of a fair claim for business use of your car with little of the record-keeping hassle.

Where to learn more

▶ Request copies of IRS Publication 334, "Tax Guide for Small Business," and Publication 917, "Business Use of a Car," from the IRS number listed in your local telephone book or call 800-829-FORM.

▶ Discuss your individual situation with your accountant.

Related topics

Accountant

Advertising

Attorney

Budgeting

Business image

Insurance

Leasing

Legal/illegal business operation

Promoting your business

Records

Separating business and personal

Tax checklist

BUSINESS USE OF HOME

What you need to know   According to the IRS, if you use part of your home exclusively and regularly as the principal place of business for your trade or business or as a place where you meet or deal with customers in your business, you can deduct the expenses for that part of your home. Also, you may be allowed to deduct expenses for use of part of your home as a day-care facility or as a place to store inventory you sell in your business, even if that part of your home is sometimes used for personal purposes (IRS Publication 334, p. 78). The IRS is distinctly unfriendly to the home-based business person. In a recent case, the Supreme Court ruled, in January 1993, that necessary and exclusive use of the home is not enough to constitute principal, and if you do more work outside the home than in, you are not entitled to a home office deduction. If you spend most of your business time in a home office or operate as a sole proprietor filing Schedule C (Form 1040), you can deduct the direct expenses of painting or repairing the home office and such indirect expenses as real estate taxes, deductible mortgage interest, casualty losses, rent, utilities and services, insurance, repairs, security systems, and depreciation. In each case, everything is prorated to reflect the part of your home used for business. Use IRS Publication 587, Form 8829, and the accompanying worksheet to calculate your home office business expenses, and keep the necessary records to back them up. In the unlikely event of an audit, you have to demonstrate the use you claim. Remember that the IRS has recapture rules, and the business use of your home is excluded from the private use benefits of rollover on resale and after-age-55 sale shelters. Before taking the home office deduction, verify with your accountant that it is wise in your circumstances.

Why you need to know it   About four million people take the home office deduction. The many other millions entitled to it do not take it because they fear an IRS audit. If you actually run a serious business enterprise from your home, there is no reason not to claim the deduction. The exclusive use of the corner of your den may not be worth the trouble, but a full room or more, clearly devoted to the pursuit of profit, is. Know the rules and make a reasonable effort to comply, then go about your business and make a realistic claim on your tax return. With the number of home-based businesses mushrooming and the level of their sophistication keeping pace, the IRS is finding it less profitable to examine them with the expectation of finding fraud behind every claim.

Where to learn more

▶ Request copies of IRS Publication 334, "Tax Guide for Small Business," and Publication 587, "Business Use of Your Home," (Appendix E) from the IRS number listed in your local telephone book or call 800-829-FORM.

▶ Bookstores and libraries have books on the tax consequences of home office use, but be cautious of their currency in this fast-changing field. One to consider is Thomas Vickman's *Home Office Tax Deductions* (800-554-4379).

▶ Monitor the changing requirements for the deduction with the assistance of your accountant.

Related topics

Accountant	Legal/illegal business operation
Advertising	License
Business address and location	Promoting your business
Business cards	Psychological factors
Business image	Records
Computer equipment	Regulations
Computer on-line services	Separating business and personal
Computer software	**Tax checklist**
Computer use	Telecommuting
Family	Telephone equipment
Franchises	Telephone services
Insurance	**Zoning**

BUYING A BUSINESS

What you need to know   The advantage of buying an operating business is that it has a track record, a tangible set of financials, and past performance you can use to build its future. This makes financing easier than it is for a business start-up. You can probably also count on the seller's doing part of the financing—taking the purchase price over a period of years. The risks and uncertainties of the start-up can be reduced or avoided. Before you buy a business, be certain that it has a proven product or service and someone to sell it to and that its problems are the kinds you are well equipped to solve. Look for existing businesses in the industry or situation that interests you, and approach them directly or through a business broker. Don't limit yourself to reading the business opportunities sections of newspapers. Be hard-nosed and very rational about the business potential and the price you can afford to pay for it. Use zero-based valuation—calculate what the business is worth, rather than negotiate from the asking price. Avoid an emotional decision. Be cautious about basing your offer on national averages and ratios that may have little relevance in your setting. A sensible basis for estimating the value of a company is to establish its total earnings, deduct the fair value of what it would cost to hire a replacement for the owner/manager, back out what you would earn on the purchase price if you invested elsewhere, and apply a reasonable multiplier—2 to 3 times, or 4 at the most. Add the fair value of the tangible assets you get in the deal and you should be approaching a reasonable price. (Buying a business opportunity or franchise is another matter entirely. See BUSINESS IDEAS and FRANCHISES.)

Why you need to know it   Of the various ways to begin in business, one of the least risky is buying a going company that you can improve. Some conventional businesses can be converted into home-based operations. One successful pattern is to bring the marketing and management functions into the home and have the manufacturing and shipping (if relevant) done off-site. Regardless of the particulars, you need to approach the task with a systematic and rational way of establishing the value of the business being considered. Too many businesses are bought because the buyer falls in love with it, is able to strike a deal with the seller, or otherwise goes forward because the deal is possible, not because it is a winner. You need to be prepared to look at as many situations as necessary to find the one that has actual potential for you.

Where to learn more

▶ Gary Schine's *How You Can Buy a Business without Overpaying* fleshes out the general approach described above, which is based on Schine's article, "How to Buy a Business without Overpaying," in the August 1993 issue of *Home Office Computing* magazine. Check your library or contact: Reprint Manager, *Home Office Computing*, 730 Broadway, New York, NY 10003; 212-505-3580.

▶ Look for business brokers in your telephone book, and let them know what you are interested in examining.

▶ Familiarize yourself with methods used to place value on businesses. Research the topic at a library or ask a business professor at a local college to suggest some sources.

Related topics

Accountant	Financial planning
Agents and brokers	**Franchises**
Attorney	Insurance
Bartering	Legal/illegal business operation
Budgeting	License
Business address and location	Loans, credit, and venture capital
Business ideas	Marketing and market research
Business image	Negotiating
Business name	Projections
Cash flow	Regulations
Competition	Telephone equipment
Environmental considerations	Telephone services
Equipment and furniture	Undercapitalization
Escrow	Zoning

CAMERA-READY COPY

What you need to know   Camera-ready copy is anything you give a printer that is ready to be printed without further preparation. The printer doesn't have to set the type, do the artwork, or screen images. There are degrees of completion that are referred to as camera-ready copy. For instance, all of the type might be set but the printer may have to prepare some photos for shooting. Before modern computers and desktop publishing software, the preparation of camera-ready copy was a painstaking operation that involved carefully aligned rub-on letters and special typewriters that achieved the desired spacing. Now anyone can produce camera-ready copy with a computer, some commonplace software, and a printer. The quality of your final product depends on your artistic talent, the variety of type and art options available, and the quality of your computer systems printer. The printer's process camera will not improve poorly prepared copy. A dot-matrix or inkjet printer with 300 dpi (dots per inch) resolution will be readable, but not professional. A laser printer of the same resolution will be considerably better. For commercial work, you should use a 600-dpi laser printer or better. The standard for truly professional copy is 1200 dpi. The best approach is to use a modem or disk to deliver your finished computer work to a service bureau that will produce the actual camera-ready copy via a commercial-grade printer. Adding photos and other images is best left to the professionals, although popularly priced scanners are improving. You can at least use your scanner and software to crop and place the image so the professional knows exactly what you want.

Why you need to know it   On any documents or communications that represent your business, you want to project a professional image at a reasonable price. With your computer and a little talent, you can prepare camera-ready copy for printed materials ranging from business forms and brochures to advertising copy. The more you can do in the final preparation of these materials, the lower your cost for the finished products. You also get what you want without struggling to communicate a concept to a third party. The risk in preparing your own copy lies in not knowing at what point to turn the job over to a professional. Keep the door open to objective criticism, and establish realistic criteria for deciding where your creative efforts end and those of a professional should begin.

Where to learn more

▶ Libraries, bookstores, graphic art supply stores, and catalogs have books on the preparation of printers' copy. An example is *No-Sweat Desktop Publishing* by Steve Morgenstern. To order, call: 800-325-6249.

▶ Printers will give you specifications for what they need, if you plan to provide them with camera-ready copy. Ask your printer for guidelines and advice.

▶ Software manuals for graphics and desktop publishing products are excellent sources of technical advice for preparing camera-ready copy.

▶ Magazine and newspaper advertising departments will supply you with specifications for the sizes and quality of the mechanicals they require, if you intend to give them your own camera-ready copy or that of a third party.

▶ Courses in desktop publishing and related topics can provide useful information on the preparation of camera-ready copy. For recommendations, ask your local computer users group or the customer service unit of your software or equipment supplier. You might also examine back issues of computer magazines for advertisements. Appendixes C and D will give you some good leads.

▶ "Preparing Pages for a Print Shop," in the September 1992 issue of *Home Office Computing* magazine, gives the essentials of readying materials for an outside printer. Check your library or contact: Reprint Manager, *Home Office Computing*, 730 Broadway, New York, NY 10003; 212-505-3580.

Related topics

Advertising	**Desktop publishing**
Business cards	Forms
Business image	Newsletters
Computer equipment	Paper
Computer software	**Printing**
Copiers	Proposals
Copyright, patent, trademark,	Reducing expenses
and service mark	

CASH FLOW

What you need to know   The stream of money through your business is rarely even and balanced. In one month, you will take in more than you spend; in the next month, you will spend more than you receive. Cash flow is the term businesses use for the constant cycle of income and expenditures. They monitor the cash flow to ensure that there is sufficient overlap of income to cover expenditures and enable the business to meet its obligations. You can approach your cash flow problems in a number of ways that vary in complexity but accomplish the same goal. Using a pad of paper and a calculator, project your budget into the future a year or so, to show you what kind of balancing acts you will have to perform and when. Depending on your facility with computers and the software you own, easier and more sophisticated approaches are possible. (1) Create a spreadsheet that lists your expected income and expenses over the next 12 months or more. By changing income and expenses in particular months or quarters of the year, you can see how the bottom line adjusts across the period. What opportunities might capture a cash reserve to get you past a future shortfall? At what time of year might you need to borrow short-term to reach the more lucrative months that will follow? (2) Set up a checkbook accounting program in which you enter all anticipated revenues and expenses for the coming year. The minus signs will show you the shortfalls you'll have to overcome.

Why you need to know it   Cash flow problems are common in business, but they are seldom fatal if they can be anticipated. Begin with the assumption that your cash flow ends the period with a positive balance. If this test is not met, you do not have a profitable business that can sustain itself. Determining whether your business passes this test should be your first objective in business planning. Assuming you project a profitable year, you have to plan how you will bridge the shortfalls that are a normal part of the business cycle. You can do it in several ways: (1) renegotiate your obligations, and pay them when your income materializes; (2) sell your receivable accounts to a third party for a fee (factoring), and pay your bills on time; or (3) borrow against your accounts receivable, pay your bills now, and reimburse the loan when the income materializes.

Where to learn more

‣ Read the budgeting chapter of any small business textbook. You can get one at a library or a college or commercial bookstore. If you want more personal advice, call a professor who specializes in small business classes at a local college and ask for suggestions. Take a course on the subject if you feel the need for more financial management knowledge. Audit the class (take it for no grade and no credit) if you don't want tests or degree credit.

‣ Small business and computer publications periodically have articles on using spreadsheet software for cash flow management. An example is "Will It Be a Good Year?," in the December 1993 issue of *Home Office Computing* magazine.

‣ Small business financial software packages have manuals that tell you how their products help you to manage cash flow. One program that addresses cash flow directly is *Up Your Cash Flow* by Granville Publications Software. It includes CPA Harvey A. Goldstein's best-selling book by the same name. (Order for about $80 from *Power Up Direct*: 800-851-2917.) Microrim's comprehensive small business accounting program, *In the Black*, is also useful.

‣ Read Robert Gehorsam's "Start-Up Diary," in the September 1993 issue of *Home Office Computing* magazine—an excellent, realistic account of what you can expect to encounter in starting a serious business. Check your library or contact: Reprint Manager, *Home Office Computing*, 730 Broadway, New York, NY 10003; 212-505-3580.

Related topics

Accountant
Accounting
Banking services
Bankruptcy
Bartering
Bookkeeping
Budgeting
Business plan
Checking accounts

Computer software
Credit cards
Credit unions
Debt collection and creditworthiness
Electronic banking
Evaluating your business
Financial planning
Investing
Leasing

Loans, credit, and venture capital
Money management
Overhead expenses
Projections

Separating business and personal
Success and failure
Tax checklist
Undercapitalization

CHAMBER OF COMMERCE

What you need to know   About 5,000 local Chambers of Commerce represent the business interests of communities around the country. They are lobbying organizations and business advocacy groups that often have links to local government through economic development councils and other promotional bodies. Their influence is generally positive. Many of the local Chambers and individual businesses belong to state and national Chambers of Commerce as well. The role of the movement is to provide information on businesses and represent their interests before public policy and other influential groups. Dues paid by members are generally prorated depending on the number of employees. Chamber membership cannot be used in advertising, but a displayed decal or plaque on the business premises can indicate membership. Chambers of Commerce issue information packages that usually include a list of member businesses, complete with CEO, number of employees, products and services, mailing address, and telephone number. The packet also contains demographic information on the service area as well as quality-of-life factors such as the availability of schools, the denominations of places of worship, the cost of buying a home, and similar regional data.

Why you need to know it   If you are going to be part of the business community, you should consider being a dues-paying member of the organization that represents it. Dues are usually modest for small companies that employ only a few people. Membership buys you the respectability of belonging to the group and the opportunity to network with other members. By association, you are part of the local business scene. Together with the Better Business Bureau, the Chamber of Commerce represents a painless step into the business establishment for home-based or other small business persons. If you operate statewide or nationally, consider membership in the broader-based Chambers as well. Association with them is often worth the modest price of membership, and your dues pay for lobbying efforts that represent the interests of small business before state and national legislatures.

Where to learn more

▶ Call your local Chamber of Commerce and inquire about membership. Ask for contacts at the regional, state, and national levels of the Chamber of Commerce organization, if they are applicable in your circumstances.

▶ Nationally, the U.S. Chamber of Commerce, 1615 H Street, NW, Washington, DC 29962 (202-659-6000), is your point of contact.

Related topics

Advertising
Better Business Bureau (BBB)
Business associates
Business image
Competition
Conferences, seminars, shows,
  and workshops
Customer relations
Ethics

Information sources and research
Marketing and market research
Media relations
Networking
Promoting your business
Public relations
Service Corps of Retired Executives
  (SCORE)

CHECKING ACCOUNTS

What you need to know   Advice varies on checking accounts for small businesses. The conventional wisdom says a separate account is essential—anything else would amount to commingling funds and can cause problems. If you use modern checkbook software—for example, Intuit's *Quicken* or Microrim's *In the Black*—commingling doesn't have to be a concern. It is entirely possible to have a single checking account serving multiple purposes and still keep it all straight. You assign your income and expenses to the proper categories, and the program tracks and summarizes them. You can, for example, prorate the amount of rent that accrues to business and personal use as you issue one check. Easily designed and executed reports show where all your subaccounts stand. There are certain economies in maintaining a single, higher-balance personal account as your small venture is getting off the ground, but only if you are not compromising your business image. Order separate checks (through an independent check-printing service, not your bank) with a business imprint, leaving the account number coding the same as for your personal account. What matters is that you are able to separate business and personal activity for accounting and tax purposes. As soon as you start doing enough business to call yourself a company, it is still wise to have a separate business account. Ethically, you would not want to make heavy business use of a personal account because you would be denying your bank the higher fees associated with a business account. Ask about "relationship banking" that lets you link private and commercial accounts to meet balance minimums.

Why you need to know it   It is essential that your financial records accurately reflect the flow of money into and out of your company. Your checking account is a primary record of this flow. Whether it is a separate account is less important than the fact that it must be maintained accurately and completely. If you are audited, the IRS will want to see your check register. You can expect the agent to total all your deposits and ask you to justify anything that exceeds the amount you reported. Whether you run your business from your personal account until it is complicated enough to warrant a separate account or whether you begin separately, be sure the entries reflect the true history of your transactions and match the bookkeeping entries that are the basis for your tax returns.

Where to learn more

▶ Inquire at several banks about the options available and the costs involved for small business checking accounts.

▶ Learn the limitations of and differences among commercial banks, savings banks (S&Ls), and credit unions. As your business grows, you may want retail credit and other services that are available mainly through a full-service commercial bank. The earlier you establish a relationship, the more receptive the bank will be to serving you.

▶ Establishing your business banking relationship is part of your networking process. Take the occasion to meet an officer of the bank, make her or him aware of your company, and lay the groundwork for a commercial reference and future dealings.

Related topics

Accounting
Banking services
Bookkeeping
Budgeting
Business address and location
Business basics
Business image
Business name
Cash flow

Computer software
Credit unions
Electronic banking
Financial planning
Loans, credit, and venture capital
Money management
Payroll
Printing
Records

COMPETITION

What you need to know   Competing in the small business market involves the same forces that are in action among major companies. The Harvard Business School's five-forces model sees competition affected mainly by: (1) rivalry among existing companies, (2) threat of new entrants, (3) threat of substitutes, (4) buyer power, and (5) supplier power. Reducing these to the small business level, the home-based business has a potential advantage in a number of areas. A small business can be selective in choosing its market and customers. It can pick the most profitable situations and leave its larger rivals to battle over the larger marketplace. Similarly, small firms pose little threat as they enter new markets. Small operators can offer lower-priced substitutes, especially for business services, because they lack the overhead of their established competitors. Buyer power, the ability of the buyer to force lower prices, usually works to the advantage of the small firm operating with lower expenses. Supplier power, the ability of suppliers to affect price, is less of a factor in small businesses because prices conform to what the larger customers are paying their suppliers. What a small company lacks in competitive advantage accruing from economies of scale and scope, it regains in improved learning-curve positioning. The owner's expertise is the small company's knowledge base, and the ability of a small business to focus its owner's specialized knowledge on selected segments of the market gives it a unique advantage to identify and serve needs not yet viable for larger competitors.

Why you need to know it   To succeed as a small business, you have to be competitive with larger firms. Your most likely route to success is to serve niche markets not appreciated by your larger competitors. Small business occupies a tactical position in which guerrilla warfare succeeds better than set offensives. You are not apt to go head-to-head with a "big eight" consulting firm, but you may be able to live well off of the crumbs from its table. Competition with peer small businesses is different. The playing field is level, and you have to be more attractive in price, service, image, and everything else that attracts and holds business. Specialization is your greatest advantage, so it is important to select your niche well. By specializing in the right way, you reduce competition by being the only company doing what you do in the way you do it.

Where to learn more

▶ Business texts and articles spell out competitive theory. If you feel you should approach the problem academically, go to a library or ask a business professor for recommended readings.

▶ To determine where you might best compete as a small business, know the professional literature in your specialty and analyze it with competitive forces in mind.

▶ Talk to people who would buy the services you plan to sell, and ask about the competition.

▶ Talk to your competition. Allow for the guarded nature of such conversations, but get some idea of whether the field is open or saturated. Inquire about buying the competing business, and see what kind of reaction you get. If everyone is ready to sell, it might indicate a less than lucrative field.

Related topics

Advertising
Bidding
Bonding
Business address and location
Business cards
Business name
Business plan
Buying a business
Copyright, patent, trademark,
    and service mark

Credit cards
Customer relations
Diversification
Ethics
Expense sharing and joint ventures
Fees and pricing
Franchises
Marketing and market research
Promoting your business

COMPUTER EQUIPMENT

What you need to know   Popularly priced computers come in two basic varieties: (1) IBM/DOS/Windows and clones and (2) the Apple Macintosh. Within the two groups, computers break down by physical size into desktops and notebooks. Another discriminator is a combination of power, capacity, and speed of operation. These are mainly functions of the microprocessor chip. Currently, the top of the line is a Pentium in the IBM world, a PowerPC in Macintosh, but 386s and 486s, and 68030s and 68040s, respectively, are still respectable. The clock speed of the processor—anywhere from 16 to 60 or more MHz—is important and relates to the 16- to 32-bit data bus that limits how fast the data can flow within the computer. A minimum of 4 MB RAM is needed for the computer to do its internal "thinking." Math coprocessors speed functions needed not just for mathematics but also for the graphics programs that rely on math algorithms. Most popular computer models now come with a 1.4 MB floppy disk drive for loading and removing data. This is the minimum needed to switch work between Mac and IBM platforms without cables or a modem. Some computers have a CD drive that also inputs data and has a much higher capacity. Hard drives ranging from about 80 MB to well over 100 MB are the standard for storing everything a computer uses and produces. Floppy disks and tapes back up the hard disks in case they become defective. Beyond this basic computing unit, you should consider at least an inkjet printer if not a laser printer; a telephone modem for communicating with on-line services, and possibly a fax-modem that turns your computer into a fax machine; and a scanner that allows you to turn images and printed pages into digital data for your computer to use.

Why you need to know it   You put yourself at a tremendous disadvantage if you do not know the basics of small computers today. Not only are computers the standard for performing the routine tasks of most professions, but the language of computers is the benchmark for the literate person in the modern business world. If you haven't been educated by osmosis in the workplace, take a class, read some books, buy an inexpensive system, and learn what the revolution is all about. A reasonably full-featured system in either the Mac or MS-DOS/Windows environment can be purchased for under $2,000.

Where to learn more

▶ Depending on your own learning style: buy a computer and read the manuals; join a local users club; call the technical support numbers; buy instructional tapes and videos; read books, computer magazines, and catalogs; take a class at a community college or a computer reseller; let a computer-literate friend help you; read and participate in the on-line services bulletin boards that support your system.

▶ To request current information, visit your computer reseller or contact the manufacturers directly: Apple, 800-776-2333 or 408-996-1010; Compac, 800-345-1518 or 713-370-0670. Many other choices exist; these are merely representative of the two main operating systems. (Appendixes B, C, and D will give you additional leads.)

Related topics

Answering machines and voice mail	Ergonomics
Camera-ready copy	Insurance
Computer on-line services	Leasing
Computer software	Multimedia
Computer use	Office planning and decorating
Desktop publishing	Printing
Disaster planning	Telecommuting
Electronic banking	Telephone equipment
Environmental considerations	Telephone services
Equipment and furniture	

COMPUTER ON-LINE SERVICES

What you need to know   With your computer and a modem to hook it to a telephone line, you can access on-line services that connect you to the world. The Internet is becoming the best known and farthest reaching computer network: 15 million users are on-line and a million are being added monthly. Internet was developed for government, large company, and university use and is not very user-friendly. Your more likely route to networking is through one of the large commercial services: Prodigy, CompuServe, American Online, GEnie, and Delphi. Prodigy has nearly 2 million members, CompuServe over 1 million, and the others several hundred thousand members each. All work in the MS-DOS and Macintosh environments; most support Windows. Many of the on-line services offer their own front-end software that makes them easier to use. Fees vary from flat rates for basic services to time and functional charges for individual services. The larger systems have local telephone numbers for accessing them toll-free from hundreds of cities; the smaller ones route you through a fee-based line. Most have hundreds of special-interest forums or bulletin boards. All have shareware and freeware libraries available— tens of thousands in many cases. Computer software and hardware vendors maintain on-line product support services bulletin boards on most of the systems.

Why you need to know it   You can use on-line computer services to send and receive e-mail and faxes, shop for all kinds of merchandise, schedule travel, do research, check stocks and the weather, and get help using your computer and its software. Thousands of databases on every subject imaginable are available for your use. Special-interest forums on hundreds of topics let you participate in discussions. Many on-line services offer access to the Internet. Heavy use of the most sophisticated services, such as Dow Jones News/

Retrieval, can be very costly. If all you want is an e-mail address, buy a less expensive service. It probably crosses over to the e-mail services of the other systems anyway. If a particular bulletin board service or research database is what you need and only the pricey systems have it, buy the more complete service. On-line services can be powerful tools for the home-based business person, but they can also be a black hole in which you spend time and money unnecessarily. Be selective in choosing only what you need, and limit your on-line time to profitable applications. It is easy to succumb to the rapture of being on-line, but you could waste a lot of time and money that would be better spent pursuing the conventional aspects of your business.

Where to learn more

▶ America Online, Vienna, VA: 703-448-8700 or 800-827-6364.

▶ CompuServe, Columbus, OH: 800-848-8199.

▶ Delphi, Cambridge, MA: 617-491-3393 or 800-695-4005.

▶ GEnie, Rockville, MD: 301-340-5397 or 800-638-9636.

▶ Prodigy, White Plains, NY: 914-993-8000 or 800-776-3449.

▶ Computer magazine reviews of on-line services: see Appendix C.

▶ Books specializing in the various services are in libraries and stores.

Related topics

Advertising
Banking services
Bulletin Board System (BBS)
Business address and location
Business image
Business travel
Computer equipment
Computer software
Computer use
Conferences, seminars, shows, and workshops
Continuing education
Copyright, patent, trademark, and service mark

Customer relations
Electronic banking
Ethics
Fees and pricing
Information sources and research
Legal/illegal business operation
Marketing and market research
Merchandise buying services
Networking
Promoting your business
Public relations
Regulations
Small Business Administration (SBA)

COMPUTER SOFTWARE

What you need to know   Computer software refers to the programs that tell your computer how to run (operating systems software) and how to do useful things like keep books, write checks, do taxes, and so on (applications software). There are two popular operating systems: Macintosh (about 15 percent of the market) and MS-DOS or MS-DOS/Windows (85 percent of the market).

The next version of Windows will operate independently of DOS and will re-place it as the predominant IBM (and clones) operating system. Windows is the visual interface system that looks and acts like the easy-to-use Mac sys-tem. It is still more awkward to use than the Mac, but it is apparent that the two will soon be virtually the same. In 1993, programs written for Windows became the top selling software, followed by MS-DOS and Mac. Word proces-sors, spreadsheets, databases, and presentation graphics are the best-selling business software applications. Integrated software packages combine a word processor, a spreadsheet, a database manager, a communications module, and a graphics component into a single program. The advantages of integrated soft-ware packages include a lower purchase price and the ability of the modules to work together smoothly. Beyond these basic kinds of business software ap-plications, there are specialized programs for graphics and design, video and sound, multimedia, learning and games, networking and communications, per-sonal finance and investing, and almost anything you can name. Shareware is another source of applications software; you generally pay less and do it on an honor system basis. On-line services and catalogs published on software guide you to hundreds of choices in this less commercial market.

Why you need to know it Software is the brains of your computer. Whatever you want to do has to begin with applications software that instructs your computer on how to accomplish specific tasks. It is essential that you select an operating system and applications software that do not intimidate you. Using the system should be easy and comfortable. Macintosh once ruled supreme on this dimension, but Windows is quickly closing the gap. Applications vary widely in ease of use and capacity. You have to know enough about software to strike a balance between sophistication and user friendliness that lets you function most effectively.

Where to learn more

‣ Computer magazines are published for different kinds of user interests. Sample them until you find some that address your needs. Monitor them for the latest software products. (Appendix C can be of help here.)

‣ Computer catalogs—*MacConnection, PC Connection,* or many more advertised in user magazines—are good sources of software information. (See Appendix C also.)

‣ Computer stores and super stores have software packages on display—sometimes running and available for customers to try. Third-party books on popular appli-cations are also displayed, so you can explore their capabilities from another perspective.

‣ Computer store clerks and customers can provide a wealth of feedback about software, but you have to consider the source and make your own judgments.

‣ On-line services have bulletin boards on which software is critiqued and dis-cussed by users. Call 603-446-0100 for information on downloading demos of the latest software products.

▶ The Software Publishers Association, 1730 M Street, NW, Washington, DC 20036 (202-452-1600), offers guidance on the legal use of software products.

Related topics

Answering machines and
voice mail
Billing
Bookkeeping
Budgeting
Bulletin Board System (BBS)
Business basics
Business cards
Business plan
Camera-ready copy
Cash flow
Computer equipment
Computer on-line services
Computer use
Conferences, seminars, shows,
and workshops
Copyright, patent, trademark,
and service mark
Desktop publishing
Direct mail and mailing lists
Ethics
Evaluating your business
Fax
Financial formulas
Financial planning
Forms

**Getting organized and
managing information**
Information sources and research
Investing
Legal/illegal business operation
Loans, credit, and venture capital
Mail order
Managing growth
Marketing and market research
Media relations
Money management
Multimedia
Newsletters
Office planning and decorating
Payroll
Personnel policies
Presentations
Printing
Projections
Promoting your business
Proposals
Records
Separating business and personal
Tax checklist
Telecommuting
Time management

COMPUTER USE

What you need to know

Copying software: Software is copyrighted and strictly controlled. You are not at liberty to make copies beyond your backup copy, and the penalties for doing so can be severe. The reason for the restriction is to preserve the incentive for developers to continue producing innovative software.

Other restrictions: Be alert to possible copyright, trademark, and service mark infringement on scanned artwork, research downloaded from on-line services, and registered company and product names.

Viruses: Protecting yourself from computer viruses, the bugs that hackers create to destroy files, is another necessary computer user habit. Although on-line services and manufacturers screen for them, viruses still pass from user to user.

When importing information from outside sources, use software designed to detect and destroy viruses.

Saving files: Computers can easily move your work to permanent storage. Unless you save your files, you have only an unstable storage that disappears if your computer fails. Make it a habit to hit the "save" key combination often. By doing so, you limit your losses from a power or system failure to the last point at which you saved data.

Backup files: Permanent storage media occasionally fail, so a second copy of the data on floppy disks, tape, and so on, is needed to ensure against loss. Specialized software recovers some "lost" data, but you can't always rely on it.

Ventilation: Heat buildup is the leading cause of computer failure. Don't limit the air circulation by blocking vents with papers, other equipment, or furniture.

Maintenance: Computers are increasingly easy to upgrade and adapt, but unless you are confident of the procedure and willing to risk your warranty, have your computer serviced professionally.

Focus: Remember that a business person's computer is a tool for making money. It is easy to become enraptured and invest too much time and money pursuing computer fads. Discipline yourself to review developments, stay current, and acquire what you need, but avoid unprofitable hours spent on-line or adding equipment and software that contribute little to your profitability.

Help: Available from on-line services, local resellers and user groups (Appendix C), manufacturers' help lines (Appendix D), your professional associates, and even on television ("MacTV"; see below).

Why you need to know it   Computers are indispensable aids to the home office small business person. They are relatively easy to use, but certain protocols need to be observed to get the most from them. Computers are prone to periodic failures that are minor in terms of the equipment but devastating in terms of work lost, unless you follow the simple rituals that can protect you. Computers tempt you to break intellectual property laws, and that can be embarrassing and costly. Finally, computer users can waste more time and money than they save if the device becomes an obsession that makes disproportionate demands on their time and resources.

Where to learn more

▶ Computer equipment and software are designed to be understood and operated by owners. Manuals, help menus, and telephone-based technical service representatives (see Appendix D) tell you what you need to know.

▶ Specialized third-party books on equipment, software, and services are available in bookstores and through computer book clubs. They sometimes simplify and highlight shortcuts not stressed in the original documentation.

▶ Computer resellers demonstrate and explain their products, but their expertise varies widely. Before investing, get a second opinion and do independent research in user magazines.

▶ "The Computer Guy Show" (214-746-5339) is a syndicated computer version of "This Old House."

▶ "MacTV" is an hour-long weekly show that appears Monday through Friday on satellite and cable (Galaxy 7, Channel 10, 8:00–9:00 A.M. Eastern; on cable's Mind Extension University/The Education Network—check local listings). For information, call 800-800-6912.

▶ The Software Publishers Association, 1730 M Street, NW, Washington, DC 20036 (202-452-1600), offers guidance on the legal use of software products.

Related topics

Answering machines and
  voice mail
Billing
Bookkeeping
Budgeting
Bulletin Board System (BBS)
Business basics
Business cards
Business plan
Camera-ready copy
Cash flow
Computer equipment
Computer on-line services
Computer software
Conferences, seminars, shows,
  and workshops
Copyright, patent, trademark, and
  service mark
Desktop publishing
Direct mail and mailing lists
Ethics
Evaluating your business
Fax
Financial formulas
Financial planning
Forms

**Getting organized and
  managing information**
Information sources and research
Investing
Legal/illegal business operation
Loans, credit, and venture capital
Mail order
Managing growth
Marketing and market research
Media relations
Money management
Multimedia
Newsletters
Office planning and decorating
Payroll
Personnel policies
Presentations
Printing
Projections
Promoting your business
Proposals
Records
Separating business and personal
Tax checklist
Telecommuting
Time management

CONCERNS ABOUT WORKING FROM HOME

What you need to know   Working from home should be a stimulating and positive experience, but you may have to overcome some natural doubts. Your main concerns will be in these areas:

Isolation: Being your own boss and operating in the relative isolation of your home office calls for discipline, focus, and a positive view of your self-worth and commercial value. Loneliness is relative, and people who choose to work at home usually value their privacy. But everyone requires social interaction to remain alert to the realities of running a business. Stay in touch with the world by telephone, fax, and computer, and make regular forays into the business community. Screen the possibilities and select functions that match the needs of your business and personal style. Social interaction contributes to maintaining business contacts and a favorable perspective. In the absence of day-to-day at the office colleague interaction, surrogates for your former face-to-face contacts (like telephone and E-mail associates) can help to mirror your thinking and stimulate fresh insights. Balance is the key to successful adjustment to working from home. Reappraise your situation regularly, and recalibrate your outside contacts according to your needs and priorities. Initiative can keep you comfortably and productively in the professional mainstream without office politics, ritual meetings, and excessive travel.

Selling: Expect to be a salesperson for your business. It is unlikely that business will come to you with sufficient volume and regularity to make you successful with self-promotion. The key is to do things your way and avoid the stereotypical salesperson approach that makes people uncomfortable. Think of this activity as "business development" rather than sales. Turn your natural enthusiasm for what you do into a disciplined, regular practice of asking for new business, and you will have established a sales routine that matches your style.

Task avoidance: Exposure to the routine distractions of operating a home and managing a family provides endless excuses to avoid work. Disciplined separation of work from household routines is the answer. Give your work the priority it requires to produce the results that pay the bills.

Business skills: Except for the support tasks that are natural for you, don't try to do things that others can do better and more cost-effectively. Focus your energies on your business specialty and pay others to do legal, tax, accounting, and other specialized tasks. Appraisers apply to real estate a test called "highest and best use"—a struggling farm in the path of widespread commercial development fails the test. So do you, if you spend time doing what others can do better instead of clocking the maximum number of billable hours in your specialty.

Why you need to know it
Your greatest enemies in implementing a sound business idea that is adequately financed and within your professional capabilities are distraction and self-doubt. It is legitimate to have concerns; deal with them rationally and don't dwell on them to the point where they dilute your ability to perform. Assuming the basic viability of your business, there is no routine concern that cannot be compartmentalized and dealt with effectively without causing you to break your stride. You need a safety valve for concerns that threaten to persist, and the best one is labeled "confrontation and action." Don't allow any concern to become so irrational that it goes beyond its legitimate boundaries. Take a realistic measure of each problem, and do whatever is within your capabilities to remove it as an obstacle.

Where to learn more

▸ Review your business plan frequently, to verify that you are on course.

▸ Talk one-on-one with business associates and members of your network who either may have experienced similar problems in growing their businesses or have the professional expertise to suggest rational solutions.

▸ Join a business incubator or other small business support group that is designed to address the kinds of concerns you are having.

Related topics

Attitude
Bankruptcy
Budgeting
Business address and location
Business associates
Business image
Competition
Debt collection and
    creditworthiness
Financial planning
Independent contractor status
**Loans, credit, and venture
    capital**

Regulations
Retirement
**Separating business and
    personal**
Start-up
Stress and overworking
Success and failure
Tax checklist
Time management
Transitioning
Undercapitalization
Vacation, work styles, and schedules
Zoning

CONFERENCES, SEMINARS, SHOWS, AND WORKSHOPS

What you need to know   Home office workers are indistinguishable from others in their specialties at professional gatherings. Take advantage of this level playing field, and network with peers, customers, and clients. Professional gatherings offer formal opportunities to add your name to programs and lists of participants—documents that you and others use to identify possible business associates long after meetings end. Gain recognition by presenting at sessions that will be advertised, attended, and reviewed by potential clients and associates. Conferences, seminars, shows, and workshops are the ultimate networking opportunities. Their formal agenda is punctuated with informal conversations and social contacts that link people who have common business interests. Presentations are opportunities for free advertising in the form of publication in the newsletters, journals, and magazines of your interest group. Select the kind of participation that best suits your business needs and personal style, but use professional gatherings as a hunting ground for future business and a listening post for what is of interest to your clients.

Why you need to know it   Opportunities to meet with others in your field are especially valuable because your ability to network daily is limited. You can approach professional meetings pragmatically, targeting only events and people likely to be beneficial. As an independent business person, you have the privilege of coming and going at will at such events. Your only criterion is a successful gleaning of the information and contacts that look profitable. If you were formerly in a traditional business or bureaucratic setting, it may require conscious effort to unabashedly "cherry pick" these events and not waste time with irrelevant sessions and people. The only politically correct concerns for the small business person are serving clients well and making a business prosper; there is no requirement to get a card punched or to endure deadly sessions just to show the company flag. If an event can mean dollars now for you, make an effort to be there. If you are uncertain about the value of an event, make telephone inquiries to satisfy yourself on whether attendance will be worthwhile. If the sponsors and planners are nebulous, and specific business outcomes for you are lacking, don't go. Generally, pay attention to trade shows. They are excellent vehicles for an efficient hands-on review of computers and other equipment you may be considering purchasing or producing.

Where to learn more

▶ Join professional groups and monitor their publications for annual meetings and special events that interest you.

▶ Gale's *Directory of Associations* lists dates and locations of organizations' upcoming meetings. Review the publication at a library.

▶ Business magazines advertise specialized meetings that cross individual professional lines. Request detailed information, talk with others who have attended previous sessions, and appraise each event's potential value before attending.

▶ Ask for a calendar of upcoming events at conference centers and hotels that cater to the kinds of meetings that interest you and are held within your geographic area. Chambers of Commerce and economic development councils are also worth checking, as are the adult and continuing education divisions of universities and colleges.

▶ College professors tend to stay informed on professional activities in their fields. Call a college, ask for the department that represents your interests, get the name of a faculty member who might share your interests, and ask him or her for suggestions.

Related topics

Advertising

Attitude

Business cards

Business ideas

Business image

Business travel

Buying a business

Competition

Consulting

Continuing education

Evaluating your business

Expense sharing and joint
   ventures

Fees and pricing

Government customers

**Information sources
   and research**

Marketing and market research

Media relations

Motivation

Networking   Public relations
Newsletters   Separating business and personal
Presentations   Success and failure
Professional help   **Training**
Promoting your business   Vacation, work styles, and schedules

CONSULTING

What you need to know   More than one out of ten home-based businesses
is a consulting business, according to popular surveys. When you sell specialized knowledge, your office location is less important than your expertise and
your ability to deliver it. Technology puts the delivery mechanisms into a home
office as readily as into a high-rise corporate tower. The same is true for research to support a consulting practice. On-line services and CD-ROM libraries bring specialized data banks and communications to your home office
with an ease that used to be hard to find outside the Library of Congress. Independent consulting is about two-thirds using your expert knowledge and one-
third running a business. Assuming the use of professional accounting and legal
services, the biggest headache for must consultants is marketing—getting business on a regular, manageable, profitable basis. Specific consulting business
skills like proposal writing are needed. You may find it desirable to work
through a broker or in a group practice. Consultants have sidelines—specialized software or publications, for example—that they sell along with their services. The secret to successful consulting is finding a service that is needed and
providing it for a fee. Examine the software market for a product you are willing to become an expert at using, and sell either a service based on it or, as a
trainer, your knowledge of how to use it.

Why you need to know it   Consulting is fertile ground—a most likely
independent business for a professional person with marketable specialized
knowledge. You probably have contacts from your salaried years that can be
converted into consulting clients and sources of referrals. Working in a large
organization lends itself to identifying niches that are overlooked. You might
be able to exploit them profitably. Those who succeed approach consulting as
a business and expect to be business people as well as knowledgeable experts.
Fortunately, consulting is a much written-about field. Read some books on it,
and avoid relearning old lessons on succeeding and failing in a highly individualized business that is based on a common set of approaches.

Where to learn more

▶ If you have the opportunity and are so inclined, learn consulting from the inside.
Join an established group practice for a while, and build your knowledge of the
business and your reputation.

▶ Libraries and bookstores have a selection of how-to consulting books. Examine
them until you find one that addresses your needs. Herman Holtz's series on the

subject includes *How to Succeed as an Independent Consultant, The Consultant's Guide to Winning Clients, The Consultant's Guide to Proposal Writing,* and *The Consultant's Guide to Hidden Profits.* Herbert Bermont's *How to Become a Successful Consultant in Your Own Field* is another possibility. (800-221-7945).

▶ Software catalogs and computer magazines describe a constant flow of new and improving software that lends itself to consulting practices based on the products. For example, Microsoft Corporation runs a certification service for people who qualify as experts on its products (206-635-7200). (See Appendix C.)

Related topics

Agents and brokers	Customer relations
Associations	Ethics
Attitude	Expert witness
Bartering	Foreign markets and languages
Business address and location	**Government customers**
Business associates	**Information sources and**
Business cards	**research**
Business image	Insurance
Business name	License
Business travel	**Marketing and market research**
Competition	**Networking**
Computer use	Newsletters
Conferences, seminars, shows,	**Promoting your business**
and workshops	**Proposals**
Continuing education	Regulations
Contracts	Tax checklist
Copyright, patent, trademark,	Vacation, work styles, and schedules
and service mark	

CONTINUING EDUCATION

What you need to know   Formal education is generally obtained in traditional classroom settings and presented at a full-time student pace. Continuing education, the working adult version, is decidedly more practical in the content and scheduling of the courses. Continuing education classes are everywhere—at colleges and retailers, on cable television channels and on-line computer services. You can earn a degree or take specialized courses intended to introduce you to a new skill or to keep you apprised of the latest developments in your field. Colleges and universities often have special "adult and continuing education" divisions where registrants encounter few of the rigid admission tests and rituals associated with traditional college admission. The courses offered tend to stand alone, and it is almost secondary that many of them might also serve degree-seeking students. Content is business- and technology-oriented, and the faculty are often moonlighting professionals who bring on-the-job experience to the classes. Depending on your needs, a noncollege setting might be just as useful. Computer stores often offer excellent courses on using the equipment and software products they sell. Commercial workshops and conferences on every imaginable subject are held around the major cities on a rotating basis. Professional organizations and publications advertise educational opportunities that are of interest to their members and readers. Video and audio cassette courses are available on a variety of subjects ranging from how to upgrade your computer memory or operating system to learning a foreign language.

Why you need to know it   To be successful in a home-based business, you must be aware of the latest trends, knowledge, and technology. The continuing education community hones your awareness with courses offered at convenient times and with a pragmatic emphasis that respects your time and scheduling limitations. You can usually get the knowledge you need by reimmersing yourself only briefly into specialized continuing education courses. Their "cafeteria" selectability has none of the intimidating formality or protracted length that you might associate with full-time college attendance.

Where to learn more

▶ Call colleges and school systems and ask for schedules of adult education offerings. Many advertise and send direct mail schedules.

▶ Call resellers of computers and other specialized products and services and inquire about available training classes. As an example, Micro Center®, a major computer and software reseller in the Washington, DC, area, offers an extensive user education program (703-204-8409).

▶ MacConnection, the mail-order computer catalog firm, will tell Macintosh users what product-related programming is on satellite or cable TV (800-800-6912). The same firm (and others like it) supplies videos, instruction booklets, and tools needed to upgrade computer memory (800-800-2222). Trade publications are filled with articles and advertising on the subject of continuing education. (See Appendix C.)

Related topics

Associations
Bulletin Board System (BBS)
Business associates
Business ideas
Computer on-line services
Computer use
Conferences, seminars, shows, and workshops
Diversification
Evaluating your business
Financial planning

Information sources and research
Investing
Marketing and market research
Negotiating
Networking
Newsletters
Service Corps of Retired Executives (SCORE)
Small Business Administration (SBA)

CONTRACTS

What you need to know A contract creates a mutual obligation to perform certain duties that the parties agree to, and failure to perform them has remedies in law. The contract has to have the genuine assent or agreement of both parties, as evidenced by an offer and acceptance. Additionally, a valid contract requires that the parties making the agreement must be competent (able to understand the agreement), the subject matter must be legal (or it is unenforceable), there has to be consideration (payment), and participation and obligations have to be mutual. Parties to a contract have reciprocal rights to demand that the promises made by the other be kept. A legal contract can take various forms including written, oral, or some other understood medium like sign language. Oral contracts are sometimes limited to agreements of a certain dollar value; check the laws of your state. Contracts can be express (all the terms are spelled out) or implied and based on the actions of the parties—for example, ordering and accepting merchandise implies agreement to pay for it even without a written document as proof. Although the general content of a contract may seem obvious, review by an attorney is usually necessary because state laws vary and an important legal nuance may escape your untrained eye. In specialties like writing, an agent might be responsible for contract review and the negotiation of modifications.

Why you need to know it You encounter contracts as you establish and conduct your business. With a home office, you may avoid an office lease but incur one on equipment or services. The form of the contract (or the absence of a contract) when you perform assignments for clients may have implications for your ability to use what you produce in future projects. Work-for-hire contracts, for example, give the client ownership of the copyright on your work. Your attorney should review all but the most routine contracts. Far more is negotiable than you might imagine, and an attorney can help balance contracts that generally begin tilted in favor of the originator.

Where to learn more

▶ Business stationers sell preprinted standard contracts for ordinary transactions like leases, installment purchases, and so on.

▶ Libraries and bookstores contain standard legal references like *Black's Law*, which list typical formats and wording for a variety of conventional contracts. A less formal guide is Chilton's *Business Agreements: A Complete Guide to Oral and Written Contracts*.

▶ Professional associations and societies publish suggested legal contracts for the use of their members.

▶ Computer software is available that contains readily adaptable contracts. An example is *It's Legal* by Parsons Technology, One Parsons Drive, P. O. Box 100, Hiawatha, IA 52233-0100; 319-395-9626 or 800-223-6925. Price: about $40.

▸ EZ Legal Books, 384 South Military Trail, Deerfield Beach, FL 33442 (305-480-8933/Fax 305-480-8906), sells series of perforated forms books including *301 Legal Forms and Agreements*.

Related topics

Agents and brokers	Forms
Attorney	**Franchises**
Banking services	Homeowners' associations
Bidding	**Independent contractor status**
Billing	Insurance
Bonding	Leasing
Buying a business	Loans, credit, and venture capital
Consulting	**Negotiating**
Direct mail and mailing lists	Printing
Escrow	Proposals
Ethics	Sales representatives
Expense sharing and joint ventures	Syndication
Financial planning	

COPIERS

What you need to know   Two categories of copying machines are of potential interest to the home-based business person: (1) desktop and (2) office. The differences between the two involve purchase price, operating cost, and capacity. The task of selecting the one that is right for your business begins with the number of copies you are apt to make—at one time, and in an average month. Copiers are rated on what manufacturers call their duty cycles—the number of copies the unit can comfortably be expected to make per month. The ratings are conservative, but they are an indication of the machines' relative capacities. Don't expect to run the full duty cycle in one day. You would be taxing the equipment beyond its limits. Your decision will probably go beyond a copier's ability to produce a good copy—all of them do that now. The important variables include: (1) copies per minute—4 to 12; (2) duty cycle or total copies per month—200 to 1,500 desktop/tens of thousands office; (3) purchase price—$400 to $1,800 desktop/$4,000 to $8,500 office; (4) cost per copy—3 to 5 cents; and (5) operating features like reductions, two-sided (duplex) copying, collating, and so on. Among other characteristics to consider are weight, portability, and whether the copier occupies a fixed area or has to have extra space to move back and forth as it prints. Experts say anyone regularly making 500 or more copies per month will find the larger machines more economical in the long term.

Why you need to know it   Unless you know your needs from past experience, you should expect to start your business using a local copy service. Gradually, you can establish a baseline of what you will ultimately require in a copying machine. Although owning a machine can be a worthwhile convenience that pays for itself by saving the billable professional hours you spend running errands to the copy center, it can also represent a sizable bad investment if you purchase it before you know what you need and what is available.

Where to learn more

▶ Check product review publications like *Consumer Reports* at your library or bookstore. Read Daniel Grotta's December 1993 article in *Home Office Computing* magazine, "Duplicate and Multiply!", a review of small business copiers. Check your library or contact: Reprint Manager, *Home Office Computing*, 730 Broadway, New York, NY 10003; 212-505-3580.

▶ Office supply stores and catalogs rate copiers and describe their features. Discount office supply sources and price clubs sell name brands at off price.

▶ Name brands list consumer information 800 numbers in the telephone yellow pages. A few of the leading companies are Canon U. S. A., Inc. (800-828-4040), Sharp Electronics Corporation (800-237-4277), and Xerox Corporation (800-832-6979).

Related topics

Business image
Camera-ready copy
Copyright, patent, trademark, and service mark
Desktop publishing
Environmental considerations
Equipment and furniture
Fax
Forms
Leasing

Merchandise buying services
Newsletters
Office planning and decorating
Overhead expenses
Paper
Printing
Promoting your business
Supplies
Time-share offices

COPYRIGHT, PATENT, TRADEMARK, AND SERVICE MARK

What you need to know   You can legally protect your intellectual property using copyright, patent, trademark, and service mark law. Each of these terms applies to a different situation: (1) a copyright protects textual materials, including music, film, and electronic media; (2) a patent protects an invention; (3) a trademark protects the right to distinguish your products from those of others by using a certain word, phrase, symbol, or design—or a combination thereof; and (4) a service mark is the same as a trademark except that it identifies and distinguishes the source of a service instead of a product. In each case, you secure the protection by making application to the appropriate federal agency and paying an application fee that might range from $20 to several hundred dollars, depending on the circumstances. You also have to provide drawings and a copy of the work or product being registered. The government provides useful publications to assist you in filing; it doesn't advise individual applicants. If more help is necessary, you must hire an attorney who specializes in the kind of protection you seek. The starting point for pursuing any of the categories of protection is securing the government publications and application forms. They provide answers to many questions, including how to conduct a search of existing claims; how much protection you might have without registering; fees; time periods involved in the process; and the kinds of professional help to seek.

Why you need to know it   As a home-based business person, you need to be aware of intellectual property protection laws from two perspectives: (1) you might create properties of commercial value that you want to protect, and (2) you need to appreciate the vulnerabilities you have for misusing items already protected by others. One of the most common examples is the illegal sharing of copyrighted computer software. What seems like a minor offense in isolation becomes a giant concern of industry groups like computer software producers' trade organizations, which regularly prosecute violators. Similar concerns exist for the small business person who builds a successful operation and either fails to protect it or finds that it is using information or processes already assigned to others who, at a minimum, issue a cease-and-desist order or, at worst, launch a ruinous lawsuit. Before committing substantial resources to an enterprise that is linked to these laws, clarify the rights and limitations they impose.

Where to learn more

▶ Copyright information is available from the Library of Congress at 202-479-0700 (information specialists) and 202-707-9100 (forms and publications).

▶ Patent, trademark, and service mark information is available from the Department of Commerce at 703-557-4636.

▶ Attorneys specializing in these kinds of law are listed in the telephone yellow pages. Referrals from bar associations are also available.

Related topics

Advertising
Attorney
Bulletin Board System (BBS)
Business ideas
Business name
Buying a business
Camera-ready copy
Competition
Computer equipment
Computer on-line services
Computer software
Conferences, seminars, shows,
    and workshops

Copiers
Desktop publishing
Direct mail and mailing lists
Ethics
Franchises
Information sources and research
Legal liability
Legal/illegal business operation
License
Negotiating
Newsletters
Proprietary information
Regulations

CREDIT CARDS

What you need to know   Merchant credit card accounts allow you to collect from customers via their credit cards. To obtain such an account, you apply to a bank or credit card company, which will charge you a percentage of your sales to make its profit. Visa and MasterCard are marketed through banks. American Express, Diners Club, and other independent cards are approached directly. Small businesses need a stable record of operations to secure a merchant account. Home-based and small mail-order businesses find it nearly impossible to secure merchant status with banks because they are viewed as marginal businesses that might cost the banks money through customer charge-backs. If you have a solid financial record and banking relationship, your bank may provide the service. If not, approach a small local bank, savings and loan, or credit union, which might be more flexible. Offer to move your account to a bank that will support your credit card needs. Investigate the possibility of securing a merchant account through a trade association for your industry. Professional businesses can sometimes take advantage of bank card services made available to doctors. If all else fails, consider an independent sales organization (ISO), an intermediary between small businesses and the card-issuing banks. Expect to pay extra fees, and be very cautious of fraudulent operations. Once you have merchant account status, either directly or through an ISO, be aware that you have a valuable credit reference to protect. If your account is terminated, you get effectively blacklisted in the credit card industry and will find it quite difficult to secure merchant status again.

Why you need to know it   Doing business by credit card can double the amount of your average sale, according to some small business persons. The credit card industry claims that increases ranging from 10 to 50 percent are realistic expectations. There is also an endorsement quality about being able to offer a universally recognized credit card. It enhances your business image and implies that you are reputable. The sheer convenience to the customer stimulates impulse buying and removes one more obstacle to doing business. On the negative side, credit card surcharges can cost you from 3 to 7 percent of sales, and considerably more if you have to operate through a third-party ISO. There is also the administrative inconvenience of verifying the legitimacy of the card and processing the credit card purchases.

Where to learn more

▶ Approach the bank where you maintain your business account and ask about its credit card requirements.

▶ Inquire as to whether the trade associations for your industry offer merchant account arrangements. (To find them, look in Gale's *Encyclopedia of Associations* at your library.)

▶ Ask your Chamber of Commerce for suggestions.

▶ Cautiously respond to ISO advertisements in small business publications, or contact one of these companies: (1) Security Merchant Service, 404 Dakota Trail,

Irving, TX 75063 (214-401-1437); (2) Teleflora CreditLine, Credit Card Operation, 12233 West Olympic Boulevard, Los Angeles, CA 90064 (800-325-4849 or 310-826-5233, ext. 4000); or (3) Modern Business Services, Attn: George Rawlins, 615 Harper Road, Perry, GA 31069 (Fax 912-988-3017; include your telephone number).

▶ R. Howard Direct, Agent, 7070 Belleview Plaza, Suite 101-B, Fairfield, AL 35064 (205-781-3585), sells *PhoneCheck*, a check approval service that offers an alternative to taking credit card purchases.

Related topics

Banking services	Franchises
Bankruptcy	**Loans, credit, and venture capital**
Bookkeeping	Managing growth
Budgeting	**Money management**
Business basics	Profit
Cash flow	Reducing expenses
Electronic banking	Separating business and personal
Evaluating your business	Undercapitalization
Financial planning	

CREDIT UNIONS

What you need to know   Credit unions are financial consumer cooperatives that offer savings, loan, checking, credit card, and other services to members. Membership is based on employment with certain kinds of organizations—government agencies, major private companies, and so on. The criteria for membership have broadened in recent years, as have the services offered. Credit unions now exist for almost anyone who is diligent enough to identify a kindred group, and that includes the self-employed. Once membership is secured, participation can be continued indefinitely, even after leaving the class of employment that originally qualified you.

Why you need to know it   Credit unions provide an alternative to large regional banks and sometimes offer both more favorable terms and more individualized treatment. Not all credit unions are geared for commercial banking services, even the relatively small-scale requirements of home-based businesses. If you qualify for credit union membership or have an established account, inquire about the support it might provide you as a small business person.

Where to learn more

▶ Credit unions are listed in the telephone yellow pages.

▶ National trade associations include the Credit Union National Association, Inc., 805 15th Street, NW, Washington, DC 20006 (202-682-4200), and The American

Federation of Community Credit Unions, 1722 7th Street, NW, Washington, DC 20009 (202-328-9805).

▸ The federal agency overseeing the industry is the National Credit Union Administration, 1775 Duke Street, Alexandria, VA 22314-3428 (703-518-6300).

▸ The National Association for the Self-Employed (see Appendix B), with a membership fee of $48, operates a credit union for the self-employed. Inquire among other trade and professional groups that might offer credit union services that would be attractive in your situation.

Related topics

Associations	Managing growth
Banking services	**Money management**
Checking accounts	Reducing expenses
Credit cards	Regulations
Electronic banking	Separating business and personal
Financial planning	Undercapitalization
Loans, credit, and venture capital	

CUSTOMER RELATIONS

What you need to know   Customer relations is mainly stimulating communications. Ask your customers for feedback, and keep them informed about your company. Solve problems and evaluate what you do for customers by taking the initiative and asking their opinions when you present a bill, deliver merchandise, or submit a completed project. "Ask for the sale!" is a shopworn but masterfully effective adage in selling. Its corollary in customer relations is "Ask what the customer thinks!" Some customer relations work is passive; that is, you can depend on what trade organizations and big companies have already learned. Read business publications and ask trade associations to send you copies of surveys and studies on the subject of interest. But the most effective customer relations for your business is your personal solicitation of customers' or clients' opinions on how well you are satisfying their needs and how you might still improve your service. People like to be thanked. They like to have their opinions asked. Clients like to be remembered. All these can be accomplished with a personal touch when your business is small. Postcard mailings, periodic personal telephone calls, diligent response to complaints and inquiries, newsletters, and announcements of new products and services are examples of small businesses activities that can enhance public relations. Ask whether your product or service was received in good condition. Are there any questions you might answer or is there additional information you might provide? Was your product or service satisfactory? Would the client use your company again or recommend it to others? How might you personalize your service next time? Shortly after the point of sale is the ideal time to initiate a customer relations effort, while the transaction is fresh in the customer's mind.

Why you need to know it   Customer satisfaction yields repeat business and favorable word-of-mouth publicity, which are essential to building a successful small business. The conventional wisdom is that a satisfied customer spreads the word to about five other people, and a dissatisfied customer will cover almost four times that many friends and associates. Customer relations is not difficult or time-consuming, and it doesn't have to be a formal activity for a home-based business. Recognize its importance and make it a habit, a daily attitude that lets you optimize the many opportunities that come from being a one-person (or several-person) enterprise that deals intimately with its clients.

Where to learn more

▶ Gale's *Directory of Associations* is an ideal source for identifying groups that share your client base and might be approached for studies and advice about customer relations. Some have codes of good practice that can form a core for your own policy and the outreach effort that flows from it. Check the business reference section of your library.

▶ Look at customer relations surveys and practices you encounter as a consumer, and adapt them to your business.

▶ Consultants who specialize in customer relations are available. Check your telephone yellow pages and directories. (See also Appendix B.)

Related topics

Advertising	Desktop publishing
Answering machines and voice mail	Environmental considerations
Attitude	Ethics
Bulletin Board System (BBS)	Franchises
Business cards	Mail order
Business image	**Newsletters**
Conferences, seminars, shows, and workshops	**Promoting your business**
	Public relations
Debt collection and creditworthiness	**Telephone use**

DEBT COLLECTION AND CREDITWORTHINESS

What you need to know   Debt collectors act as agents for companies that are owed money and have been unsuccessful in collecting it. As his or her fee, the debt collector receives up to 40 percent of the sum collected. Because of abuses, the debt collection business is now highly regulated, and anyone who violates the rules can be arrested for assault or sued for libel, slander, or invasion of privacy. A collection agency can contact persons suspected of owing money, and take reasonable steps to locate them, including contacting friends and acquaintances, but they are not allowed to mention the indebtedness or harass and threaten. Debtors have a specific right to a written statement of the claim against them and of what they can do if they wish to dispute the claim.

Proper notice to the collector can also greatly limit further contact. There is no imprisonment for debt in the United States, but fraud or forgery carries a sentence. If your concern is determining the creditworthiness of a company you are considering doing business with, the information is available for a fee through on-line computer services and directly from firms like Dun and Bradstreet and TRW. These are not inexpensive services, and the typical home-based business may find the costs prohibitive. A less expensive alternative is to use a standard business reference at your library and query the firm's banking and accounting references informally to determine the firm's present financial health. Collection efforts for the small business center around mailed notices that escalate in abruptness. These are followed by referral to an attorney and a collection agency, in that order. Before exhausting your goodwill, take advantage of the intimacy of being a small business and consider creative solutions such as barter.

Why you need to know it

A small business owner can end up on either end of the debt collection and creditworthiness equation—as the one collecting or the one who is the subject of the collection action. In either instance, it is prudent to know the rights of both parties and proceed accordingly. Debt collection tends to be an emotional exercise, and the potential for legal missteps and a resulting liability is real. After you send the routine sequence of debt collection notices, it is wiser to consult your attorney rather than a collection agency. The best approach is to deal only with creditworthy clients, but that isn't always possible, and today's AAA-rated firm can develop problems tomorrow.

Where to learn more

▶ Inform your state attorney general's office or the Federal Trade Commission (202-326-2222) if you are the subject of debt collection abuse. Potentially relevant legislation includes The Fair Debt Collection Practices Act, The Fair Credit Billing Act, and The Fair Credit Report Act.

▶ Engage an attorney to pursue a debt collection on your behalf or to defend you from abusive collection procedures.

▶ A useful book containing information on debt collection rights is Lawrence R. Reich and James P. Duffy's *You Can Go Bankrupt without Going Broke* (New York: Pharos Books, 1992).

▶ Credit reporting services include Dun & Bradstreet sales (800-234-3827) and TRW sales (800-344-0603).

▶ Computer on-line services offering credit reporting include: NewsNet (800-345-1301); CompuServe (800-848-8990); and Dialog (800-334-2564).

▶ EZ Legal Books, 384 S. Military Trail, Deerfield Beach, FL 33442 (305-480-8933/8906 Fax), sells *Credit Manager,* a complete credit and collection system of over 150 letters, agreements, notices, memos, and other documents to help you get paid every time. Price: about $25.

◗ Performance Source II, Ltd., PS II Building, 1448 Old Skokie Road, P. O. Box 1905, Highland Park, IL 60035-7905 (708-831-5080/5050 Fax), is a national collection agency that works on a contingency fee basis.

◗ The professional association for collectors is the American Collectors Association, P. O. Box 39106, 4040 West 70th Street, Minneapolis, MN 55439; 612-926-6547.

◗ *CashCollector* (about $140, from Jian Tools) is a computer software product used for debt collection. Call 800-442-7373 or 415-941-9191.

◗ R. Howard Direct, Agent, 7070 Belleview Plaza, Suite 101-B, Fairfield, AL 35064 (205-781-3585), sells *PhoneCheck,* a check approval service.

Related topics

Accountant	Customer relations
Accounting	Escrow
Attorney	Ethics
Bankruptcy	**Evaluating your business**
Bartering	Fees and pricing
Billing	**Financial planning**
Bonding	**Forms**
Bookkeeping	Legal/illegal business operation
Budgeting	Loans, credit, and venture capital
Business image	Money management
Buying a business	**Negotiating**
Cash flow	Records
Computer software	Reducing expenses
Contracts	Regulations
Credit cards	Tax checklist

DESKTOP PUBLISHING

What you need to know   With a desktop computer, appropriate software, and access to a laser printer, anyone can produce printed materials that rival commercial newsletters and other printed products. The range of sophistication (and price) of publishing software is extremely wide. At the inexpensive level is *PagePlus for Windows* at about $60 (800-697-3743); at the pricey level is Aldus *Pagemaker* at just under $600 (800-800-5555). Alternatively, an upscale word processing program and basic page layout and graphics capabilities may be enough for your needs. Clip art has long been available via ads in computer magazines and through mail-order houses. Now you can buy editorial material as well. An example is *ClipEdit* (from Dartnell, 800-621-5463)—ready-to-publish articles, on disks, that cover a variety of subjects and can serve as filler in your publications. Scanners that let you turn photographs and drawings into images for your computer (assuming you have obtained the permission to use them) are available at popular prices. You can build publications by importing graphs, tables, and text from other programs. The ability to select different type faces, size and crop images, and add finishing touches like borders and dividing lines lets you achieve a professional look.

Why you need to know it

As a home-based business person, you will need printed materials. If you have the equipment and a degree of talent, and haven't reached the point where your time is worth more, desktop publishing can save you money and improve your business. Controlling the creative process yourself and having the ability to modify at will puts in your hands considerable power that otherwise would go to others. Cost savings can be substantial. Whether you produce a finished consulting report that you have formatted for maximum impact, or a mailing piece to advertise your goods or services, or a catalog for your mail-order business, the potential is realistically there for preparing it yourself—even if you turn the job over to a printer for large numbers of copies.

Where to learn more

▶ Computer software manuals contain most of what you need to know about desktop publishing.

▶ Computer and small business magazines contain articles on desktop publishing. Page through current issues or do a key word search at the library, to compile an up-to-date list. (See Appendix C.)

▶ Bookstores sell specialized works on desktop publishing. An example is Steve Morgenstern's *No-Sweat Desktop Publishing.* Call 800-325-6149 to order it for under $25.

▶ EF Communications, 6614 Penrod Avenue, St. Louis, MO 63139 (Fax 314-647-1609; orders only, 800-264-6305), sells *Advertising from the Desktop,* a 425-page book on desktop design, for about $25.

▶ A free booklet on scanners is available from UMAX. Call 800-562-0311 or 510-651-8883; Fax 510-651-8834.

Related topics

Advertising
Business cards
Business image
Camera-ready copy
Computer equipment
Computer software
Conferences, seminars, shows,
   and workshops
Copiers
Copyright, patent, trademark,
   and service mark

Ethics
Expense sharing and joint ventures
Forms
Marketing and market research
Newsletters
Paper
Printing
Promoting your business
Reducing expenses

DIRECT MAIL AND MAILING LISTS

What you need to know   Direct mail promotion of your business involves a mailing list and a mailing piece (the letter and/or advertising copy you send your prospects). Professional services contract such projects for a fee, but a computer with a good word processing program, and possibly database and publishing software, will let you do the job yourself. There is software that prints postal bar codes; specialty papers let you publish professional quality mailing pieces (see PAPER); and you can sort address labels in zip code order and save postage on large mailings. Most of your home business mailings would consist of a letterhead to identify your business and convey its image, a greeting in letter format or an introductory heading that makes the subject clear, a statement of the problem you intend to solve for your customer, a list of benefits to be derived from using your services, a description of your services and your qualifications to provide them, an offer, and an invitation to respond. Mailing lists can be built from your own contacts and research or rented for one-time use. CD-ROM disks are sold that list the names and mailing addresses of most businesses and individuals in the country, and they can be sorted by industry and zip codes. Mailing list companies are more sophisticated and can provide precise demographic selection for a price.

Why you need to know it   Home-based businesses often lend themselves to direct mail because they have a specific, easily targeted clientele. Although mass mailings may be too costly and inappropriate, the efficient use of direct mail to selected markets can work well for the microbusiness. A secondary source of income is rental fees from a well-managed mailing list. Don't overlook the barter possibilities with small business people who cater to the same clients you do, offering a different product or service. Exchanging your lists can be mutually beneficial and cost you nothing. There is a lot of potential for small businesses in general, and home-based businesses in particular, to work cooperatively in sharing lists and doing combined direct mailings. Check your network and computer bulletin boards for possibilities.

Where to learn more

▶ Consult the telephone yellow pages under "Mailing Lists and Mailing Services." National mailing list firms include: Hugo Dunhill (800-888-8030), Americalist (800-321-0448), Bell Atlantic (800-333-7980), and TRW (800-527-3933).

▶ Check software catalogs and computer magazines for software that supports direct mail projects. Many full-featured word processing programs include bar code, mail merge, list maintenance, and other capabilities. An example of a special mailing program is *DAZzle Plus for Windows,* a mailing utility that prints addresses, bar codes, and custom messages, and verifies zip codes. Order for about $70 from Power Up! (800-851-2917).

▶ CD-ROMs with 11 million business listings gleaned from over 5,000 directories cost about $80 at Power Up! (800-851-2917). A CD-ROM set, available for about $90 from DAK (800-325-0800), contains 9.1 million business and 70 million residential listings nationally. Pro CD, Inc., 8 Doaks Lane, Little Harbor, Marblehead, MA 01945 (617-631-9200), offers a "national phone directory" consisting of 70 million residential and 7 million business listings on 7 CDs for about $150.

▸ The Direct Mail/Marketing Association, 6 East 43rd Street, New York, NY 10017, is the industry's professional association.

Related topics

Advertising	Environmental considerations
Agents and brokers	Ethics
Associations	Expense sharing and joint ventures
Bartering	Fax
Business address and location	Information sources and research
Business image	**Mail and overnight delivery**
Business name	**services**
Competition	**Mail order**
Computer equipment	Marketing and market research
Computer software	**Newsletters**
Computer use	Paper
Copyright, patent, trademark,	Printing
and service mark	Professional help
Customer relations	**Promoting your business**
Desktop publishing	Regulations
Direct selling and multilevel	
marketing	

DIRECT SELLING AND MULTILEVEL MARKETING

What you need to know   One legitimate, low-capital way to start a business is direct selling, including multilevel marketing, if the opportunity is sound and your expectations are realistic. Unfortunately, get-rich-quick schemes and exaggerated claims abound in this business, and new, ill-conceived companies set up shop and solicit associates regularly. A high percentage of direct selling companies fail, leaving their sales organizations without a product to sell or, worse, with a supply of worthless merchandise. There are several hundred established, legitimate direct selling and multilevel marketing companies, and they account for the vast majority of the sales in this multibillion-dollar industry. If you are considering a direct selling opportunity, determine that the company has a verifiable record of making money for its dealers through the sale of its merchandise, not the up-front membership fees associated with pyramid schemes. Avoid opportunities that call for much in the way of an initial investment or inventory. Direct selling has an evangelical character; expect to be motivated in what might strike you as crude and unsophisticated ways. Expect to constantly recruit others to sell your company's products. Understand that successful products introduced by direct selling are quickly emulated in the retail market at lower cost. Realize that the reputable companies have already heavily penetrated the consumer market and it will take great effort to find new recruits and customers. With those cautions in mind, there *is* opportunity for determined people who are capable of systematically offering a salable product. Sales success is ultimately determined by the numbers of contacts made. Make enough contacts and you will make money. Technology can help; one of the most popular software developments in recent years has been "contact management" software that makes systematic selling easier.

Why you need to know it   The most popular rip-offs in the business opportunities marketplace involve direct selling. You need to be an intelligent consumer and not be taken advantage of as you launch or expand a home-based sales business. Avoid the pulp magazine ads showing beautiful people and fast cars. Don't pay dearly for a business plan you can acquire much less expensively by buying a discount-price computer and reading a few readily available books on how to offer popular services. Watch out for technology-based schemes that promise painless direct selling via telemarketing machines (which are rapidly becoming illegal to operate). Be careful not to buy an oversold idea like computer-based scholarship searches. By the time such ideas reach the mass market business opportunity mailers and magazines, you must ask hard questions (of yourself and potential buyers—*not* the promoter, who will have an endless selection of success stories) about their viability. On the other hand, if you are willing to put your energies into one of the established, household-word direct selling companies and can do what needs to be done, there is always an opportunity to prosper in sales.

Where to learn more

▶ Direct Marketing Association, 1101 17th Street, NW, Washington, DC 20006; 202-347-1222.

▶ Better Business Bureau in your region and in that of the company offering the direct selling opportunity.

▶ State attorney general's office, consumer affairs division, in your state and in that of the company offering the opportunity.

▶ Amway, Mary Kay, Shaklee, Watkins, and others can be found in your telephone book or in national business directories available at your library.

▶ *PROSELL* (800-444-9945) is an example of computer "contact management" software; another is Symantec's *ACT!*, which is available through software resellers, including mail-order sources in Appendix C.

Related topics

Advertising	**Competition**
Agents and brokers	Computer equipment
Associations	Computer software
Bartering	Computer use
Business address and location	Copyright, patent, trademark,
Business image	and service mark
Business name	Customer relations

Desktop publishing
Direct mail and mailing lists
Ethics
Fax
Information sources and research
**Mail and overnight delivery
   services**

Mail order
Marketing and market research
Newsletters
Promoting your business
Regulations

DISABILITIES

What you need to know   Home-based businesses are ideal for people
   with disabilities. The problem of commuting is eliminated, and the use of
   customized equipment is more convenient. Another advantage is that the
   physically challenged individual need not make his or her limitation known
   to clients, thus leveling the playing field and doing away with any stigma or
   unequal treatment. Remote-access software extends the reach of anyone
   working at home. By combining it with a telephone modem, a person working at home can access and manipulate computers in other locations. One
   physically challenged entrepreneur in New England runs a home-based company (Special Access Computer Enhancements, Derry, NH) that adapts
   computers for special use by other disabled people via remote-access software. Government agencies and private industry groups make a special effort to assist in providing the physically challenged with access to technology
   (see below).

Why you need to know it   Home-based businesses are viable alternatives
   for physically challenged people with entrepreneurial leanings. Whether you
   are in that category yourself or interested in assisting someone who is, familiarity with the home-based business movement is helpful. Another motivation
   might be to employ a physically challenged person whose talents and abilities
   fit your home-based business needs—either remotely from his or her home or
   in person at your office.

Where to learn more

▶ For help in starting a technology-related assistance program, call the Technology-
   Related Assistance for Individuals with Disabilities program in Washington
   (DC), at 202-205-5666.

▶ The Easter Seal Society and IBM run a cooperative program designed to provide
   technology to qualified physically challenged people at deep discounts. It is
   called Computer Assistive Technology Services (CATS) and can be reached at
   312-726-6200, 312-726-4258, or 800-221-6827.

▶ The Electronic Industries Association, Consumer Electronics Group, 2001 Pennsylvania Avenue, NW, Washington, DC 20006 (202-457-8700), offers a booklet
   that lists companies making special computer-related products and services for
   the physically challenged.

Related topics

Bulletin Board System (BBS)

Business address and location

Business associates

Business travel

Computer equipment

Computer on-line services

Computer use

Customer relations

Electronic banking

Employees

Equipment and furniture

Ergonomics

Insurance

Labor laws

Legal/illegal business operation

Loans, credit, and venture capital

Personnel policies

Public relations

Regulations

Telephone equipment

Telephone services

Telephone use

Vacation, work styles, and schedules

DISASTER PLANNING

What you need to know   Fire protection experts say nearly one third of companies that have a serious fire are out of business within a year, and nearly three quarters of them fail within five years. Anything that is a threat to your home is also a danger to the survival of your home-based business. Specialists in business contingency planning suggest going through your home office acting out a typical business day and anticipating everything that could go wrong. Their primary advice is to make backup copies of important data and records regularly, and to store them off-site in a safe deposit box or, at least, at another location. Equipment is often covered by insurance and almost anything can be insured for a price, but lost records and work in progress are virtually irreplaceable. Anticipate problems like water damage or kitchen or heating system fires, and try not to situate your business where it would be in the direct path of possible destruction—below a flooding bathroom, sharing a wall with the furnace room, or near the kitchen's cooking appliances. Be sure you have adequate insurance, and know its limitations. Verify that your business activity doesn't somehow void your homeowner's insurance. Your cheapest and best protection is to update your files regularly and store them safely off-site. A good inventory of your equipment will be helpful if you must file an insurance claim—a video camera offers an easy way to record the contents of your office. Keep the video tape in a safe place off the premises. Contingency planning might include informal arrangements to continue operations in the facilities of one of your business associates. An adequate financial reserve to cover an unanticipated disruption is also essential.

Why you need to know it   Your home business is vulnerable to everything from natural disasters to accidents and theft—more so than a well-designed and managed commercial building. Cash flow for small businesses depends on continuous operations and on the files that are the lifeblood of the enterprise. Believing that "It can't happen to me" offers no protection when it does. Have a firm contingency plan, and form the habit of regularly backing up your invaluable files and storing them safely, in a fireproof box, at another location.

Where to learn more

▶ Consult current computer magazines and catalogs for data backup systems that would work in your situation. Buy one that is simple (so that you will use it regularly) and portable (so that you will store it properly). (See Appendix C.)

▶ Ask your insurance agent what coverage is available, and at what cost, to protect the business you operate.

▶ Using computer magazines, catalogs, and resellers, familiarize yourself with computer utilities that recover apparently lost data. If you are uncomfortable with the procedures and valuable data are at stake, pay a consultant to execute the recovery. (See Appendix C.)

▶ Using computer magazines, catalogs, and resellers, familiarize yourself with surge protectors and power backup systems that can protect your operation at reasonable cost. (See Appendix C.)

Related topics

Cash flow
Computer equipment
Computer on-line services
Computer software
Computer use
Customer relations
Debt collection and creditworthiness
Direct mail and mailing lists
Diversification
Employees
Evaluating your business

Information sources and research
Insurance
Investing
Loans, credit, and venture capital
Office planning and decorating
Security
Tax checklist
Telephone equipment
Telephone services
Telephone use
Undercapitalization

DIVERSIFICATION

What you need to know   Dependence on a single large client can be ruinous to a small business if that source of revenue is withdrawn. Home-based businesses often begin with a single focus and gravitate toward ever-larger dependence on several clients. It is more comfortable to expand existing accounts with people you know than to generate new business, but the ultimate cost of giving up diversity for comfort can be manipulation by the primary client or a painful recovery when that client no longer chooses to do business with you. No small business should spurn large clients. The recommended tactic is to make a realistic appraisal of the value of the relationship and enter it with your eyes wide open. Beneficial contacts and in-depth industry knowledge can often be gained by working for certain large clients. A caution: Maintain your operating independence and have your business positioned to expand in other directions when it becomes necessary. One approach is to service the account but subcontract enough of the work to allow you to take on additional clients. If the large account goes, you have other business in place. Have several months' worth of operating reserves ready to bridge the gap between the loss of the lucrative single account and the acquisition and cultivation of new ones. Diversity can also take the form of a client mix that crosses economic and geographic sectors, to lessen the impact of regional recessions on your company.

Why you need to know it   Your business survives on the revenue stream from its customers or clients. If it is vulnerable to the whims of a single individual or company, you can find yourself out of business unless you have other business to turn to or enough reserves to keep you afloat until new clients can be developed. Economic downturns can also be ameliorated to some extent if your business lends itself to a mix of industries and regions. As you plan and grow your business, opt for diversity when it can be accommodated. Diversity is insurance against technological obsolescence. If you keep pushing your service into innovative niches, you might find a natural replacement for a primary line that is growing stale or oversold.

Where to learn more

▶ As you read the magazines and trade journals in your specialty, look for new customers and approaches that might allow you to broaden your operation.

▶ Talk with clients about additional services they need and are finding in scarce supply.

▶ In working projects, identify other contractors whose work you respect, and network with them where complementary possibilities exist for client, services, or product development.

Related topics

Budgeting
Business address and location
Business ideas
Business image
Business plan
Buying a business
Cash flow
Conferences, seminars, shows,
   and workshops
Consulting
Continuing education

Evaluating your business
Expense sharing and joint ventures
Financial planning
Foreign markets and languages
Information sources and research
Loans, credit, and venture capital
Managing growth
Marketing and market research
Syndication
Tax checklist
Zoning

ELECTRONIC BANKING

What you need to know   Electronic banking used to mean a direct tie-in with your bank. That is still a possibility; determine what is available from the banks in your area. Any bank will accommodate a regular fixed payment by electronic funds transfer. But to the computer- and modem-equipped home-based business person, electronic banking is more apt to mean a user service add-on to his or her money management and check writing program. With services like *CheckFree*, you can have your bills paid directly by a central service bureau for a modest monthly fee. If you are using *Managing Your Money* (MECA Software) or *Quicken* (Intuit) to manage your checking account, it is an easy step to make arrangements with *CheckFree* to receive your bill paying instructions via modem and pay them on your behalf, debiting your account electronically and saving you postage and time. The cost is currently $9.95 for 20 payments a month, $3.50 for every 10 checks thereafter. You give up the security of receiving canceled checks, but you receive a detailed monthly statement. Payment isn't limited to large electronic funds transfer payees; checks can be personally mailed to individuals as well. Depending on your situation, it may be worthwhile to pay your clients and suppliers this way. It is businesslike and it increases the certainty of timely payment. Errors still occur, of course, and there is a complaint resolution procedure.

Why you need to know it   Two of your concerns as a home-based business person are your business image and the highest and best use of your time. Anything you can do inexpensively to enhance them deserves consideration. If the time you spend balancing a checkbook, writing checks, and stuffing and stamping envelopes could be applied to doing more business, you should do it. Image is intangible, and any check that doesn't bounce is welcome, but there is something to be said for how electronic payment conveys an image of a progressive small business person who is on the cutting edge of financial management. The combination of computerized money management and electronic bill fulfillment is worthy of your consideration.

Where to learn more

‣ Information on contacting *CheckFree* is included with *Managing Your Money* and *Quicken* money management software packages. Alternatively, you can call 617-898-6000 or connect via CompuServe EasyPlex (mailbox 72537, 2156) or MCI Mail (checkfree).

‣ Call the customer service desk of a local bank to see what electronic banking facilities are available and whether they might serve your needs.

‣ ScanFone (800-578-7226, ext. 11) is an electronic bill paying, merchandise ordering, and banking service that leases a special telephone equipped with a credit card reading device that lets you conduct business from your telephone.

Related topics

Banking services	Financial planning
Bookkeeping	Loans, credit, and venture capital
Cash flow	Managing growth
Checking accounts	**Money management**
Computer equipment	Reducing expenses
Computer on-line services	Telephone equipment
Computer software	Telephone services
Computer use	**Telephone use**
Credit cards	Time management
Credit unions	

EMPLOYEES

What you need to know   The main consideration with employees, aside from the economic justification for hiring them, is their correct tax treatment. You are legally bound to properly meet the federal and state tax withholding requirements. The simple rule is: the government considers anyone who is paid regularly to assist you to be an employee subject to withholding unless you can prove otherwise. The IRS has a series of categories with which you should be familiar. Complicated tax withholding laws make possible the home-based businesses of many "independent contractors." Companies will often buy your services if you can help them demonstrate that you are not their employee. In general, you have an employer–employee relationship when the person paying for the service controls both what must be done and how it must be done. If the employer has the legal right to control both the method and the result of the services, it is an employer–employee situation for tax purposes. That relationship is further established by providing the place to work and the tools for doing it. It does not matter whether the person works full- or part-time, how the person is paid, or what he or she is called. The only safe approach is to consult with your CPA and be certain you are satisfying the withholding requirements. The picture is not entirely negative. Ask your accountant about the several thousand dollars you can pay your dependent children if they do legitimate work for your company, without losing them as deductions or incurring heavy taxation.

Why you need to know it   You are subject to substantial back taxes and penalty payments if you misjudge your withholding obligations. For example, if you misclassify an employee as an independent contractor and do not withhold income, social security, and Medicare taxes from his or her wages, you may be held personally liable for a penalty of 100 percent of such taxes.

Where to learn more

▶ From the IRS: Publication 334, "Tax Guide for Small Business"; Publication 15, "Circular E, Employer's Tax Guide"; Publication 505, "Tax Withholding and

Estimated Tax"; and Publication 937, "Employment Taxes and Information Returns." For forms and other publications, call 800-829-FORM; for assistance, 800-829-1040.

▶ See your accountant to verify your tax withholding obligations.

Related topics

Bonding
Bookkeeping
Business image
Business travel
Concerns about working
    from home
Continuing education
Customer relations
Disabilities
Disaster planning
Ergonomics
Ethics
Family
Financial planning
Insurance

Labor laws
Legal liability
Legal/illegal business operation
Office planning and decorating
Payroll
Personnel policies
Records
Regulations
Retirement
Tax checklist
Telephone use
Temporary help
Time management
Vacation, work styles, and schedules
Zoning

ENVIRONMENTAL CONSIDERATIONS

What you need to know   Small businesses have taken steps to make their companies more environment-friendly. And their greatest motivation is "doing the right thing," not government regulations. Almost none of them receive government assistance to improve their environmental posture. The key avenues open to home-based businesses that want to be environmentally responsible are recycling and conservation. Recycling has two approaches: (1) sorting and disposing of your office waste products in a way that makes them available for future use, and (2) buying recycled paper, toner cartridges, and other products that preserve resources. Recycled paper takes intelligent buying, to avoid the mere appearance of doing the right thing. The trick is to look for 20 percent "post consumer waste," and not just mill scrap and envelope clippings. Not all recycled papers work well with toner and printers, so do your homework before buying. Energy conservation is another way to help. Most home-based businesses are energy-intensive, albeit in a small way compared to larger enterprises. To improve the economy of your operation and the health of the environment, turn off unneeded lights and equipment. There is a trend toward government-mandated conservation standards that will reach the home office indirectly. Computer companies are installing sleep-mode features on their equipment and earning the Environmental Protection Agency's Energy Star designation. To meet the standard, computers and monitors drop power consumption to 30 watts or less in sleep mode versus the 100 to 200 they normally use.

Why you need to know it   You can run a profit-making small business and still advance the cause of the environment. Singly, home-based businesses don't have much of an impact, but with millions of similar operations, enormous amounts of energy, paper, toner, and other office products are consumed. On the business development side, your small business can benefit by touting its "green" image. It has become good business to be environmentally sensitive.

Where to learn more

▶ Quill Corporation, 100 Schelter Road, Lincolnshire, IL 60069 (708-634-6693), publishes a 20-page catalog of recycled paper and business products. It also recycles toner cartridges.

▶ Dataproducts (800-232-2141) and Qume's Eco-recycling center (800-421-4326) remanufacture and return toner cartridges to you at prices that are about 25 percent below list.

▶ Hewlett-Packard (800-232-2141) provides prepaid return labels for toner cartridges and donates $1 to conservation organizations for returns.

▶ Recycled paper sources include: Paper Direct (800-272-7377); PaperAccess (800-727-3701); Domtar Fine Papers (800-267-3060); and Mohawk Paper Mills (800-843-6455).

Related topics

Advertising
Business image
Computer equipment
Computer use
Copiers
Desktop publishing
Direct mail and mailing lists
Equipment and furniture
Ethics
Financial planning
Forms

Government customers
Legal liability
Legal/illegal business operation
Lighting
Managing growth
Media relations
Noise
Public relations
Regulations
Supplies
Tax checklist

EQUIPMENT AND FURNITURE

What you need to know   In surveying its readers, *Home Office Computing* magazine (September 1992) found that everyone had a desktop computer, 83 percent owned answering machines, 70 percent used a mouse or trackball, 66 percent had a dot-matrix printer, 44 percent a cordless phone, 40 percent a laser printer, 40 percent a modem, 35 percent a fax board or modem, 29 percent a fax machine, 29 percent a copier, 27 percent a multiline phone, 20 percent a cellular phone, 17 percent a scanner, and 15 percent a notebook or laptop computer. Twenty-two percent planned to buy a CD-ROM drive, and 17 percent a tape backup drive. These statistics indicate the kinds of equipment home-based businesses use. In addition to the items mentioned, consider a 300-watt or larger uninterruptible power supply if your electrical supply is subject to failure. These cost several hundred dollars but allow you to save your data and shut down your computer without losing data. You will need two telephone lines in most cases. A stand-alone fax machine is money well spent. Well-designed working tables, chairs, and lighting fixtures are essential because you will spend long hours using them.

Why you need to know it   The modern home office phenomenon is based on the power of commercial-grade equipment that is available at consumer prices. You need to make good use of the technology that multiplies the impact of your home-based business.

Where to learn more

▶ Reliable Office Supply is a good company for office supplies and equipment by mail; call 800-735-4000 or 312-666-1800. The company's catalog is informative.

▶ Quill Corporation, 100 Schelter Road, Lincolnshire, IL 60069 (708-634-6693), is another first-rate supplier.

▶ ScanCo (800-722-6263 or 206-481-5434) sells specialized office tables and chairs.

▶ BackSaver Products (800-251-2225 or 508-429-5940) sells expensive but very effective ergonomic office chairs.

▶ Levenger (800-362-0880 or 407-276-2436) is a source for high-quality lighting fixtures.

▶ Appendix C lists more suppliers and sources of specialized advertising.

Related topics

Accounting	Disaster planning
Answering machines and voice mail	**Ergonomics**
Bartering	Fax
Bookkeeping	**Insurance**
Business image	Leasing
Business use of car	Legal liability
Buying a business	Merchandise buying services
Computer equipment	**Office planning and decorating**
Contracts	Reducing expenses
Copiers	Separating business and personal
Desktop publishing	**Tax checklist**
Disabilities	Telephone equipment

ERGONOMICS

What you need to know   Ergonomics is the science of adapting equipment to the functional constraints of the human body. Much attention has been focused on computer workstations. Here is what you need, according to most experts: (1) a seat that keeps your neck and back straight; (2) support for the lower back; (3) a wrist rest; (4) a stand to hold documents at screen height; (5) an arrangement that avoids screen glare; (6) placement of your keyboard in a range of 24 to 27 inches from the floor, so it is below desk level; (7) several feet of clear leg room and possibly a foot rest; (8) 16 to 18 inches space between your eyes and the screen; and (9) a viewing angle of 10 to 30 degrees down from eye level. A wide variety of manufacturers cater to ergonomic requirements. One of the recent, attention-worthy innovations is Apple Computer's split keyboard, which spreads at the center to accommodate a more natural wrist position for its user. The other universally recommended (and available) item is the wrist rest. Cushioned, height-adjustable models in colors to match your decor are available anywhere you can buy a mouse pad. An inexpensive experiment worth trying is to roll a towel into a comfortable support an inch or two thick and see whether it adds to your keyboarding comfort.

Why you need to know it   Painful tendonitis and carpal tunnel syndrome can cost you productivity and even a surgeon's bill—although several months in an awkward wrist support is the more likely outcome. These conditions can be avoided by respecting the subtle stresses you put on your body systems when you operate home office equipment. False economy in the selection of a desk and chair can cost you dearly in discomfort and the lost productivity that accompanies it.

Where to learn more

‣ MicroComputer Accessories, Inc., A Rubbermaid Company, will send you a free booklet on making your workplace more ergonomically correct. Call 800-876-6447 and ask for *The User Friendly Office—What You Need to Know about Computer Ergonomics.*

‣ Reliable Office Supply (800-735-4000 or 312-666-1800) is a good company for office supplies and equipment by mail. The company's catalog includes ergonomic designs.

‣ Quill Corporation, 100 Schelter Road, Lincolnshire, IL 60069 (708-634-6693), is another first-rate supplier.

‣ ScanCo (800-722-6263 or 206-481-5434) sells specialized office tables and chairs.

‣ BackSaver Products (800-251-2225 or 508-429-5940) sells expensive but very effective ergonomic office chairs.

‣ Levenger (800-362-0880 or 407-276-2436) is a source for high-quality lighting fixtures.

‣ Apple, 20525 Mariani Avenue, Cupertino, CA 95014 (408-996-1010 or 800-776-2333), sells the Apple Adjustable Keyboard (about $200). Available locally.

‣ Ergodyne WorkSmart (800-323-0052) sells wrist rests.

‣ Computer resellers and office supply stores can be found locally and via catalog. (See Appendix C.)

Related topics

Computer equipment	Lighting
Copiers	**Office planning and decorating**
Desktop publishing	Stress and overworking
Employees	Telephone equipment
Equipment and furniture	Vacation, work styles, and schedules

ESCROW

What you need to know   Escrow is the deposit of something of value with a neutral third party under terms of a contract or agreement, the disposition of which depends on satisfaction of the agreement. The most common use of escrow is where a real estate deed and/or purchase money is held until the title is cleared or some other condition is met. When the contract's terms are satisfied, the escrow agent conveys the money or property. If the deal falters, the property or money is restored to its owner. The agent gets a fee for his or her services. Escrow is used more broadly than real estate transactions. Theoretically, any deal that requires payment or the exchange of property or services contingent on performance of specific conditions can be managed by a third-party escrow agent. The depositor has no control over the items placed in escrow. It is a useful way to bring enough confidence to a buyer and seller to close an agreement. The seller is assured of getting his or her price, and the buyer is assured the seller will honor the agreement and not accept a subsequent offer. General escrow services are sometimes referred to as performance escrow. Arrangements processed via escrow should be examined by your attorney, and you should verify the reliability of an escrow agency before entrusting it with your funds or property.

Why you need to know it   The creative use of escrow can help a small business person deal positively with customers who might lack confidence in his or her financial stability. In the absence of a published business credit rating, the home-based business can convince clients that a deal can be brought to closure without deposits or purchase money being at risk. Arrangements can be made for payment to an escrow agent who will not release the funds to you until you have satisfied the conditions in the contract. An example might be an advertising publication where the home-based publisher needs a firm commitment of funds before incurring the cost of printing a book or buying space in a newspaper or periodical, and the advertisers are reluctant to pay before publication. The escrow compromise is an agreement under which payment is made to the agent, who doesn't release the funds to the publisher until the advertising is produced and distributed.

Where to learn more

▶ The telephone yellow pages list "Escrow Service" or "Title and Escrow." Inquire as to whether an escrow agent is limited to real estate title exchanges or handles broader agreements. If limited, ask for a referral to a general escrow agency. If you are in a small town, go to your library and check the yellow pages in nearby larger cities' telephone books.

▶ Ask your attorney, accountant, or independent insurance agent to recommend an escrow agent

Related topics

Agents and brokers	Buying a business
Attorney	Contracts
Banking services	Expense sharing and joint ventures
Bonding	Financial planning
Bookkeeping	**Insurance**
Business image	Managing growth
Business plan	**Money management**

ETHICS

What you need to know   Ethics are the moral behavioral expectations that we have of one another. Anyone performing within the standards set for the group he or she belongs to is said to be an ethical member. Interest groups form organizations, and an expected mark of such federations is a published set of ethical standards. Infractions of ethics may have little recourse under law, but they are enforced within organizations whose endorsement is valuable to members who perform services for the public. Belonging to a recognized professional group carries its tacit endorsement, and members share an image and public confidence based on its ethical standards and positions on issues. Your ethical behavior as a small business person is manifested in honesty, fair treatment of clients and customers, equitable billing, timely payment of obligations, respect for information shared in confidence, performance to the best of your ability, and nonacceptance of business for which you are not qualified.

Why you need to know it   Good ethics is good advertising—it is the basis for the word-of-mouth communication on which your success ultimately relies. Bad ethics is bad business—a false economy that creates short-term gains at the cost of repeat sales. As a home-based business person, you rely even more on your ethical reputation than would a national firm, whose image is homogenized by a large number of representatives and broad advertising. Large firms cannot ignore ethical weakness, and it consumes small businesses even more rapidly.

Where to learn more

▶ Research the professional associations in your field, using Gale's *Directory of Associations,* and request copies of their ethical codes.

▶ Pay attention to ethics statements and customer relations policies published in catalogs, printed on the back of billing statements, and included with the promotional literature of your business associates. Much of it can be generalized and adapted for use in your own circumstances.

▶ Chambers of Commerce and Better Business Bureaus can help with broad ethics codes.

▶ The Wharton School of the University of Pennsylvania sells a complete business ethics video seminar through Kantola Productions, 55 Sunnyside Avenue, Mill Valley, CA 94941; 800-989-8272. Price: about $190.

Related topics

Accountant
Advertising
Agents and brokers
Attorney
Banking services
Bankruptcy
Bartering
Bidding
Billing
Bonding
Business basics
Business image
Computer software
Computer use
Consulting
Contracts
Copyright, patent, trademark, and service mark
Customer relations

Debt collection and creditworthiness
Direct mail and mailing lists
Direct selling and multilevel marketing
Environmental considerations
Expense sharing and joint ventures
Fees and pricing
Financial planning
Insurance
Loans, credit, and venture capital
Profit
Projections
Promoting your business
Proposals
Public relations
Sales representatives
Separating business and personal
Tax checklist

EVALUATING YOUR BUSINESS

What you need to know   Success standards vary, but certain criteria should be examined periodically to verify that your business is worthwhile. Here are some benchmarks to check. (1) Cash flow is an obvious test. Are you meeting your obligations? If you are borrowing to do it, are there realistic prospects of future profits that will clean the slate? (2) Are you progressing? Are the trends in your business favorable—revenues up, expenses down, client contact rising and producing new business? (3) Ratio analysis is tricky to apply in small businesses, especially home-based businesses, but it can be useful if you realize the ratios were established on larger operations. Business references in libraries, college business department faculty, and bank lending officers can tell you what businesses in your industry are doing in comparisons like liquidity ratios, asset management ratios, and debt ratios. Ask your accountant what ratios would be useful in your situation, learn what they mean, and set up a spreadsheet to monitor them. (4) Your business income versus the salary and benefits you could be earning as an employee is a good measure of how you are doing, but you have to factor in growth potential and life-style. (5) "Highest and best use" is a real estate appraisal term that you can apply to your talent. Are you concentrating on the things that bring you the greatest return? Give adequate consideration to your values—money may not be the only measure of success. (6) Return on investment is worth considering. Would the money you have invested in the business earn more in the stock market? Would you be as happy with the result?

Why you need to know it   Although you don't want to fall prey to "analysis paralysis"—the tendency to spend more effort analyzing your business than working to make it succeed—you do need to examine meaningful snapshots of its performance on a regular basis. If this is a task that doesn't come naturally to you, pay for the service and benefit from the objective evaluation of your accountant and his or her probably conservative opinion about how to redirect your efforts and resources.

Where to learn more

- Michael Tyran and Fred Dahl's *The Vest-Pocket Guide to Business Ratios* (Prentice-Hall, Inc., 1992) lists hundreds of business ratios, some of which might be adaptable to your business.

- Kenneth R. Ferris, Kirk Tennant, and Scott Jerris's *How to Understand Financial Statements: A Nontechnical Guide for Financial Analysts, Managers, and Executives* (Prentice-Hall, Inc., 1992) does what the title implies *and* includes computer software to generate cash flow analysis and 19 graphic financial ratios.

- Popular bookkeeping software like *Managing Your Money, M.Y.O.B.,* and *Quicken* offer varying degrees of analysis and evaluation, as does accounting software like Microrim's *In the Black.* Research them in computing magazine reviews and catalogs or at your local reseller.

- Spreadsheets like Excel, Lotus 1,2,3, and many other competitive products are reviewed in computer magazines and described in catalogs or at your local reseller. (See Appendix C.)

- Ask your accountant about a practical, targeted approach to monitoring the performance of your particular business.

▶ SCORE representatives can be helpful *if* they have a significant background in small business management. (See Appendix B.)

▶ Eric Siegel et al.'s *The Ernst & Young Business Plan Guide* contains useful methodologies for evaluating businesses. (See the Bibliography.)

▶ The Wharton School of the University of Pennsylvania sells a video seminar on finance and accounting for nonfinancial managers through Kantola Productions, 55 Sunnyside Avenue, Mill Valley, CA 94941; 800-989-8272. Price: about $190.

Related topics

Accounting	Forms
Billing	Franchises
Bookkeeping	**Insurance**
Business address and location	Leasing
Business associates	**Legal liability**
Business basics	**Legal/illegal business operation**
Business image	**Managing growth**
Business name	**Marketing and market research**
Business organization	**Money management**
Business plan	Overhead expenses
Cash flow	**Profit**
Computer equipment	**Projections**
Computer software	Promoting your business
Computer use	Public relations
Contracts	Reducing expenses
Customer relations	Regulations
Debt collection and creditworthiness	Retirement
Diversification	Separating business and personal
Employees	**Tax checklist**
Environmental considerations	Telephone equipment
Equipment and furniture	Telephone services
Expense sharing and joint ventures	**Telephone use**
Financial planning	Undercapitalization

EXPENSE SHARING AND JOINT VENTURES

What you need to know   Not every project is completed by a single firm. On the macro scale, thousands of subcontractors around the world contribute to the manufacture of a Boeing 747, for example. On the micro scale, small businesses pool their efforts to accomplish projects they could not manage alone. The degree of formality involved varies with the project. It can be simple: two or three home businesses agree to independently pay shares of salary and benefits for an employee who splits his or her time proportionately among them. The same concept can be applied to advertising: businesses with similar client bases share the costs of an ad. American Express does this with restaurants and other establishments that accept the Amex card; so do publishers and booksellers who advertise books together. The home-based business parallels are obvious. At the more formal end of the expense-sharing spectrum is the joint venture that is structured enough to bring not only shared effort and profit, but also shared liability. Many joint ventures become formal partnerships with all the legal and tax ramifications of that business form. Examine your network of clients, competitors, and professional associates for ways to share costs and grow your businesses together, and be alert to the need for managing combined risks.

Why you need to know it   Small and home-based businesses come with built-in limitations that can be overcome by expanding their horizons beyond the view from their own operations. Without spending more, you can secure a multiplier for your business by astutely affiliating with others in complementary situations. Joining with others calls for judgment, and you lose a little bit of your independence, but the possibilities for profit and growth may make the connection worthwhile.

Where to learn more

▶ Networking is the best way to learn of opportunities for expense sharing and joint ventures.

▶ Just as a salesperson asks for the sale, make it a habit to ask about sharing the business effort when you talk with competitors, clients, and professional associates.

▶ Computer bulletin boards can link you to other entrepreneurs who have complementary skills and needs and may have good ideas about what joint effort might work locally.

▶ Small business magazines showcase joint ventures that you might clone successfully in your environment. (See Appendix C.)

▶ Barter services can link you in specific exchanges which, in time, might grow into joint ventures between similarly motivated business people.

Related topics

Accounting	Equipment and furniture
Bartering	Forms
Bookkeeping	Information sources and research
Business associates	Mail and overnight delivery services
Business plan	**Managing growth**
Computer use	Newsletters
Conferences, seminars, shows, and workshops	Overhead expenses
	Public relations
Consulting	**Reducing expenses**
Debt collection and creditworthiness	Security
Employees	Telephone use

EXPERT WITNESS

What you need to know   Expert opinion is a marketable commodity in courtroom settings and elsewhere. It is a form of consulting, and there is a market for many specialists who, as disinterested experts, are capable of rendering authoritative opinions to people who are about to invest in a costly product, service, or procedure. Executive recruiters are contacted to describe employment and compensation practices in cases involving employment law. Engineers of every stripe comment professionally on questions relating to their specialties. Arbitration panels seek expert witnesses to help them resolve disputes. Writers and others who establish themselves as experts in a field are paid to represent it. Expert witness work is consulting, but it is more sporadic and focused—rarely a full-time undertaking. Fees are based on a day-rate that takes into consideration the time necessary to prepare.

Why you need to know it   Specialists tend to start home-based businesses, and they should recognize the built-in potential for selling their expertise as another profit center. As an expert witness, you can inject short bursts of profitable activity into the established routine of your primary consulting or other knowledge-based business.

Where to learn more

▶ Network with professional colleagues and practitioners in related fields who might have periodic need for your expert opinion. Discuss the possibilities with practicing professionals in specific areas and with generalists such as attorneys and accountants.

▶ Contact professional associations and describe yourself as someone who is interested in receiving referrals from those seeking the expertise you possess. This can be done locally, regionally, and nationally, depending on your circumstances.

▶ Watch the professional news in your field and identify people who regularly surface as expert witnesses. Contact them and offer to assist when they are overextended or encounter situations that tax their knowledge or are otherwise unappealing to them.

Related topics

Accountant
Agents and brokers
Associations
Attorney
Business associates
Business image
Consulting
Diversification

Legal liability
License
Media relations
Presentations
Professional help
Promoting your business
Public relations

FAMILY

What you need to know   One reason parents work at home is to be more intimately involved in the raising of their children. Children and productive work, however, don't mix without rules, discipline, and special arrangements. Professional image is shattered when a child cries or lifts a phone and contributes to an important client conversation. Even the anticipation of what children (or others) in the house may do can destroy a working routine. Solutions range from detached studios to nannies and child care. Unrealistic expectations lead the list of problems to overcome. A media image of the perfect family or reflections on how things were when one parent worked and the other was the homemaker can lead to exhaustion, guilt feelings, and failure unless coupled with realistic helping arrangements. Experts say you're lucky to get three hours of work done per day while caring for an 18-month-old or younger child and four hours with a 3- to 5-year-old child. You shouldn't expect to approach an eight-hour day until your children go to school full-time. Serious, professional-grade work suffers from any interruption, and the only effective solution is a nanny and strict rules that separate parent and child during working hours except for emergencies and rare opportunities to present outstanding good news. Teamwork with children can help if it includes meaningful chores and progressive, earned participation in your professional life as the child grows more capable. Safety is a major factor. Be aware of your limitations in monitoring a young child while you are engaged in your work. Physical precautions like blocking access to equipment, for the safety of both the child and your data, are important.

Why you need to know it   Home offices attract millions of workers, many of whom have young children. More than 6 million child safety devices, ranging from door knobs that twist harmlessly unless squeezed by an adult grip to padding for desk corners, are being sold each year. The success of your at-home business depends on a realistic approach to the mutual needs of both sides of your home-based life. Business planning for home-based businesses should include child care expenses in terms of both dollars and time.

Where to learn more

▶ Research some associations that address the needs of at-home working parents—for example, Juvenile Products Manufacturers Association of Marlton, NJ. Find it and similar organizations in Gale's *Directory of Associations* at your library.

▶ Child-oriented stores like Toys "R" Us and home equipment stores like Lowe's, Hechinger's, Home Depot, and others, stock products designed to protect children from hazards in the home and shield adult valuables like computers from the intrusion of children.

▶ Specialty magazines and catalogs directed to the parents of young children are good sources for identifying manufacturers of child safety products.

Related topics

Answering machines and voice mail
Business image
Business travel
Business use of home
Computer use
Customer relations
Employees
Insurance
Noise
Office planning and decorating

Psychological factors
Retirement
Role
Separating business and personal
Tax checklist
Telephone use
Temporary help
Vacation, work styles, and schedules
Values
Women's programs

FAX

What you need to know   Fax machines provide almost instantaneous hard-copy communications around the world at low cost. Things to consider when buying a fax include: (1) plain versus thermal paper; (2) multipage document feeder versus one sheet at a time; (3) a cutter for incoming pages; (4) redialing and memory for frequently called numbers; (5) stand-alone unit versus a computer add-on fax/modem; (5) print quality as measured by gray-scale transmission rating; and (6) a switching device to share a single telephone line, or a separate line. The preferred choice for each item is evident, and the costs of fax machines vary accordingly from several hundred to several thousand dollars. A respectable unit can be purchased for less than $700. If you choose a fax/modem, you have the convenience of faxing directly to and from your computer, but you'll need optical character recognition software and a scanner in order to send and receive messages the way you can with a stand-alone unit. Technology is changing rapidly; for example, there are now devices that let your fax/modem and laser printer combine to become a plain paper fax. Regulations limit sending "junk fax" or unsolicited faxes, so examine the laws before you take to broadcast faxing. If you need to send a large-scale fax to many recipients, consider using a service bureau. Fax has also become an effective response device for customer service and information; special equipment and a dedicated computer are needed. There are fax mailboxes for people who travel and need to call in and have their faxes rerouted to another location.

Why you need to know it   The fax machine ranks with the telephone and computer as great equalizers for the home-based business person. With the right setup, you can function like a major corporation, sending and receiving client fax communications whenever and wherever you go. Having to explain that you have no fax, when asked for your fax number, definitely puts you in the minor leagues as a business person. Spend the money for a decent fax and a dedicated telephone line (or reliable switching equipment) if you need fax services.

Where to learn more

‣ Read product reviews in business publications and catalogs, for example, Crutch-field, 1 Crutchfield Park, Charlottesville, VA 22906 (800-388-7700). *Home Office Computing* magazine reviews equipment and software. (See Appendix C.)

‣ Delrina's *WinFaxPro* with OCR uses your modem to send, receive, edit, and broadcast faxes with your computer. Purchase from resellers or catalogs. (See Appendix C.)

‣ Remote-access answering machines for your fax include EMI's SmarterFAX Mailbox Manager (about $700; call 214-340-6789) and Macronix's Vomax 2000 (about $500; call 408-453-8088).

‣ Fax mail is another alternative for receiving your faxes remotely. You subscribe to the service through your regional telephone company or long-distance carrier. Call AT&T (800-446-2452), Ameritech (800-343-8200), US West (612-944-0655), or Envoy Global (503-224-6505).

‣ Fax response systems for replying to requests for information are available from FaxQuest (415-771-0923 or 800-995-9141) and Ricoh Corporation (408-432-8800 or 800-524-1801). To see how they work, try BizFAX (800-227-5638).

‣ The Federal Communications Commission's information number for the regulations under the Telephone Consumer Protection Act is 202-632-7554.

Related topics

Advertising

Business image

Competition

Computer equipment

Computer software

Computer use

Copiers

Customer relations

Direct selling and multilevel
   marketing

Information sources and research

Leasing

Legal/illegal business operation

Marketing and market research

Merchandise buying services

Networking

Paper

Promoting your business

Public relations

Reducing expenses

Regulations

Telephone equipment

Telephone services

Telephone use

FEES AND PRICING

What you need to know   Fees and pricing have to be based on realistic estimates of the annual revenue needed to pay overhead, a salary, and benefits, and to yield a profit for the business that is at least comparable to what you would earn if your business investment were in a reliable mutual fund. The process begins by calculating how many billable hours or days you will have each year. Multiply 40 hours per week times 52 weeks per year (2,080 hours). Subtract realistic amounts of time for vacations and holidays (180 hours?), sick leave (40 hours?), time to generate new business (400 hours?), unbillable professional activities and administrative time (360 hours?), and another 100 hours for miscellaneous down time, and you end up with 1,000 billable hours per year. On the other side of the equation, calculate what you need to earn. Begin with your old salary, say $55,000; add a third to cover overhead and taxes ($18,000) and a 15 percent return on the $50,000 you have invested in the business ($7,500). Your needed revenues for the year are $80,500. Divide by the 1,000 hours you plan to bill, and you have to be charging clients $80 an hour. Variations include working the same kind of cost estimates against daily billings that reflect the same realistic expense and revenue requirements. Validate your charges against what your competition charges, what acquaintances pay when they buy similar services, what trade groups recommend, and what an employer pays and charges to perform similar services. The same approach works with pricing products if you consider how many you can produce and sell per year and what it costs to do it.

Why you need to know it   It is entirely possible to be very busy, work very hard, collect a fair amount of money, and still go broke in short order. There is no substitute for knowing what your business is really costing you to operate, how much you need to take from it to live an acceptable life-style, and charge your clients accordingly. It just doesn't work to go into business and charge what people want to pay you, unless the bottom line equals a living wage and reasonable return on your investment. The only way to know whether that is happening is to run the numbers, and no great sophistication is needed to calculate what it costs to do business, pay your expenses, and extract a salary and profit. Do it before rushing into business, and be candid with yourself on the question of whether you can command the fees you need and bill the necessary hours. If you can't make what you end up with as an employee, forget the business, unless you have other motivations that make it worthwhile, even with less income.

Where to learn more

▶ Check professional associations and publications in your field for reports and articles on salary surveys.

▶ Inquire among acquaintances, competitors, and potential clients regarding the going rate for services like yours.

▶ Use your present salary and benefits—or the package you could command—as an earnings target for your calculations.

▶ Ask an executive recruiter or employment agency what compensation you could expect for your services working full-time.

Related topics

Accounting	Bartering
Advertising	**Bidding**
Associations	Billing
Bankruptcy	Budgeting

Business basics

Cash flow

Competition

Contracts

Customer relations

Debt collection and creditworthiness

Direct selling and multilevel
  marketing

Ethics

Financial formulas

Financial planning

Franchises

Managing growth

Negotiating

Overhead expenses

Payroll

Profit

Projections

Promoting your business

Proposals

Reducing expenses

Regulations

FINANCIAL FORMULAS

What you need to know   The need to contend with awkward formulas has been replaced by the convenience and ease-of-use of popular computer spreadsheets. If you are not into computers and spreadsheets, inexpensive financial calculators are helpful. Concentrate on understanding the concepts behind the particular financial calculations you need and how to interpret the results, not the arcane calculations themselves. If you can do it yourself by reviewing the documentation that comes with software and calculators, fine. If financial formulas are alien, ask your accountant to give you a layperson's briefing on what you need to know and why. Have the accountant provide a few measures that you can monitor and review with his or her assistance until you understand their meaning and significance. Here are some of the topics for which you might find financial formulas useful in managing a small business: (1) loans—the cost of borrowing, balance due, amortization table, accelerated payback, interest variations; (2) business analysis—break-even point, inventory costs, sustainable growth rate, sales-to-profit relationships, discounting, rates of return; (3) personal planning—inflation, retirement; (4) miscellaneous—present and future value, depreciation, real estate, leasing, and statistics. These and many more are built-in functions on modern financial calculators and in popular business software packages.

Why you need to know it   Certain aspects of your business lend themselves to standard calculations as aids in planning and price determination. Someone else has almost certainly taken the time to compute whatever quantitative data you have in mind, and with modern spreadsheets and financial software you don't need extensive mathematical training to use these tools. If you concentrate on the concept behind a formula and its results, and not the calculations themselves, mathematical tools for business can be easy to use.

Where to learn more

▸ Practical applications appear in articles in small business publications. An example is Stephen L. Nelson's "Solve 13 Common Money Problems" in the October

1992 issue of *Home Office Computing*. It provides spreadsheet formulas and illustrates their use. Check your library or contact: Reprint Manager, *Home Office Computing*, 730 Broadway, New York, NY 10003; 212-505-3580.

▶ *The Numbers You Need*, edited by Nigel J. Hopkins, John W. Mayne, and John R. Hudson (ISBN 0-8103-8373-X), includes financial formulas in its extensive collection of fully explained mathematical calculations. Check your library or call 800-877-GALE.

▶ *Executive Calculator Guidebook*, Texas Instruments, Lubbock, TX 79408; 800-858-1802 (national), 800-741-2646 (Texas), or 806-741-2646.

▶ Read computer magazines and catalogs for information on spreadsheet and small business financial software. The manuals that accompany these products are excellent sources of financial formula information.

▶ Computer and business sections of bookstores contain many books on using financial software in innovative ways. Examine them until you find one that matches your needs.

▶ The Wharton School of the University of Pennsylvania sells a video seminar on finance and accounting for nonfinancial managers through Kantola Productions, 55 Sunnyside Avenue, Mill Valley, CA 94941; 800-989-8272. Price: about $190.

Related topics

Accounting	Leasing
Bidding	Loans, credit, and venture capital
Billing	Payroll
Bookkeeping	**Profit**
Business plan	**Projections**
Cash flow	Proposals
Computer software	Reducing expenses
Financial planning	Retirement
Insurance	Tax checklist
Investing	

FINANCIAL PLANNING

What you need to know   The financial plan is a component of the overall business plan used to chart the creation and management of a business and gain financial backing. In an established business, the financial plan is based on past performance altered to reflect expected changes. A new enterprise has to rely on conservative adaptations to standards accepted for similar businesses. The degree of formality in your business plan depends on its purpose—self-management and planning, or securing financial backing. Here are the accepted components of a business financial plan: (1) a statement of the assumptions underlying the projections: What is the basis for the numbers you present? Why should the reviewer believe them? (2) projected income statements for a period of three to five years, quarterly for at least three years;

(3) detailed cash flow statements for two years, then quarterly for years three through five; and (4) an initial balance sheet and projected year-end balance sheets for the duration of the plan. Break-even analyses are also helpful to show minimal performance required at different levels of operation. An existing business would be expected to show historical financial performance. The financial plan serves as the basis for budgeting and evaluating the progress of a business.

Why you need to know it   You need to know how your business should be performing to meet its obligations and make it grow. If you require the use of other people's money, your business plan has to convince them that you will be able to pay them back or make their shares valuable. Whether justifying your place in a joint venture or applying for a line of credit at your bank, you must show the people involved that you are following a pattern of responsible financial behavior. The data in your business plan are also needed if you plan to sell your business, take on a partner, or sell stock. Understanding and maintaining your own financials is important, but gaining the ability to analyze those of others with whom you do business is equally vital.

Where to learn more

▶ *The Ernst & Young Business Plan Guide,* listed in the Bibliography, contains a thorough section on financial planning. Check your library or bookstore for this and similar publications.

▶ Your accountant is your counselor for both your initial financial planning and the ongoing evaluation needed to monitor your enterprise.

▶ Bankers provide a necessary conservative critique of your financial planning.

▶ College business faculty can recommend readings and serve as consultants, but be careful to check out their currency and real-world experience levels.

▶ SCORE can provide helpful consultants on financial planning, depending on the appropriateness of their background. Be sure to get your small business advice from someone who has been successful in such enterprises. (See Appendix B.)

▶ The Wharton School of the University of Pennsylvania sells a video seminar on finance and accounting for nonfinancial managers through Kantola Productions, 55 Sunnyside Avenue, Mill Valley, CA 94941; 800-989-8272. Price: about $190.

▶ Palo Alto Software sells a *Business Plan Toolkit* that takes you through the steps of creating a business plan on your personal computer. A similar software product is Jian's *BizPlanBuilder.* They cost about $75 and are available in both Macintosh and PC versions from your software reseller or PC or MacConnection catalogs. (See Appendix C.)

Related topics

Accountant	**Business plan**
Attorney	**Cash flow**
Bookkeeping	**Computer software**

Evaluating your business	**Projections**
Fees and pricing	Proposals
Insurance	Reducing expenses
Investing	Retirement
Loans, credit, and venture capital	Tax checklist
Profit	

FOREIGN MARKETS AND LANGUAGES

What you need to know   Under the North American Free Trade Agreement (NAFTA), Canada, the United States, and Mexico will establish a committee on small businesses within 12 months of ratification to help them take advantage of government contract procurement in each of the three countries. Small firms will provide software, equipment, and services as the Mexican economy in particular catches up in the use of enhanced communications, data processing, networks, databases, and electronic mail. Bidding on government agency contracts greater than $50,000 and state corporation (like Pemex) contracts greater than $250,000 must be open to all three countries. There is expected to be a market for engineers (especially environmental experts), animal breeders, consultants, lawyers, systems analysts, and meteorologists, to name a few. Licensing is to be reasonably reciprocal, and all requirements are to be clearly published and monitored to prevent discrimination. Electronic bidding networks for the North American continent are envisioned, with Canada's Open Bidding System, a computer bulletin board operating since 1989, leading the way. Experts say you need to know the language and be sensitive to the culture if you plan to do business in Mexico. Successful consultants are already operating from paired home-based offices in the United States and Mexico, and the future looks good for others who have marketable skills and the ability to learn Spanish and the Mexican culture.

Why you need to know it   Home-based businesses are adaptable, and they lend themselves to focusing on specific needs with surgical precision. NAFTA and pending arrangements that open trade in Mexico and Canada bode well for entrepreneurs with professional skills that are relatively commonplace here but are rare in those markets. If the cultural and language challenges are not too forbidding, there is also great opportunity for selling services on the world market.

Where to learn more

▸ Small Business Administration help lines guide you to offices being set up within the government to exploit NAFTA. (See Appendix C.)

▸ Contact the embassies and consulates of Canada and Mexico for assistance in making government and private business contacts in their countries.

▸ Colleges and private schools offer formal instruction in Spanish and French, which would be useful in NAFTA-related commerce. There are also commercial tapes, CDs, and videos that teach the languages and cultures independently. Visit a bookstore or library. Travel, business, and in-flight magazines advertise these products. Berlitz, for example, offers programs in many languages in the following price ranges: seven audio cassettes, $165; six to eight CDs, $185, or seven CD-ROM disks, $199—with a 30-day money-back guarantee. Call 800-362-5500.

▶ AT&T Language Line offers interpreter services in German, French, Spanish, and Japanese for $3.50 a minute. Call 800-752-6096 for information or 800-843-8420 to use the service in the United States or Canada. For overseas help, ask for the service using AT&T USA Direct or call 408-648-7174.

▶ Computer software called *The Language Assistants* (about $80) translates written documents, in both directions, for French, German, Italian, and Spanish. Available from Power Up! Direct, 800-851-2917.

Related topics

Agents and brokers

Associations

Attorney

Business associates

Business image

Business travel

Computer on-line services

Computer use

Conferences, seminars, shows, and workshops

Consulting

Fax

Government customers

Mail and overnight delivery services

Professional help

Promoting your business

Regulations

Sales representatives

Telephone use

FORMS

What you need to know   There are three ways to get the business forms you need: (1) go to a library or bookstore and find a book of standard business forms that can be copied directly or adapted; (2) buy standard forms from business supply catalogs or stores; or (3) purchase software that generates business forms and allows you to design your own forms or customize the models to meet your individual requirements. (See Appendix A.) Many software packages besides those specializing in forms offer report formats that might serve as form templates. Advantages of computer-generated forms include not having to order or store them; they can be modified without having to discard your existing stock as your needs change. Many of the forms can be filled in with the help of built-in formulas and transmitted electronically. You can access other databases and generate summaries and reports. The more sophisticated applications literally automate your business via your use of electronic forms.

Why you need to know it   Depending on the nature of your business, you will find it necessary to use forms to deal with clients and customers.

From shipping and receiving products to billing and following up on late accounts, you need forms to manage your business. With computer-generated forms, you can avoid the expense of printing, storing, and discarding (when forms become obsolete). They make it possible to approach paperless office status with all the related convenience and savings in space and resources. Backup files become all the more important, however, when you depend on electronic forms.

Where to learn more

▶ Appendix A provides additional information on computer-generated forms and contacts for the companies that sell the dominant software, Delrina's *FormFlow* and WordPerfect's *InForms*.

▶ Appendix C lists representative companies that supply printed forms by mail.

▶ Check your business supply store and software reseller for local sources.

Related topics

Accounting	Environmental considerations
Billing	Fax
Bookkeeping	Franchises
Business image	Insurance
Camera-ready copy	Legal liability
Computer software	Loans, credit, and venture capital
Contracts	Paper
Copiers	Promoting your business
Copyright, patent, trademark, and service mark	**Records**
	Reducing expenses
Debt collection and creditworthiness	Tax checklist
Desktop publishing	**Time management**

FRANCHISES

What you need to know   Franchises are tested businesses you buy into for an initial fee and ongoing royalty and advertising fees. Your chances for success are great, according to the Small Business Administration, because the business has been shaken down by others and you have a proven plan to follow. In this era of downsizing, when many managers with experience and severance money are being put on the street, franchises are more popular than ever. The odds of acceptance are long on many of the big names: McDonald's—over 15,000 applicants for 150 openings annually; General Nutrition Centers—20,000 for 250; Decorating Den—20,000 for 260; Mail Boxes Etc.—30,000 for 330; Travel Network—900 for 63; and Merry Maids—3,500 for 95. The investment is substantial—McDonald's expects you to train without pay in one of its restaurants, and bring $200,000. Merry Maids or Decorating Den investments run in the $18,000 to $35,000 range. Expect to have rigorous interviews, a close look at your net worth, the right kind of personality for the company culture, and a solid record of achievement. They can be as low as $1,500, but franchise fees more commonly run $10,000 to $30,000. Franchising choices run the full spectrum, however, and many are readily available in all price ranges. One third of all retail sales are made by franchises, they create over 100,000 jobs a year, and the industry is stable—over 90 percent of the parent franchise companies formed in the past ten years (not necessarily the individual franchisees) are still in business.

Why you need to know it   Franchising offers real opportunities, but you need to be realistic. If you've spent years as a professional or a manager, are you sure you can face endless days as a cold-calling executive recruiter or making donuts before dawn? Any franchise requires you to sell. You're told what to say, but *you* pick up the phone and say it enough times to pay the bills. Do you have the resources to pay the start-up costs, service the debt, and let the business get established before having to rely on it for a substantial salary? Be clear on your territorial rights, any noncompete clauses you might be signing, lawsuits pending to which you might become a party, your training, and resale/termination rights if you want out. Be sure the franchise is properly registered in your state. Step back and count to ten—temper the rapture of hearing only the good news by facing the down side of any business you consider. Don't pay for a franchise and take on its obligations for something you already know how to do or can readily learn. Consider working for a franchisee before buying a unit of your own. It will be well worth the effort and, should your real-world experience prove favorable, it will impress the parent company.

Where to learn more

▶ Attend a franchise fair; they are scheduled regularly in major cities. Inquire at convention centers about upcoming events or contact a franchise organization and ask where it will be appearing in the coming year.

▶ International Franchise Expo, P. O. Box 1780, Winter Park, FL 32790 (800-IFE-INFO or 407-647-8895), promotes franchise shows.

▶ Request a Uniform Franchise Offering Circular from each company you consider.

▶ Talk with present and past franchisees. Ask them for the names of people they know who tried and failed in the business. Franchise training classes become fraternal: some applicants succeed, others don't, and everyone talks about it for a few years. Get the perspective of people who didn't make it.

▶ International Franchise Association, 1350 New York Avenue, NW, Suite 900, Washington, DC 20005 (800-543-1038 or 202-628-8000), is a national trade association of over 800 franchisors that publishes *Franchise Opportunities Guide* (updated every six months).

▶ U.S. Department of Commerce (202-783-3238) publishes *Franchise Opportunities Handbook*, a listing of over 1,400 franchisors.

▶ Business magazines run articles on the latest in franchising. Check the current issues, run a key word search at the library or via your on-line service. Here are a few examples: Gregory Matusky's "The Best Home-Based Franchises," *Home Office Computing,* and Jean Sherman Chatzky's "Body Slammed," *Smart Money,* both December 1993; Wesley J. Smith's "Business in a Box," *Home Office Computing,* October 1992. If you can't find them in a library, ask about reprints: *Smart Money,* 800-444-4204; Reprint Manager, *Home Office Computing,* 730 Broadway, New York, NY 10003; 212-505-3580.

▶ Bookstores and library books cover franchising. Lynnie Arden's *Franchises You Can Run from Home* lists more than 100 possibilities, complete with basic information and points of contact.

Related topics

Advertising	Forms
Associations	Information sources and research
Attorney	Insurance
Business address and location	Legal/illegal business operation
Business associates	License
Business ideas	Loans, credit, and venture capital
Business image	**Marketing and market research**
Business name	Professional help
Business plan	Projections
Computer use	Promoting your business
Conferences, seminars, shows, and workshops	Public relations
	Regulations
Continuing education	Success and failure
Contracts	Tax checklist
Copyright, patent, trademark, and service mark	Telephone use
	Training
Customer relations	Undercapitalization
Fees and pricing	Zoning
Financial planning	

GETTING ORGANIZED AND MANAGING INFORMATION

What you need to know   Home offices are infamous for being disorganized, perhaps because few outsiders see them. *Home Office Computing* magazine ran a contest for the most disorganized, and a contestant described his "historical" method of filing: the closer to the floor, the older the item—the way the earth is naturally organized. Limited space and a lack of clerical help make home offices good candidates for new approaches to getting organized. Add the likely existence of a computer, and software solutions are attractive. Good habits like filing things neatly and discarding no-longer-needed materials are useful, but software can help. Personal information managers like

Symantec's *ACT!* are "contact managers" that include a contact database, an activity scheduler, a report generator, a word processor, an autodialer, a mail merge, to-do and meeting lists, calendar alarms, and more. Enter notes on clients and they are at your fingertips during your next call. If you don't need that much help, there is calendar and to-do software, electronic card file and contact list software, file retrieval software, and traditional databases. There is software that scans text into electronic files, and there is electronic forms software. (See Appendix A.) Use your notebook computer to take it all with you, or invest in a new generation of personal digital assistants like Apple's Newton for a more limited version in an even more portable unit.

Why you need to know it   If you can't find information or you forget commitments to clients, your business suffers. You must stay in touch with clients and systematically pursue new business. You are both the planner/ strategist and the action officer who picks up the phone and makes the calls, sends the follow-up letters, bills regularly, and pursues late payments. Integrated personal information manager software can do wonders for your business.

Where to learn more

▶ Read organizational software reviews in business and computer magazines, catalogs, or computer store displays. *Touchbase Pro* and *Datebook Pro* are two "organize your life" products. (See Appendix C.)

▶ If you prefer a pen-and-paper system to the computerized versions, call The Executive Gallery, Inc., and ask for information on Executive ScanCard Systems, 814 West 3rd Avenue, Columbus, OH 43212; 800-848-2618.

▶ The National Association of Professional Organizers, 655 Alvernon, Suite 108, Tucson, AZ 85711 (602-322-9753), will help you locate a consultant who will organize your office for a fee.

Related topics

Answering machines and voice mail	Goal setting
Banking services	**Managing growth**
Bookkeeping	Marketing and market research
Business organization	Money management
Business plan	**Office planning and decorating**
Cash flow	Professional help
Computer software	**Records**
Computer use	Separating business and personal
Debt collection and creditworthiness	Stress and overworking
Disaster planning	Tax checklist
Financial planning	Telephone use
Forms	**Time management**
	Vacation, work styles, and schedules

GOAL SETTING

What you need to know   There are as many approaches to goal setting as there are purveyors of success literature. Certain recurring points, however, are fundamental and invaluable. To succeed, you need priorities and planning—goals, and schedules for meeting them or altering your approach. Success is the result of forming good work habits, among them goal setting, self-monitoring, and self-evaluation. You must do more than just set goals; they have to be made tangible and turned into specific tasks that can be pursued doggedly through trying times. Everyone from Napoleon Hill (*Think and Grow Rich*) to Ken Blanchard (*The One-Minute Manager*) emphasizes the necessity for goals to be quantifiable, written down, and set for a target date: "I will have $50,000 invested in mutual funds by New Year's Day three years from now." Follow through on these commitments with a personal written recipe or a set of specific steps you will take to accomplish your goals. Be efficient; always look for common goals that can be advanced with shared effort. Stay adaptable; be ready to alter your routines for getting things done, if you find they have become outdated obstacles. Software can help you plot and monitor the time lines for achieving your goals.

Why you need to know it   Goal setting is a valid and necessary activity for any successful home business person. If you are a transplant from an organization that used prescriptions like Management by Objectives (MBO), try to overcome your aversion to make-work goal setting, and define a system that is real and valuable to your new situation. Some people do it naturally; others need to formalize the process. Do an honest self-appraisal, and get help if you need it. The first sign of suffering from poor goal setting is a lack of visible progress and an operation that moves in fits and starts. If that is where you find yourself, make a commitment to practical goal setting, and give it an honest try for a year.

Where to learn more

▶ Bookstores and libraries have books on goal setting, including the classics mentioned above.

▶ Popular books have audio tape versions that some people favor. Zig Ziglar's *The Goals Program* (The Zig Ziglar Corporation, Carrollton, TX 75006) is an example.

▶ SMI International, 5000 Lakewood Drive, Waco, TX 76710, offers a catalog of tapes.

▶ Attain Corporation's *In Control* and Portfolio Systems, Inc.'s *DynoNotepad* are popular to-do-list software packages that help manage goals. *AllClear Trade-up* is a diagramming program that can chart progress toward goals. Other project manager software products also lend themselves to personal and business goal management. (See Appendix C.)

Related topics

Bidding
Billing
Budgeting
Business plan
Computer software
Computer use
Customer relations
Debt collection and
   creditworthiness
Diversification
Expense sharing and joint
   ventures
Financial planning

Getting organized and managing
   information
Investing
Loans, credit, and venture capital
Managing growth
Marketing and market research
Money management
Networking
Projections
Promoting your business
Reducing expenses
Retirement
Tax checklist

GOVERNMENT CUSTOMERS

What you need to know   Depending on how they are tallied, there are between 30,000 and 80,000 government entities throughout the country. In just the federal government, there are at least 100,000 employees whose jobs are to spend about $200 billion a year on goods and services. Some government purchasing is highly centralized, but much of it is disbursed throughout the many agency contracting offices. What most government procurement systems have in common is a set of guidelines crafted by the American Bar Association known as the Uniform Procurement Code. The *Commerce Business Daily* is the federal government's official notice of what it wants to buy. There are categories for almost anything you care to name, from medical, scientific, and social research to training services. Governments have a reputation for favoring the low bidder, but that isn't necessarily true. Modern government purchasing often entails separate technical and cost proposals so that decisions can be made on value and merit rather than cost alone. Bids may be weighted in favor of women, minorities, small businesses, and various social causes. When you identify contracting offices that use your services, file a Standard Form 129, Application for Bidders List, to ensure that you will receive some solicitations. You still need to check for notices that might not be sent because of your position on a rotating list or because your interests and capabilities were misjudged.

Why you need to know it   Marketing is one of the greatest challenges for a small business, and government represents a huge potential customer. Government is everywhere, and it constantly consumes goods and services of every description. You have the added advantage of special programs intended to encourage agencies to do business with small companies.

Where to learn more

▶ *Commerce Business Daily* is available at libraries or by subscription from the Superintendent of Documents, Government Printing Office, Washington, DC 20402-9371; 202-783-3238 (credit card orders). CBD Online makes the service available via computer on-line services.

▶ General Services Administration Business Service Center, Building 41, Denver Federal Center, Denver, CO 80225. Regional offices also exist in Boston, New York, Philadelphia, Washington, Atlanta, Chicago, Kansas City, Fort Worth, Los Angeles, San Francisco, and Auburn (WA).

▶ Each federal department publishes information about its procurement needs and procedures. Go to the library and check Matthew Lesko's *Information USA* for addresses and points-of-contact, or call your representative's or senator's office. (See Appendix C.)

▶ Herman Holtz's books on consulting emphasize doing business with the government. Check your library or bookstore for *The Consultant's Guide to Proposal Writing* and *The Consultant's Guide to Hidden Profits.*

Related topics

Bidding
Bonding
Business image
Competition
Computer on-line services
Computer use
Consulting
Contracts
Disabilities
Diversification
Environmental considerations
Fees and pricing
Foreign markets and languages

Forms
Information sources and research
Marketing and market research
Negotiating
Networking
Newsletters
Presentations
Profit
Promoting your business
Proposals
Regulations
Women's programs

HOMEOWNERS' ASSOCIATIONS

What you need to know   Public zoning regulations are not your only limitation when establishing a home-based business. You may also have to comply with the private rules, regulations, and covenants of the homeowners' association where you live or rent. Most residential property leases have a clause that specifies that the use will be a single-family residence. Some leases go so far as to proscribe business use. The practical reality is that if you run a low-profile business that doesn't come to anyone's attention, only a grudge complaint is apt to cause you trouble. Should a formal complaint arise, you face, at best, the awkward situation of having to plead for a waiver by the board that governs your building, or, at worst, the rental of office space or a time-share office and the formality of moving your business from its residential setting. With that done, and assuming you are genuinely not disruptive, you can resume working at home, but with the added expense of an off-premises office. You have the right to a computer, telephone service, a fax machine, and a reasonable amount of business-related activity stemming from your residence, so the net result of such complaints is usually inconvenience and added expense.

Why you need to know it   Resist the urge to brag to other residents that you are operating a world-class business enterprise right under their noses. Most would cheer you on and wish you well; one in three businesses now are run from home, and almost everyone does some business at home. But you never know when someone will challenge your formal rights under the lease or ownership covenants.

Where to learn more

▶ "Cut Through the Red Tape" and "The 10 Best Cities for Running a Home-Based Business," *Home Office Computing*, January and November 1993, respectively. Check your library or contact: Reprint Manager, *Home Office Computing*, 730 Broadway, New York, NY 10003; 212-505-3580.

▶ Examine your lease and ownership agreements.

▶ Talk with your attorney.

Related topics

Agents and brokers
Attorney
Business address and location
Business image
Business use of home
Contracts
Customer relations
Employees
Insurance
Leasing

Legal/illegal business operation
Managing growth
Negotiating
Public relations
Regulations
Separating business and personal
Telephone use
**Vacation, work styles, and
    schedules**
Zoning

INDEPENDENT CONTRACTOR STATUS

What you need to know   According to the IRS, an individual is an independent contractor if the employer has the right to control or direct only the result of the work and not how it is accomplished. From that point on, the definition gets complicated. The IRS takes the position that no one is an independent contractor if IRS agents can establish any case that the "contractor" is actually a common-law or statutory employee—one who works at the direction of an employer. Why does that difference matter? Many home-based business people, consultants in particular, sell their services on the basis of saving the employer about 35 percent of the costs if a salaried employee were doing the same job—costs arising from social security taxes, unemployment insurance, pension contributions, workers' compensation insurance, and the Family Leave Act and Americans with Disabilities Act (ADA). Mandatory health insurance may also be on the list. Experts, like attorney/author Robert L. Davidson III, recommend the following approach to protect independent contractor status: get paid by the job, not the hour; set your own hours; have your own primary place of work; get written contracts for each job; publicly solicit more than one client; keep your own records; hire your own staff; don't respond to "help wanted" ads; use your own business forms, cards, and stationery; have your own liability insurance, business and professional licenses, and permits; work separately from the client's employees; define the project in writing; don't become an extension of the client's business or a pseudo full-time employee; continue to contract with others; use your own tools; provide your own fringe benefits; refuse employeelike favors; vary your work pattern; avoid using clients' symbols or logos; don't make regular use of a client's office space or accept expense reimbursements outside the contract; don't participate in client staff meetings; don't accept employeelike work instructions.

Why you need to know it   Much of your attractiveness as a home-based independent consultant or worker is in the tax and benefit cost savings you provide your clients. To protect that status, you and those who purchase your services have to maintain a plausible (in the eyes of the IRS) case for your not being a salaried employee.

Where to learn more

▶ Robert L. Davidson III's *Contracting Your Services* (New York: John Wiley & Sons, 1990).

▶ IRS Publication 334, "Tax Guide for Small Businesses." (See Appendix B.)

Related topics

Accountant

Attorney

Bidding

Billing

Bookkeeping

Business address and location

Business organization

Business plan

Business travel

Computer equipment

Computer use

Consulting

Contracts

Copyright, patent, trademark, and service mark

Customer relations

Diversification

Employees

Equipment and furniture

Ethics

Evaluating your business

Expense sharing and joint ventures

Fees and pricing

Financial planning

Forms

Insurance

Legal liability

Legal/illegal business operation

Money management

Negotiating

Networking

Overhead expenses

Personnel policies

Promoting your business

Proposals

Records

Regulations

Tax checklist

Vacation, work styles, and schedules

INFORMATION SOURCES AND RESEARCH

What you need to know   Traditional research sources have been augmented by the computer age. Whether you rely on others to perform the research or do it yourself, it is unlikely that you can avoid the now ubiquitous "key word" search. Walk into a university library and you will be confronted by computers with simplified instructions on how to do routine searches. The same is true in many public libraries where books and periodicals can be searched on CD-ROM disks covering regional library consortium holdings. Even the Library of Congress is close to being on-line nationally. If you use computer on-line services or just have a modem, you can often do searches from your home or office, by yourself or through paid service companies. You have to balance the value of your time against the cost of the services. Regardless of your ultimate approach, be aware of the wealth of databases, CD-ROM disk libraries, and on-line services that might have the answers you seek. Fax is an increasingly useful research tool. Companies set up computers with software and modem support that lets you order reprints and get responses to frequently asked questions almost instantly, via your fax.

Why you need to know it   Most home-based businesses thrive on information. You can't page through card indexes and readers' guides while your competition is running circles around you with a few keystrokes. Either learn the art of computer research techniques—at least well enough to appreciate what is available—or establish contact with those who will do it for you for a fee. When you buy a CD-ROM drive for your computer, check the latest information on the advantages of the faster drives, those that let you handle photo input, and other innovations.

Where to learn more

▸ Gale Research, 835 Penobscot Building, Detroit, MI 48226 (313-961-2242, 800-877-4253), sells hundreds of specialized directories. Ask a librarian to let you review the Gale catalog. Examples include *Business Organizations, Agencies, and Publications Directory,* a 1,400-page bible of business contacts and information including specialized organizations and research sources, and *Gale Directory of Databases,* an extensive guide to on-line services.

▶ About 4,000 CD-ROM disks are available and the number is growing rapidly. Check computer magazines, catalogs, and software resellers, including those listed in Appendix C.

▶ Census and other government data are available on CDs; call the relevant departments and inquire. Use the Washington (DC) telephone book (available in many libraries) government pages or a government information guide, or ask your congressional staff for help (inquire at your representative's local office). (See Appendixes B and C.)

▶ Ask libraries if you can access their catalogs and other services via your computer modem.

▶ Ask information sources that are important to you about the availability and cost of fax research. *Home Office Computing* magazine, for example, has a service called BizFAX, available at 800-227-5638.

▶ Executive Book Summaries, 5 Main Street, Bristol, VT 05443-1398 (800-521-1227), provides monthly eight-page summaries of leading business books on a subscription basis.

Related topics

Accountant
Agents and brokers
Attorney
Bulletin Board System (BBS)
Computer on-line services
Computer software
Conferences, seminars, shows, and workshops
Consulting
Continuing education
Copyright, patent, trademark, and service mark

Expert witness
Fax
Multimedia
Networking
Newsletters
Professional help
Regulations
Sales representatives
Tax checklist
Telephone use

INSURANCE

What you need to know   Inform your insurance carriers of your business activities. A loss originating from commercial activity could, at best, not be covered, and, at worst, void your residential policy. Auto insurance needs to strike a balance between costly primarily-business-use coverage and occasional commercial errands in your personal vehicle. The determination depends on the percentage of use more than on the miles driven. Homeowner's and renter's coverage for a home office can usually be handled with an inexpensive rider unless you have frequent business visitors, employ others in your home business, or maintain valuable inventory. Supplemental coverage can be added for computers and software or for specialized equipment and liability exposures. Your basic coverage should include loss (material and business activity) and liability. Errors-and-omissions insurance is a good idea for a business in which an error in judgment could cause someone else a loss and result in being held liable. Disability insurance protects against lost income, but as a small business, your financial records would have to substantiate a history of earnings at a certain level. Legal, dental, eye care, key person, and other specialized insurance is available, but after covering catastrophic losses it is prudent to self-insure against some risks. "Independent" agents are generally your best bet: they shop from a number of companies to find you the best deal. "Captive" agents representing a single company can do a good job too, but they are limited to one menu of products. Fraternal, professional, and alumni associations may have economical group policies tailored to your profession. Insurance is also sold by direct marketing and by reduced-fee agents. The more you know about what you need, the less advice you should pay for, but cheap coverage that doesn't pay when you need it is no bargain. Unless you are familiar with a company, call the Better Business Bureau and the Consumer Affairs Office of the state attorney general's office where you live and where the company is based.

Why you need to know it   Insurance is something you can easily have too much or too little of, especially as a small business. There is also a possibility of costly, and even dangerous, overlap between personal and business liabilities and coverages that must be sorted out and dealt with appropriately. There are many ways to purchase insurance (see below) and you should be aware of your options, especially where the coverage you need is straightforward.

Where to learn more

▸ Jean Sherman Chatzky's "Everything You Ever Needed to Know About Insurance, But Were Too Confused to Ask," an excellent overview of insurance products and services, appeared in *Smart Money* magazine in October 1993. If you can't find it in a library, call 800-444-4204 and ask about a reprint.

▸ Check the telephone yellow pages or ask business associates for recommendations on effective agents. The Association of Independent Insurance Agents (703-683-4422) will make referrals. Direct-selling companies that can be less expensive include Geico (800-841-3000) and America Mutual (800-242-6422) for home and auto, Ameritas (800-552-3553) and USAA (800-531-8000) for life insurance. Check professional and fraternal associations. USAA, for example, also sells auto insurance if you are a military officer (or family member). SelectQuote Insurance Services (800-343-1985) and Quotesmith (800-556-9393) will quote several top-rated, lowest-priced policies; call for details and fees. Low-load insurance marketers like Fee For Service (800-874-5662) will advise you in selecting policies for a fee.

▶ Alliance for Affordable Health Care, 1725 K Street, NW, Suite 310, Washington, DC 20006, offers health insurance plans for the self-employed.

▶ National Association for the Self-Employed offers group health insurance for members. (See Appendix B.)

▶ Design Benefit Plans, 1750 East Golf Road, Schaumburg, IL 60173 (800-947-9000, ext. 508; Fax 800-289-2895), offers policies that can be customized to meet the individual needs of the self-employed.

▶ Call HMOs and Blue Cross–Blue Shield providers; many offer individual plans. Consider arranging a transition with your present plan, before leaving a traditional position for self-employment. Ask whether individual coverage is available to departing group-plan participants. The Consolidated Omnibus Budget Reconciliation Act (COBRA) requires that you be allowed to extend your employer's coverage for from 18 to 36 months at your own expense. Call the Department of Labor at 202-523-8921 for an information brochure.

▶ Safeware (800-848-3469 or 614-262-0559) is a Columbus, Ohio, based computer and software insurance company.

▶ Lawphone (800-255-3352) and Caldwell Legal, U.S.A. (800-222-3035) offer legal insurance plans intended to meet the needs of small businesses.

▶ USAA (800-531-8000) is noted for its customer service excellence. Home and auto policies are available only to military officers and their families, but other kinds of policies are available to the general public.

Related topics

Agents and brokers
Business travel
Competition
Contracts
Employees
Equipment and furniture
Evaluating your business
Financial planning
Legal liability

Professional help
Records
Reducing expenses
Regulations
Retirement
Security
Separating business and personal
Tax checklist

INVESTING

What you need to know   Traditional interest-bearing bank investments produce low returns, and money passing through your business should be positioned to make the most of the available investment opportunities. Begin your investment planning with a broad perspective of what you have and what you need to achieve, both personally and in your business. Familiarize yourself with the risks, rates of return, and flexibility of the basic investment instruments. Decide how much of the process you want to manage yourself. Your options range from doing it yourself with the help of on-line financial services, analytical software, and a no-frills broker to hiring a full-service broker who will guide you toward your goals. You can choose bank savings, money market instruments, individual stocks, or mutual funds that pool the money of many investors, offer professional management, and are available with almost any focus and level of risk. An option for obtaining less biased advice is hiring a financial planner who doesn't sell investments. Whether you act individually or with professional help, define your objectives, set targets to meet them, and decide how much risk and volatility you can tolerate. Distribute your resources across the spectrum of investments, altering the mix according to the state of the markets and your circumstances. A strategy of investing consistently over good and bad times and holding those investments tends to level the risks of timing. The strategy is called dollar averaging.

Why you need to know it   One of the strategies of big businesses that lends itself well to small ones is the practice of keeping funds fully invested. With electronic investment services, used directly or with professional assistance, you have a range of vehicles available to help you optimize the balance between immediate cash requirements and longer-term holdings for expansion, retirement, and other necessities. Know enough about what is available to be an intelligent consumer of financial services.

Where to learn more

▶ Morningstar, Inc., 53 West Jackson Boulevard, Chicago, IL 60604 (800-876-5005), is the premier source of mutual fund investment information.

▶ American Association of Individual Investors, 625 N. Michigan Avenue, Suite 1900, Chicago, IL 60611 (312-280-0170), offers membership and a variety of investment publications including *The Individual Investor's Guide to Computerized Investing*.

▶ Linda Stern's "Trade In Your Old Way of Investing," *Home Office Computing*, July 1993, provides a good layperson's overview of electronic investing from the home. Check your library or contact: Reprint Manager, *Home Office Computing*, 730 Broadway, New York, NY 10003; 212-505-3580.

▶ Libraries and bookstores stock investment publications. A solid choice is *Kiplinger's Invest Your Way to Wealth* by Theodore J. Miller, editor of *Kiplinger's Personal Finance Magazine*. Other helpful personal finance periodicals include *Money* and *Smart Money*.

Related topics

Accountant
Agents and brokers
Banking services
Budgeting
Cash flow
Checking accounts

Computer on-line services
Computer software
Computer use
Conferences, seminars, shows,
    and workshops
Continuing education

Diversification
Financial planning
Goal setting
Loans, credit, and venture capital
Managing growth

Newsletters
Records
Regulations
Separating business and personal
Tax checklist

LABOR LAWS

What you need to know   As long as you are operating your home-based business without other employees, you have little concern with labor laws. Once you hire someone, full- or part-time, talk with your accountant and, possibly, your attorney about obligations you might incur. Among the better known infringements are failure to withhold social security taxes and employment of illegal aliens. There are also minimum-wage laws that can apply even to family members. The size of your business has little to do with your liability. Technically, you have to be engaged in "interstate commerce" to incur the federal liabilities, but because the term is broadly defined, you may find that your seemingly local enterprise is considered to be operating nationally. Use common sense and don't go looking for problems, but as your business grows and you add employees, consider your possible obligations under at least the following laws: (1) The Fair Labor Standards Act of 1938, as Amended (wages and hours; child labor); (2) Occupational Safety and Health Act (OSHA) (safe and healthful conditions in the workplace); (3) Social Security Act of 1935, as Amended (employment insurance and retirement); and (4) other laws of the Department of Labor that might apply if you become involved in federal contracts, offer a pension, hire the disadvantaged, are asked to garnish an employee's wages, or perform any of a number of reasonably obscure obligations. If you are manufacturing clothing, investigate laws intended to prevent homes from becoming sweat shops. State laws generally parallel those of the federal government, but you should check them as well.

Why you need to know it   Home-based businesses can grow unexpectedly and, in the rush of hiring, laws can be overlooked and penalties incurred. Your plan for managing growth should anticipate meeting the requirements of labor laws. Most of your obligations will first hit you in the form of taxes and withholding, so keep your accountant apprised of your activities. Another approach to keep in mind is the mirror image of the advantage you may be offering others—independent contractor status, which bypasses regulatory obligations *if* done to the letter of the law.

Where to learn more

▶ Matthew Lesko's *Information USA*, published by Viking-Penguin, can be helpful in identifying contacts with the federal government. Find it at your library or bookstore.

▶ Check the federal government pages of your local telephone book for field offices that can assist you with social security, wage and hour, and other employment compliance issues. If the local listing is inadequate, try the telephone book for your state capital or for Washington, DC. The Department of Labor listing is 202-523-8921. Ask your congressman's office for help if you experience difficulties.

Related topics

Attorney	Government customers
Business image	Independent contractor status
Business use of home	**Legal liability**
Competition	**Legal/illegal business operation**
Concerns about working from home	Managing growth
Disabilities	Noise
Employees	**Personnel policies**
Equipment and furniture	**Regulations**
Ethics	Sales representatives
Family	Temporary help

LEASING

What you need to know   One way to stretch tight financial resources or improve cash flow might be leasing. Equipment is generally available for purchase or lease. Office equipment or computer resellers often display dual price tags that list purchase price and monthly leasing fees. The decision to buy or lease is seldom clear-cut. Do the arithmetic and compare: (1) multiply the leasing fee by the number of months, and add the cost to acquire the equipment after the last payment; (2) multiply the monthly payments, including interest, for a fully financed purchase; and (3) calculate what the purchase price might earn in a competing investment if you were to use business capital for an outright purchase (opportunity cost). Estimate the tax consequences of each approach, and you have the basis for making a decision. The conventional advantages of leasing are capital preservation and cash flow improvement. Leasing can also turn the cost of equipment into a monthly business expense and avoid the slower recovery of depreciation. Such considerations vary with the times—purchases under a certain amount ($17,500 in 1993) can be immediately "expensed" anyway, removing the attractiveness of a lease. Luxury limits on automobile leasing make the transaction virtually the same proposition as buying. The IRS looks closely at leases and is quick to consider them "conditional sales contracts" not deductible as rent expenses if there is a strong similarity between lease and purchase outcomes. The term "lease" also applies to a contract for the use of real property where the owner retains title and the lessee gains exclusive use in return for rent.

Why you need to know it   The advantages of leasing depend on your situation. If you replace expensive equipment on a regular basis, you might justify an ongoing leasing arrangement that spreads the cost and makes paying for the successive items a routine expense of doing business. For some people, that method is easier than saving toward an expected purchase. A discussion with your accountant will reveal any tax advantages. Your main considerations are: the availability of cash and credit and the honest cost of alternatives.

Where to learn more

▶ Consult your accountant on the ramifications of leasing in your particular circumstances.

▶ The following IRS publications are useful: Publication 334, "Tax Guide for Small Business," and Publication 917, "Leasing a Car."

▶ Examine the leasing information and contracts of the suppliers of equipment you are considering buying.

▶ Your attorney should review any significant contract, including a lease.

Related topics

Accountant	Fax
Agents and brokers	Financial planning
Attorney	**Loans, credit, and venture capital**
Budgeting	Merchandise buying services
Business plan	Negotiating
Buying a business	Office planning and decorating
Cash flow	Overhead expenses
Computer equipment	**Reducing expenses**
Copiers	Start-up
Equipment and furniture	**Tax checklist**
Expense sharing and joint ventures	Telephone equipment

LEGAL LIABILITY

What you need to know   Legal liability arises when a person or business is determined, according to governing law, to be responsible for or obligated to satisfy a claim. Liability might involve the payment of money guaranteed with a negotiable instrument, or doing (or refraining from doing) something. Liability under a contract requires the parties to perform whatever obligations are contained in the agreement. Complex liabilities, including contractual, tort, and criminal liabilities, are resolved within the legal system. A business person can incur liability by engaging in dangerous activities like handling or storing explosives or chemicals, or keeping wild animals (*strict liability*); all sorts of *shared liability* with others who provide products or services associated with his or her business; and *contingent liabilities* that might occur in the future if certain things transpire. Protection from liability takes the form of insurance that is usually added to basic property insurance policies. Liability insurance spans a continuum from personal actions to specific claims arising from highly specialized situations—malpractice, product defects, operations, employers', professional (errors and omissions), libel and slander, and farmers' liability, to name a few. Your protections against liability claims are competency and attention to maintaining good practices and safe conditions that could reasonably be expected to prevent the losses for which you might become liable.

Why you need to know it   Although you should not become obsessed with legal liability, normal prudence dictates recognizing potential exposures and taking both corrective and loss-containment steps. As a home-based business owner, it is essential that you do what is possible to separate personal and business liabilities and be certain that your insurance coverage embraces both. With awareness and candor, you can prevent losses under or voiding of personal liability coverage because of business activity that had not been made a part of the policy.

Where to learn more

▶ Consult your attorney to review possible exposures, and discuss ways to reduce your liability.

▶ Consult your insurance professional to review exposures, remedy potential problems, and insure against loss.

▶ Professional associations are good sources for liability checklists and for group insurance that targets your specialty.

▶ Personal (*not* business or commercial) legal services plans exist in many parts of the country. Unlimited consultations and preset fees for standard services are provided for a monthly fee. An example, priced at about $8 per month, is Montgomery Ward Enterprises Legal Services Plan, 200 N. Martingale Road, Schaumburg, IL 60173-2096.

Related topics

Advertising	Employees
Agents and brokers	Environmental considerations
Attorney	Independent contractor status
Bankruptcy	Information sources and research
Bidding	**Insurance**
Bonding	Labor laws
Business use of car	**Legal/illegal business operation**
Business use of home	**Loans, credit, and venture capital**
Buying a business	Managing growth
Computer software	Negotiating
Consulting	Newsletters
Contracts	**Personnel policies**
Copyright, patent, trademark,	**Regulations**
and service mark	**Separating business and personal**
Debt collection and creditworthiness	Tax checklist
Disaster planning	Telephone use

LEGAL/ILLEGAL BUSINESS OPERATION

What you need to know   The law is rarely precise; there is room for prudent interpretation and risk taking. When you establish professional relationships with accountants, attorneys, and similar practitioners, you make them aware of the degree of risk you want them to take on your behalf. The law becomes unforgiving at the point where you go from making shrewd judgments in your own favor to committing fraud—false and material misrepresentations, concealment, misleading conduct, contrivance, and other illegalities. At that juncture, you stop being viewed as ignorant of the law and meriting merely a reprimand or a financial adjustment, and you start being punished. All of the obvious ethical and moral reasons notwithstanding, fraud is bad business—the risks and costs are too high. Get the necessary licenses and registrations for your business. File the necessary tax and reporting paperwork. Avoid deals that appear to be too good to be true. "Respectable" crime that can get a small business operator burned includes the illegal use of computer software. For example, the FBI busted a bulletin board service that was downloading popular software for a modest membership fee and seized subscriber records that could lead to action against individuals. The software industry, through advertisements, public notices, and a toll-free whistle-blower number, actively solicits information on fraudulent use.

Why you need to know it   You will not want to overburden your business by chasing down and conforming to obscure laws and obligations, but you should plan to meet the legitimate requirements and count the costs among your normal business expenses. Interlocking reporting requirements make it difficult to avoid your legal obligations. The cost of a substantial fine or tax settlement can be enough to scuttle a business. Anticipate your obligations and meet them in the course of growing your business. Time and energy spent circumventing the law are better applied to the straightforward practice of aggressively developing a profitable enterprise.

Where to learn more

▸ Read the licensing agreements that come with the computer software you use.

▸ The Software Publishers Association, 1730 M Street, NW, Washington, DC 20036 (202-452-1600), offers guidance on the legal use of software products.

▸ Consult your attorney when you have questions about the legitimacy of your business practices.

▸ Seek your accountant's guidance in avoiding tax-law infringements.

Related topics

Accountant

Advertising

Agents and brokers

Attorney

Bankruptcy

Bartering

Bidding

Bulletin Board System (BBS)

Business name
Business use of car
Business use of home
Computer on-line services
Computer software
Contracts
Copiers
**Copyright, patent, trademark,
  and service mark**
Debt collection and creditworthiness
Desktop publishing
Direct mail and mailing lists
Direct selling and multilevel
  marketing
Employees

Environmental considerations
Family
Fax
Independent contractor status
Labor laws
Legal liability
Loans, credit, and venture capital
Mail order
Payroll
Proprietary information
Separating business and personal
Syndication
Tax checklist
Telephone use
Zoning

LICENSE

What you need to know   Licenses are generally of two types: (1) business, allowing you to operate a certain kind of enterprise in a jurisdiction, and (2) professional, vouching for your credentials to provide a service proscribed to those not holding a valid license, and ranging from brain surgeons to beauticians and everything in between. A local business license is, more than anything else, a tax. You get one from the local municipal office where you pay your property taxes and apply for a zoning permit. Although a home-based business with a low profile might avoid business licensure for a while, eventually you are apt to be caught in cross-checks with business property tax records, sales tax permits, advertising, telephone listings, or any of a number of other nuances of doing business. The result will be an order to comply and, possibly, a penalty or back payment of licensing fees for the period during which you ignored the requirement. Not adhering to professional licensure usually carries more severe penalties. Depending on your specialty, you can lose the right to practice and incur substantial fines for doing so illegally.

Why you need to know it   Most licensure is straightforward, but not always. When you start a business or alter one to add a new service, discuss the licensing implications with your attorney and perhaps with local licensing authorities. Licensing has revenue, control, and turf-protection aspects; the latter stands the greatest chance of getting you into trouble. This is especially true with new business opportunities that slightly overlap the territory of established groups like real estate brokers and tax preparers. Acting as an independent paraprofessional—for example, a paralegal—can be OK in some places and illegal in others. Be careful to clarify your status before investing in a business that you may be technically unable to operate without undergoing extensive training.

Where to learn more

‣ Local government officials can provide advice on complying with licensing and regulatory requirements in their jurisdictions.

‣ Consult your attorney before engaging in a business that might require a license based on specialized qualifications you do not possess.

‣ Professional licensure is usually administered at the state level. Contact the appropriate office in your state capital.

‣ Consult the national association serving any paraprofessional activity you are considering, to determine the licensing requirements in your jurisdiction. Consult Gale's *Directory of Associations* at your library, or check with the group representing the primary profession—the local bar association, in the case of a paralegal.

‣ *Professional and Occupational Licensing Directory* lists licensing requirements for 250 occupations and hundreds more specific job titles. Check your library or call 800-877-GALE.

Related topics

Advertising
Attorney
Bonding
Business basics
Business image
Business name
Buying a business
Competition
Computer software
Consulting
Contracts

Copyright, patent, trademark,
   and service mark
Ethics
Fees and pricing
Insurance
Legal liability
Legal/illegal business operation
Promoting your business
Regulations
Tax checklist
Zoning

LIGHTING

What you need to know   Like other technologies, light sources are always evolving. Once-limited fluorescent bulbs (any color you wanted, as long as it was cool white or warm white) are now available in over 200 shades. They are economical and effective sources of office light, far from the cold, humming-lights image of a 1960s government office. Fluorescents are also made for lamps, bringing economy and long life to office-task lights. Halogen bulbs are popular; they are cooler and more efficient than incandescents. Motion sensors install easily in standard switch plates and save energy by limiting light use to the time your office is occupied. Keep safety in mind—for all light fixtures, building codes call for adequate ventilation and safe distances from flammables. Inexpensive emergency lights that activate when the power fails add a measure of safety to the home office. The conventional wisdom of home office lighting suggests that you make the most of natural light while avoiding glare; add backup ambients with dimmers to compensate for cloudy days and night work; use accents like track lighting only where it is desirable to achieve an intended spotlight effect; and have task lights available when close work demands them. Let lighting adjust to individual needs—the older the worker, the more light needed, for example. Avoid glossy surfaces that reflect light harshly: matte finishes are preferred for walls and counter tops. Task lights should be 15 to 18 inches above the work. Computer screens are best set about 10 percent brighter than the room's general light level. Never face a window; instead, work at a right angle from it.

Why you need to know it   Adapting a home to intensive business use requires changes in the former ways of doing things. Lighting that was fine for casual use might be unsatisfactory for high-productivity office work. Achieving focus and a business atmosphere also depends on lighting effects that are different from those considered comfortable for residential applications. Looking at lighting from a business perspective can save time and money and economically create an office where once there was casual space.

Where to learn more

▶ *The GE Home Lighting Handbook,* General Electric Company, P. O. Box 94988, Cleveland, OH 44101-4988; about $6, 800-626-2000.

▶ Levenger, a mail-order company, is a good source for high-quality lighting fixtures and bulbs suitable for the home office.

▶ Reliable Home Office, P. O. Box 1501, Ottawa, IL 61350-9916 (800-869-6000), is a direct supplier of quality home office furnishings and equipment, including stylish office lighting.

▶ Local design studios and office equipment resellers, including discounters, carry office lighting products. Dealers who buy and resell the equipment of offices that are closing or remodeling can also be sources of lighting bargains. Check the classified advertising and used office furniture listings in the telephone yellow pages.

▶ Randall Whitehead's book, *Residential Lighting: Creating Dynamic Living Spaces,* (Rockport Publishers, 1993), offers the advice of a San Francisco decorator who specializes in home office lighting.

Related topics

Budgeting	Noise
Computer use	**Office planning and decorating**
Disaster planning	Psychological factors
Employees	Reducing expenses
Environmental considerations	Security
Equipment and furniture	Stress and overworking
Merchandise buying services	Vacation, work styles, and schedules

LOANS, CREDIT, AND VENTURE CAPITAL

What you need to know   Small businesses borrow money on the credit and character of their owners. It would be naive to think of starting or expanding a small business, even a well-known franchise, without solid personal financial credentials and personal property to put at risk. Expect to cosign business notes with every personal guarantee you can muster—equity in your home, personal savings, and earning power. In borrowing, as in so many other aspects of small business ownership, you *are* your business. Forget drawing lines between business and personal obligations, whether by incorporation or other devices; it usually can't be done. Lenders don't set themselves up to watch business loans go bad while the business owners' personal assets remain untouched. Everything will be neatly tied together before the first dollar is loaned. A good business plan or an operating business, as an extension of your personal assets, will help you borrow money for your business, but, as with any loan, be prepared to demonstrate convincingly what the money is for and how you will be able to repay it under different contingencies—a business slow down or your becoming incapacitated. Understand that business loans are short-term, usually payable in two to five years, and are generally for less than $100,000. If you need more money or a longer period of time, consider remortgaging your property or seeking venture capital equity investors who will do more for a stake in the business. For smaller loans of up to about $25,000 (an average loan is $7,000), consider one of the increasingly popular microloan organizations designed to help small businesses. Another possibility is rich individuals ("angels") looking for interesting and profitable situations.

Why you need to know it   If you are at the thinking stage of starting a small business, understand how totally business financing ties into your personal assets. After that sinks in, if you are still willing to put everything on the line, you need a road map to possible lending sources. Start with your personal resources and get the money you need in as uncomplicated a way as you can. If credit cards or a home equity loan will serve your purposes, go for it. The risks are not that different from a commercial loan, but there are fewer conservative people to wave red flags if you are acting irrationally. Unconventional lending sources exist. Explore some of the possibilities listed below.

Where to learn more

▶ Paul and Sarah Edwards' article, "Little Loans, Big Benefits," in the July 1993 issue of *Home Office Computing* magazine, includes a regional directory of 47 microlenders backed by the SBA. Call 800-227-5638 (BizFAX Extension 730; price: $6.95) or 212-505-4260 for a copy. Linda Stern's "Need $10,000, $50,000, $250,000?," in the September 1992 issue of the same publication, is also informative. Check your library or contact: Reprint Manager, *Home Office Computing*, 730 Broadway, New York, NY 10003; 212-505-3580.

▶ Association for Enterprise Opportunity, San Francisco (415-495-2333), provides information on alternative funding sources.

▶ The Small Business Administration's Small Business Answer Desk (800-837-5722) can help you locate SBA-backed lending programs.

▶ The SBA's Office of Women's Business Ownership (202-205-6673) can help you identify special programs backing women entrepreneurs. The National Association of Female Executives (212-645-0770) is another source.

▶ The American Bankers Association's *SBA Lending Made Easy* (800-338-0626) gives you a banker's view of the SBA loan application and approval process and tells you what bankers want to see. Price: about $70.

▶ The MIT Venture Capital Network, in Boston (617-253-7163), links businesses to private wealthy investors for a fee.

▶ Al Research Corporation, Mountain View, CA 94041 (415-852-9140 or 800-252-7080), sells software designed to help you locate venture capital.

▶ M-USA Business Systems, Inc., 15806 Midway Road, Dallas, TX 75244-2195 (800-933-6872), sells a video called *Find and Gain Access to Capital* for about $30.

Related topics

Accountant
Agents and brokers
Attorney
Banking services
Bankruptcy
Bookkeeping
Cash flow
Contracts
Credit cards
**Debt collection and
    creditworthiness**

Financial formulas
Financial planning
Insurance
Money management
Reducing expenses
Regulations
Separating business and personal
Tax checklist

MAIL AND OVERNIGHT DELIVERY SERVICES

What you need to know   Mail and related services have become competitive enterprises offering a wide range of prices and features. Although the U.S. Postal Service (USPS) remains the backbone of tangible business communications, it is getting a lot of competition from commercial services like Airborne, DHL, Federal Express, and UPS. The starting point for small business mail service is a visit to your post office for a copy of the zone chart listing postal services and fees based on distances from your zip code. The chart includes tables that identify rates based on service, weight, and zone. With this and a scale, you are in business. The next step up is a postage meter that you reload with bulk postage and save the trouble of buying and counting stamps. From that point on, you must decide how much speed, impact, and pickup convenience you want for your mailing dollar. All of the companies, including the USPS, will come to your place of business to pick up packages for a fee. Delivery options range from same day to next day, second day, and almost any option you want to buy. Check with your carrier whether a "day" is a calendar day or a business day only. Decide what your needs are, establish accounts with one or two services, and monitor how well each works for you. Only the USPS delivers first-class letters, and it is the only organization that serves post office box addresses. Its Express Mail service delivers on every day of the year. Computer tracking and package accounting that verifies delivery are valuable services of the overnight carriers.

Why you need to know it   There are more delivery choices than you might imagine. If you will be sending and receiving packages relating to your business, you need to know what is available, how you access the services, and the costs and limitations. Along with information technology, rapid delivery services are a factor in making home-based businesses viable.

Where to learn more

- Airborne: 800-AIRBORNE; Sky Courier: 800-336-3344 for same-day delivery.
- DHL: 800-CALL-DHL; 800-DHL-ASAP for same-day service.
- Federal Express: 800-238-5355.
- United Parcel Service (UPS): 800-PICK UPS.
- U.S. Postal Service: 800-222-1811.
- Uncanceled postage stamps that failed to reach collector status can sometimes be purchased at discount from stamp collectors. To save postage, call collectors listed in the telephone yellow pages and inquire whether any are available.

Related topics

Business address and location
Business image
Competition
Computer use
Customer relations
Direct mail and mailing lists
Fees and pricing
Foreign markets and languages
Forms

Homeowners' associations
Insurance
Legal liability
Mail order
Managing growth
Merchandise buying services
Negotiating
Newsletters
Regulations

MAIL ORDER

What you need to know   Mail order is a reliable way to do business, either as a consumer or as a business that is marketing products. But because of the ease of running an advertisement or sending direct mail, mail order attracts inept and fraudulent operators who have made it suspect. Among its ironies are mail-order get-rich-quick schemes sold by mail. Although the home-based business lends itself to the mail-order format, the business is extremely competitive and costly to enter in a serious way. Ruth Owades, who started *Calyx & Corolla: The Fresh Flower Catalog* with millions of dollars in venture capital, more nearly represents mail-order reality today than does the work-at-home drop shipper. Midlevel investment and effort are still possible, but it won't be easy or inexpensive. Get solid advice from the reputable books and consultants on the subject, not the razzle-dazzle sources. Carefully estimate how much you will have to spend to generate the volume necessary to prosper with direct mail return rates that average in the low single digits (if you're lucky). Display advertising costs are available for the asking; request rate cards from magazines you expect to use. Computers make mailing list maintenance and record keeping easier, and service companies can subcontract the mailings more reasonably than you can do it at home, but it takes a popular, competitively priced, high-profit-margin item that can't be cloned by discount retailers if you are to prosper for long. Factor-in the cost of credit card and 800 number shopping—necessities for effective mail-order marketing. Also familiarize yourself with the regulatory requirements that demand shipment or notification within 30 days of receiving orders, and so on. Mail order represents a valid business opportunity, but one that constitutes a major undertaking.

Why you need to know it

You need to know how to evaluate mail-order opportunities realistically. College financial aid research was a recent "hot item" in the unending flow of mail-order opportunities that disappoint people who invest money and effort only to find the product oversold and the return too small to cover the promotion. It is possible to plan and execute a successful mail-order marketing venture, but approach the challenge rationally, and be prepared to overcome obstacles like the difficulty you will have obtaining credit card merchant status as a home-based company.

Where to learn more

‣ Julian L. Simon's *How to Start and Operate a Mail Order Business* is a basic reference for people contemplating mail order.

‣ Cecil C. Hoge, Sr. has published several guides to mail-order businesses for Ten Speed Press, including *Mail Order Know-How* and *Mail Order Moonlighting*.

‣ National Mail Order Association, 5818 Venice Boulevard, Los Angeles, CA 90019, and The Direct Mail/Marketing Association, 6 East 43rd Street, New York, NY 10017, are trade associations.

‣ *Memo to Mailers*, P. O. Box 1, Linwood, NJ 08221, is a monthly publication available from the U. S. Postal Service.

‣ The Good Catalog Company, Portland, OR 97208 (503-654-7464 or 800-828-1810), will create a catalog and run your mail-order operation for a fee.

‣ Dynacomp, Inc., P. O. Box 641, Wayne, NJ 07474-0641 (800-858-DMOM), sells *Mail Order Manager* computer software for mail-order businesses.

Related topics

Advertising

Agents and brokers

Associations

Banking services

Better Business Bureau (BBB)

Business address and location

Business image

Business plan

Business use of home

Camera-ready copy

Competition

Computer on-line services

Computer use

Credit cards

Customer relations

Desktop publishing

Direct mail and mailing lists

Diversification

Expense sharing and joint ventures

Fax

Financial planning

Forms

Legal/illegal business operation

Mail and overnight delivery
  services

Managing growth

Marketing and market research

Newsletters

Printing

Profit

Projections

Regulations

Telephone equipment

Telephone services

Telephone use

MANAGING GROWTH

What you need to know   In a successful and growing business, your time becomes worth more than many of the things you spend it on. The beginning of an entrepreneurial effort calls for the willingness and ability to do everything yourself. As the business catches hold and demand for your talents outstrips the time you have available, you must hand over the less critical tasks to others. This doesn't have to mean hiring employees. In fact, with the cost and obligations of employing people rising, look to business associates for supporting services you can barter or purchase, and explore cost-sharing opportunities in which you share personnel, equipment, or services. Another aspect of managing growth is keeping up with technology. You don't necessarily have to track innovations yourself or hire an employee. Instead, establish a relationship with a small business computer and/or communications consultant, or a colleague who keeps up with such things, and make it known that you want to try new approaches as they become available. Assume the role of the task conceptualizer who hires a consultant to set up the software/ hardware solution and a part-time operator to perform the newly established routine.

Why you need to know it   Your home-based business is a micro-organization in which tasks proliferate and their worthiness for taking up your time varies. To succeed, you need to sort the tasks by value and focus your effort on your "highest and best use." This is a problem that tends to hit small business people when they are least prepared to deal with it—their business is getting demanding, and time for reflection is at a premium. Anticipate the problem and have contingencies arranged—avenues of relief for the welcome pressures of growing. The end result will be determined by how you face growth—with frustration and failure or with deftly changed roles to accommodate your expansion and share the wealth with others who multiply your potential.

Where to learn more

▶ Identify individuals and service companies among your business associates and network who can help carry the overload as you grow.

▶ Employ a small business consultant, contact SCORE, or discuss your growth with someone who has experienced similar problems and solved them.

▶ Seek a wider base of suggestions by asking for input on a computer bulletin board service that focuses on your specialty or home businesses.

Related topics

Accountant
Attorney
Banking services
Bookkeeping
Business image
Business organization
Business plan
Cash flow
Competition
Computer equipment
Computer software
Computer use
Debt collection and creditworthiness
Diversification
Equipment and furniture
Evaluating your business
Expense sharing and joint ventures
Fees and pricing
Financial planning
Foreign markets and languages
Insurance
Investing

Legal/illegal business operation
Loans, credit, and venture capital
Marketing and market research
Money management
Negotiating
Networking
Office planning and decorating
Overhead expenses
Profit
Projections
Promoting your business
Proposals
Public relations
Reducing expenses
Regulations
Role
Security
Tax checklist
Telephone use
Undercapitalization
Vacation, work styles, and schedules
Zoning

MARKETING AND MARKET RESEARCH

What you need to know   Marketing begins with research that tells you whether there is a demand for your product or service and how to reach customers. The starting point for that kind of research is automated demographic information that is readily available through brokers or on-line services and CD-ROM subscriptions. Identify your market and become a part of it so you can identify with your customers and follow events that are important to them. Accomplish that by joining a professional association that serves them. Most organizations will welcome you as an associate member entitled to the directories, newsletters, and contacts you seek. Once inside the client population, find a way to help the members and enhance your marketing efforts at the same time. Write a newsletter feature that makes your name known, or do something else that is useful to the group. Watch for needs in your client base and rush to fill them, even if the payoff is indirect and comes later through the relationships you establish. Marketing is a word-of-mouth exercise for most businesses. Mass marketing efforts, advertising, and direct calling are effective spot initiatives that get you started and add new customers, but a business is sustained by satisfied customers and their referrals. Networking—in person and via electronic media—is a solid path to business development for the home-based business person. For basic research on growth in major sectors of the economy, check with the U.S. Department of Commerce.

Why you need to know it   Every self-employed person is in the marketing business—it is not optional. The secret of successful marketing is the systematic pursuit of leads while avoiding "analysis paralysis"—excessive market research orientation that leads to neglect of the energetic conduct of your basic business.

Where to learn more

▶ The Wharton School of the University of Pennsylvania sells a complete video seminar on marketing strategy through Kantola Productions, 55 Sunnyside Avenue, Mill Valley, CA 94941; 800-989-8272. Price: about $190.

▶ Digital Directory Assistance, Inc. (800-284-8353) sells CD-ROM products for marketing research.

▶ Marketplace Information Corporation (800-999-9497) sells metered use CD-ROM marketing information.

▶ BIZ-FILE is the business information research database of CompuServe (800-848-8199), on which you can do key word and information parameter searches and download the information you want for a reasonable fee.

▶ Gale's *Directory of Associations*, found in libraries, helps you identify national groups that share a common interest. Locally, consider your Chamber of Commerce for listings by industry group.

▶ Consult your software reseller or the catalogs listed in Appendix C for contact management products like *Act!* and marketing products like Palo Alto Software's *Marketing Plan Toolkit* and *Sales & Market Forecasting Toolkit*.

▶ American Information Exchange Corporation, 1881 Landings Drive, Mountain View, CA 94043 (415-903-1000), is an on-line service on which you can market newsletters, business information, and software for a fee.

▶ *U.S. Industrial Outlook*, part of a collection called the National Trade Data Bank, is a sector-by-sector analysis and set of growth predictions for the U.S. economy.

It is available on CD-ROM ($35) or disks ($135) from the Department of Commerce (202-482-1986), or in book form ($37) from the Superintendent of Documents, P. O. Box 371954, Pittsburgh, PA 15250-7954.

Related topics

Advertising	**Customer relations**
Associations	Direct mail and mailing lists
Business associates	Evaluating your business
Business ideas	Financial planning
Business image	**Franchises**
Competition	**Information sources and research**
Computer software	**Networking**
Computer use	Newsletters
Conferences, seminars, shows, and workshops	Professional help
	Promoting your business
Continuing education	Telephone use

MEDIA RELATIONS

What you need to know   There are at least 1,000 radio and TV talk shows, and their producers are constantly looking for personalities and ideas to fill their air time. The big-name shows are very competitive, but that barrier changes completely when you get down to the local and regional markets. If you have an interesting product or service that you would like to promote, identify shows that are likely to reach people who might become your customers if they are impressed with what they hear. Just as you would read a magazine before writing an article for it, watch or listen to the talk show before making contact. Plan your approach so you can tell the producer how your topic and background make sense for the program's audience. Build a media kit consisting of: a cover letter to remind the producer of your previous telephone conversation and the problem you intend to solve; a list of topics to cover and questions you would suggest being asked on the air; a press release that backs your claims with market research; a biography telling why you are qualified to address the subject; a list of quotes from earlier publicity; and a tape (audio or video) of a successful interview (if you have one) that showcases your personality and ease before an audience. Do follow-up telephone calls, and expect each conversation you have to be a screening interview for how you would conduct yourself on the air. Be articulate, lively, positive, and interesting. One successful interview leads to others. Persist until you break in, and then make the most of your appearances.

Why you need to know it   Not all publicity costs you money or even much time. With the proliferation of radio and television programs, there is great potential for anyone with the gumption to go before an audience. Your topic will determine how high up the ladder of household-name shows you go, but even the local versions can help market your products and services. Don't overlook your local cable-TV outlet and the public service broadcasts that all stations are obligated to air. Distance need not be a limitation. Many big-city talk-show hosts conduct what are known as "phoners"—interviews conducted by telephone.

Where to learn more

▶ Jian's *PublicityBuilder* is template software that supplements your computer word processor and helps you interact well with the media and attract reporters through sample press releases, press kit materials, telephone contact guidelines, and information on how to handle your publicity professionally. Purchase from a software reseller or call 800-346-5426. Price: about $130.

▶ Peter G. Miller's *Media Power—How Your Business Can Profit from the Media,* offers advice for press releases and making the most of the media. It is available for about $20 from Dearborn Financial Publishing, 520 North Dearborn, Chicago, IL 60610; 312-836-4400 or 800-621-9621.

▶ *Annual Broadcasting Yearbook,* the $160 who's who of the radio business, can be ordered from Reed Reference Publishing, P. O. Box 31, New Providence, NJ 07974; 908-464-6800 or 800-521-8110.

▶ Among newsletters and magazines distributed to talk-show hosts and producers are: *Interviews & Reviews,* 2218 Bamboo Street, Mesquite, TX 75150 (214-613-4033); *Newsmaker Interviews,* 8217 Beverly Boulevard, Los Angeles, CA 90048 (213-655-2793); and *Radio-TV Interview Report,* 135 East Plumstead Avenue, Suite 612, Lansdowne, PA 19050 (215-259-1070 or 800-989-1400).

▶ Al Parinello's *On the Air: How to Get on Radio and TV Talk Shows and What to Do When You Get There* is available from Career Press for about $13. Call 201-427-0229 or 800-227-3371.

Related topics

Advertising
Agents and brokers
Business image
Camera-ready copy
Computer software
Conferences, seminars, shows,
  and workshops
Customer relations
Desktop publishing
Direct mail and mailing lists

Ethics
Managing growth
Networking
Newsletters
Presentations
Professional help
Promoting your business
Public relations
Telephone use

MERCHANDISE BUYING SERVICES

What you need to know   The days of exclusive wholesale buying limited to retailers and large companies are a thing of the past. They have been replaced by membership merchandising buying services and clubs that offer special prices on everything from automobiles and major appliances to best-selling books. If you live in a major metropolitan area, you may be familiar with outlets that offer such services. Even if you are located in a less urban part of the country, you can access buying services via your computer modem or as an adjunct to credit card agreements with some banks. You might still encounter an occasional design center or a builder-oriented supplier of plumbing or electrical equipment who won't sell to individuals, but almost everyone else will. A membership fee is often involved, and you have to weigh the value of your long-term savings against the fee. The other tradeoff is service—discount merchandise stores sometimes lack point-of-sale advice and after-sale assistance. If you know what you need and how to use it, the discounters offer good value. If you expect to need assistance in selecting the right model, combining it with compatible products, and putting it into service, the higher price of a conventional reseller may be more realistic and a better net value.

Why you need to know it   So many buying options exist for home office materials and equipment that you need comparisons to determine your best buy. For the average home-based small business person, merchandise buying services offer easily accessed low prices. Use them as benchmarks for determining the value of the extras available from conventional dealers at higher prices.

Where to learn more

▶ MBNA America (800-421-2110) is a major credit card company that offers a membership buying service as an adjunct to basic card privileges. Other credit card companies do too. Call your customer service number and inquire.

▶ USAA Buying Services in San Antonio, TX (800-531-8905), offers a wide selection of computers, typewriters, Fax machines, furniture, and other items useful in operating a home-based business.

▶ Check your telephone yellow pages or those of an accessible major city for merchandise buying services retailers like Sam's Club (Wal-Mart), Price Club, BJ's, and others. Another approach is to call 800-555-1212 (information) for a headquarters listing that can, in turn, refer you to your nearest outlet.

Related topics

Associations
Bulletin Board System (BBS)
Competition
Computer equipment
Computer on-line services
Computer software
Copiers
Equipment and furniture

Fax
Mail and overnight delivery services
Mail order
Paper
Reducing expenses
Supplies
Telephone equipment

MONEY MANAGEMENT

What you need to know   The term "money management" runs the gamut from planning and budgeting to cash flow and investing. The tools can be as simple as a pencil and paper or as complex as sophisticated computer spreadsheets featuring financial analyses and projections. A happy medium for most home-based businesses is a computer and one or more software programs at the appropriate level. For anyone operating a relatively straightforward small enterprise, a check-writing program that assigns revenues and expenditures to categories and summarizes them in reports is the basic tool. As these programs have evolved, they have added budgeting, reporting, and forecasting functions that do most of what a small business person needs. Crude but effective financial modeling can be done in the simplest check-writing programs by entering future months' expected expenditures and revenues and watching the program show the succeeding balances. Add revenues (i.e., debt, sell more, borrow) and juggle dates (delay purchases, make smaller debt payments) to eliminate the negative balances. Financial survival requires having expenditures not outstrip revenues and being able to bridge the gaps with credit or reserves. Money management includes tracking and soliciting payment for the billable time and/or the products you sell. Software exists to do either. Another aspect of money management is "aging" your accounts—paying on time, but as late as you can, and collecting as promptly as you can from those who owe you. You must minimize the cost of handling money (e.g., avoid bank fees, late charges, interest and penalties, and so on) and maximize the income it generates while in your possession (e.g., open sweep accounts that move non-interest-bearing deposits into money market accounts that earn income, and so on).

Why you need to know it   However you accomplish it, you have to know where your finances stand at any given moment, now and into the future. You do that by managing your money—keeping track of it as it comes and goes as a result of the income you generate and the obligations you incur. The process has to make sense to you before it has value, so don't use a system so complex that you don't feel its ebb and flow. Effective money management results in changed behavior for business persons—they hustle all the harder to meet a revenue shortfall, and they hold back on planned spending until delayed income is safely collected.

Where to learn more

▸ Money market mutual funds are available from many sources. Among the leaders are USAA (800-531-8181), T. Rowe Price (800-541-8460), Franklin (800-342-FUND), Fidelity Investments (800-544-8888), and Dreyfus (800-373-9387).

▸ *Quicken* checkbook software tracks your finances, writes checks, produces income and cash flow statements, helps to prepare balance sheets, and links to tax preparation software. Call 800-624-8742 for details.

▶ *M.Y.O.B.* is small business accounting software that includes the cash management features of a checkbook program plus more sophisticated accounting.

▶ Timeslips Corporation offers software that tracks billable time or reimbursable expenses, issues statements, and links information to your accounting program.

▶ *Up Your Cash Flow* is a dedicated cash flow management program.

▶ Microrim's *In The Black* accounting software includes powerful money management features (Appendix F).

Related topics

Accountant	**Evaluating your business**
Accounting	Fees and pricing
Banking services	**Financial planning**
Bidding	**Managing growth**
Billing	Overhead expenses
Bookkeeping	Payroll
Business plan	Profit
Cash flow	**Projections**
Checking accounts	Reducing expenses
Computer software	Tax checklist
Credit cards	Undercapitalization
Debt collection and creditworthiness	

MOONLIGHTING

What you need to know   Moonlighting is an alternative to a full-risk small business start-up approach. Even with the reduced expenses of a home-based business, starting a venture that produces instant profitability comparable to your salary isn't likely. One way to ease the shock and minimize the chances of failure is to begin your business and develop it to the point of reliable profitability while still employed. Moonlighting is an efficient way to test your business idea with a safety net that lets you experiment and learn with the comfort of an outside income and benefits package. The personal energy demands are high when you add a serious business effort to a full-time job, but some balance is achieved in the lowered apprehension of having a safety net. Moonlighting makes borrowing easier because of your salaried income. It also maintains your existing support system—your company's training programs, the stimulation of professional meetings, the ego strength and momentum of an established career, continuing contacts that help your business, and the kinds of motivation and encouragement that come from a successful group work experience. Ethical considerations must be respected. Continue a full-energy, honest effort on your job; separate employer and personal business interests; and honor any "noncompete" agreements you would expect to face if you had formally resigned.

Why you need to know it   Undercapitalization and insufficient latitude to correct mistakes kill small businesses before they have a chance to begin. You can reduce both problems by making your business a serious effort but not a critical one. Moonlighting provides an opportunity to start your enterprise and experience the unexpected challenges without the immediate threat of financial ruin. You may be underestimating the shock of dropping the routine of traditional work before you have replaced it with satisfying associations in your new enterprise. A fledgling home business can be a lonely, unsatisfying experience for a moderately successful professional person used to the status of a respectable place in an organization.

Where to learn more

▶ The definitive work on the moonlighting approach to starting a business is David R. Eyler's *The Executive Moonlighter: Building Your Next Career Without Leaving Your Present Job.* Published in 1989, it is out of print but probably available at your library. The ISBN number is 0-471-50070-4.

Related topics

Answering machines and voice mail	Mail and overnight delivery services
Business ideas	Projections
Business image	**Reducing expenses**
Business plan	Separating business and personal
Computer use	**Start-up**
Consulting	Telephone use
Diversification	**Transitioning**
Fax	Tax checklist

MOTIVATION

What you need to know   Working alone without the demands of someone else's organization requires self-motivation. Without attempting to quantify this highly individual factor in everyone's success formula, it is important to recognize its significance in avoiding failure. However you approach personal motivation, it will be necessary to propel yourself from normal effort to the extraordinary levels required to make a business succeed. Some people do it through the force of their own will and discipline; others follow structured programs articulated by successful people, or harness religious faith to drive their business performance. Whatever works for you, understand that deliberate motivation is needed to summon the exertion needed to punch through the down times and lift your business to the next level. Make networking with positive people a regular part of your motivational program. When you sense yourself getting into an unproductive routine of associations that have become, at worst, negative and, at best, unstimulating, expand your circle. Motivation is an internal process, but it is driven by the stimulus of your outside activities and contacts. Take advantage of your ability to choose the quality of those external influences.

Why you need to know it   People tend to fall into two camps on the subject of motivation: (1) those who discount it and (2) those who become obsessed with it. The former group denies itself a useful tool that can help ease the unproductive moments that accompany the sustained effort of making a business succeed. The latter risk shifting their focus unproductively from the business at hand to the process of being motivated. As a home-based business person, you need to find the middle ground. Let yourself benefit from the organizational and energizing aspects of formal motivation while avoiding making it an end in itself.

Where to learn more

▶ Motivational tapes and books are available in bookstores and catalogs.

▶ SMI International, 5000 Lakewood Drive, Waco, TX 76710, offers a catalog of tapes.

▶ Nightingale Conant (800-323-5552) is another source of tapes.

▶ *The Perry Principles* is a 12-step motivational audio tape program by a nationally acclaimed industrial trainer. You can purchase it for about $200 via High Street Emporium (800-362-5500).

▶ *Successories* is a catalog of quality motivational art in the form of posters, cards, desk accessories, clothing, and books; available via High Street Emporium (800-362-5500). *Executive Gallery* (800-848-2618) offers similar products.

▶ Anthony Robbins' "Mastery University" (800-445-8183) conducts three seminars at resort locations over the course of a year, and features speakers such as General Norman Schwarzkopf and Sir John Templeton.

▶ Seminars featuring Mario Cuomo, Joe Gibbs (former NFL coach), Larry King, Debbi Fields (Mrs. Fields' cookies), and motivational speakers Zig Ziglar and Peter Lowe are held in Washington and other cities. Call 800-444-9159 for details.

Related topics

Associations
Attitude
Bankruptcy
Business associates
Business plan
Business travel
Cash flow
Computer on-line services
Customer relations
Employees
Family

Media relations
Negotiating
Networking
Newsletters
Presentations
Public relations
Success and failure
Telephone use
Training
Vacation, work styles, and schedules

MULTIMEDIA

What you need to know   As audio, video, telecommunications, and computer technologies merge into useful combinations, the first generation of bundled products for the consumer is called multimedia. To use the bundle, you buy a computer that is powerful enough (a 486 PC or a 68040 Mac), has enough memory (several hundred MB of hard disk storage), sufficient processing memory (at least 4 MB RAM), and the necessary input/output devices to work with CD-ROM disks, video tape, and audio of various kinds. Although the specifications can be slightly lower for minimal performance, you won't want to diminish the advantages you can gain with this potential. Multimedia capacity allows you to research vast libraries of information on CD-ROM; have photographs processed directly onto CD-ROMs to use on your system without scanning them; add your voice, music, and video clips to business presentations; and enjoy entertainment products developed for multimedia. If you are not committed to the PC, Macintosh offers a somewhat friendlier approach to multimedia use—there are fewer things to add. An attempt to bring some standardization to multimedia comes from the MPC designation of the Multimedia PC Marketing Council: Level 1 criteria define minimal performance; Level 2, more advanced capacity. The important feature is the assurance that MPC-designated software will run with MPC-labeled hardware. Do your homework: the many important considerations to explore range from the access speed of your CD-ROM drive to the quality of the color monitor. Given the rapid developments, you have to rely on standards, capabilities, and costs that are current at the time you enter the market.

Why you need to know it   As a one-person show, you can benefit from the image enhancement, professionalism, and sheer efficiency of custom-made presentations that wow clients. With multimedia and some talent, you can describe products and services quite impressively on your computer. A notebook computer, possibly with an overhead projection adapter for group presentations, puts you in the big leagues at a relatively economical price. If you have a knack for creating such productions, multimedia offers a business opportunity.

Where to learn more

▶ The CompuServe on-line service has a Multimedia Forum where you can interact with people who use multimedia products. The address is GO MULTIMEDIA.

▶ Computer magazines and catalogs are filled with multimedia information that is evolving monthly; check recent issues. If you are just beginning, read a few general articles like the multimedia special section of the June 1993 issue of *Home Office Computing* or the same publication's "Multimedia Mania" reviews in the August 1993 issue. Check your library or contact: Reprint Manager, *Home Office Computing*, 730 Broadway, New York, NY 10003; 212-505-3580.

▶ To request current information, visit your computer reseller or contact the manufacturers directly. Call Apple at 800-776-2333 or 408-996-1010; Compaq at

800-345-1518 or 713-370-0670. Many other choices exist; these are merely representative of the two main operating systems.

▶ Software products relevant to multimedia include: Kodak Photo CD Access, Microsoft Multimedia Pack for Windows, Cinemania, and much more. Visit a software reseller or explore the catalogs mentioned in Appendix C that are suitable for your operating system.

Related topics

Advertising	Customer relations
Business image	**Desktop publishing**
Camera-ready copy	Media relations
Computer equipment	**Presentations**
Computer software	**Promoting your business**
Computer use	Proposals
Conferences, seminars, shows, and workshops	Public relations
	Sales representatives
Copyright, patent, trademark, and service mark	Training

NEGOTIATING

What you need to know   Negotiations exist on a scale of informality that runs from almost total lack of structure to binding legal contracts. As an individual business person striking deals where only one end of the agreement is under your control, you have to be a skilled negotiator. Discussing terms and coming to agreement on business matters often constitutes an enforceable contract even when that was not your intent. Negotiations lay the groundwork for relationships that lead to satisfying and profitable interactions between clients and providers *if* they are well crafted and understood. A successfully negotiated agreement includes: (1) careful preparation that positions you to speak authoritatively and give and take accurately within your boundaries; (2) effective communication that leaves the parties precisely aware of the issues and terms being negotiated; (3) self-assurance that commands the respect of the other party; and (4) maintenance of an inoffensive professional distance that protects your authority and keeps you focused on your own best interests. Situations that involve the skills of negotiation go beyond formal contract sessions and include closing sales, establishing the terms of a purchase, building a working relationship with others, problem solving, and impasse resolution.

Why you need to know it   As a small business person, you are always structuring deals, from the extremes of negotiating a child's place in your home office routine to closing on a major consulting arrangement. Among your intuitive skills, negotiation is one that lends itself to improvement by learning. Given the home-based business person's nearly constant role of negotiator, this is a topic ripe for self-improvement when time and resources allow.

Where to learn more

▶ Bookstores and libraries have publications and tapes on the subject of negotiating. Tips are also found in the works of successful deal makers like Lee Iacocca and Donald Trump, to name just two.

▶ Karrass, 1633 Stanford Street, Santa Monica, CA 90404-4164 (310-453-1806 or Fax 800-232-8000/310-828-4739), is a leading training organization devoted to negotiating. Two-day seminars are scheduled in major cities around the world and cost between $500 and $600. The multimedia package for people who cannot attend in person costs about $320. Dr. Karrass's books, *Give and Take* and *The Negotiating Game,* are in bookstores and libraries or contact: HarperCollins, Mail Order Department, P. O. Box 588, Dunmore, PA 18512-0588; 800-331-3761.

Related topics

Accountant	Direct mail and mailing lists
Advertising	Direct selling and multilevel
Agents and brokers	marketing
Attitude	Expense sharing and joint ventures
Attorney	Fees and pricing
Bartering	Foreign markets and languages
Bidding	Homeowners' associations
Buying a business	**Independent contractor status**
Consulting	**Loans, credit, and venture capital**
Contracts	Personnel policies
Customer relations	Reducing expenses
Debt collection and	Sales representatives
creditworthiness	

NETWORKING

What you need to know   Networking is the process of building links to other people who can extend your reach, strengthen your knowledge, and use your services—or help you reach those who can. Staying in touch with former colleagues, clients, information providers, or literally anyone who touches your business life, constitutes worthwhile networking. Technology strengthens your ability to network effectively. Telephone networking is routine; computer on-line service bulletin boards are rapidly becoming so. Networking is a habit, a state of mind, and a by-product of honest enthusiasm for what you do. Sharing a cab across town, waiting in line for a table at lunch, enduring a cross-country flight in a crowded airplane—each offers networking opportunities. Refine the art of making contact that pleasantly but efficiently scans others for their potential worth in your ever-widening circle of business associates. Business cards are the low-technology staple of networking. Exchange them freely and integrate them into your higher-technology contact software. Treat each new business card like the required IRS meal-and-entertainment justification notes on a restaurant receipt: scribble enough reminders on the back to personalize your next contact with this new member of your network. File him or her with a key word and with notes that allow accessibility long after the particulars of your chance meeting fade.

Why you need to know it   Independent people who start their own businesses sometimes shrink from forced group activity. Don't limit your view of networking to Rotary Club meetings. Such activities are effective for many people, but civic luncheons and cocktail receptions are by no means the only way to network. Decide whether your greatest strength is in dealing with group or individual relationships, and approach networking in a format that is comfortable for you. If using frequent flyer coupons and upgrading to first class gets you more meaningful networking contacts than back-slapping at conventions, do it your way—but do it. Your business is built on the people you know and the interlocking networks those acquaintances form.

Where to learn more

▶ Symantec's *ACT!* contact manager software is an example of products available for your computer that make networking systematic and easy. Check its features (and those of competing products like Advanced Software, Inc.'s *InTouch* and *DateView*) at your software reseller or the catalog outlets listed in Appendix C.

▶ Microrim's *In The Black* accounting software package includes a contact manager.

▶ Some national links to other home-based business people in your region include: The National Association of Women Business Owners (312-922-0465), which has local organizations to which it will refer you; The Network (800-825-8286 or 909-624-2227); LeTip (800-255-3847 or 619-275-0600); or Leads Club (800-783-3761 or 619-434-3761).

Related topics

Accountant
Agents and brokers
Associations
Attorney
Banking services
Better Business Bureau (BBB)
Bulletin Board System (BBS)
Business associates
Business travel
Chamber of Commerce
Competition
Computer on-line services
Conferences, seminars, shows, and workshops

Consulting
Continuing education
Customer relations
Franchises
Information sources and research
Loans, credit, and venture capital
Marketing and market research
Newsletters
Professional help
Promoting your business
Public relations
Sales representatives
Telephone use
Women's programs

NEWSLETTERS

What you need to know   Promotional newsletters are a major industry
linking businesses with their customers by regularly communicating interesting
information that is valuable enough to the recipient that he or she thinks favor-
ably of the sender. Newsletters bridge the gap between overt advertising and
personal correspondence. The message or intent is to build and sustain a commercial relationship, but the method is providing information. The businesses,
organizations, and professions that pay for the creation and distribution of
newsletters generally look to others for the service. The principals spend their
time more profitably practicing their profession or pursuing their trade. Creating newsletters requires familiarity with computers, page layout software, a
sense of design, some graphics ability, and the initiative to coordinate the gath-
ering of information, basic research and reporting skills, printing, and mailing—all for a fee. Payment can be based on an hourly rate, a flat rate per issue,
inches of copy prepared, or anything else that works for the people involved.
Frequency of publication and sophistication of design are similarly flexible.
The market is unlimited, and the process is totally adaptable to any balance between what clients want to provide on their own and what they want to purchase. Supporting services like mailing-list maintenance and production are
readily available to the home-based person who is paid to coordinate the total
process. The same factors apply if the newsletter is done individually to promote your own home business.

Why you need to know it   Newsletters are important to the home-based
business person for two reasons: (1) they offer an in-house promotional device
that can project a professional image for your residential base, and (2) as an
application of desktop publishing, they lend themselves to being operated as a
home-based business. Either option offers the home worker an opportunity to
make the most of technology from a noncommercial setting, and the content of
the newsletter can be directed to almost any taste, interest, or level of effort.

Where to learn more

‣ Newsletter Publishers Association, 1401 Wilson Blvd., Rosslyn, VA 22201; 703-
527-2333.

‣ *Newsletters in Print* (formerly *Newsletter Directory*), published by Gale Research, Inc., Detroit, MI, is a descriptive guide to more than 10,300 newsletters
and similar publications. Check the reference section of your library.

‣ The *Newsletter on Newsletters* is published by The Newsletter Clearinghouse,
Rhinebeck, NY 12572.

‣ Bookstores and libraries offer a variety of publications on desktop publishing and
newsletter writing. Here are several examples you can find there or purchase
directly: Steve Morgenstern's *No-Sweat Desktop Publishing* (800-325-6149); Herman Holtz's *How to Start and Run a Writing and Editing Business* (212-850-
6554); and Roger Parker's *Looking Good in Print* (919-942-0220).

▸ EF Communications, 6614 Penrod Avenue, St. Louis, MO 63139 (Fax 314-647-1609; 800-264-6305, orders only), sells a bundle of newsletter business publications for about $50.

Related topics

Advertising

Associations

Bartering

Business image

Camera-ready copy

Computer equipment

Computer software

Computer use

Copiers

Copyright, patent, trademark, and service mark

Customer relations

Desktop publishing

Direct mail and mailing lists

Information sources and research

Investing

Legal liability

Mail and overnight delivery services

Mail order

Marketing and market research

Networking

Paper

Printing

Promoting your business

Public relations

Regulations

NOISE

What you need to know   An advantage of your home-based business is your control over the working environment. One of the more easily manipulated elements of that environment is sound. Begin with an informal analysis of household sounds that might distract you, and take steps to eliminate or isolate them. Next, consider the addition of positive sound that enhances your ability to concentrate and to tolerate hours alone in your home office. What works varies widely by individual and generation—some people work well to the sound of rock music, others thrive on silence or the wordless stimulation of classical music. Choosing what works for you is an important and generally inexpensive aspect of home-based work space design. Technology is increasingly helpful as computers adapt to multimedia. CD and other sound media have shrunk in physical size and cost and have become ever more adaptable to the home office setting. Design factors like where the office is placed in the home still matter, but soundproofing materials and electronic sound masking offer alternatives when physical relocation is not practical. The science of noise cancellation is just becoming available, but it is reaching the retail market. The technology is promising because specific sounds are matched with others that greatly reduce their impact; opposite sound waves combine to approximate silence.

Why you need to know it   As the primary producer in your home-based business, you cannot afford to waste energy tolerating distracting noises—or compensating for the absence of sounds you find stimulating. When you examine what makes you productive, don't overlook the contribution of sound-conditioning materials and equipment.

Where to learn more

▶ Background music and recorded sound effects suitable for the office are available from retail stores and catalogs. A few examples: Music, Halpren Sounds, 1775 Old Country Road, #9, Belmont, CA 94002; the sounds of a busy office, Zable's Business Services, 156 Wall Street, Kingston, NY 12401.

▶ Marsona is a manufacturer of "white noise" generating equipment, including desktop units with digitized sound effects. Its products are available through office equipment resellers and catalogs such as High Street Emporium (800-362-5500) and Reliable Home Office (800-869-6000).

▶ *NoiseBuster* from Noise Cancellation Technologies, Inc., 800 Summer Street, Stamford, CT 06901 (800-228-3141), is an active noise-reduction headset that matches an irritating sound with one that reduces it. Price: about $150.

Related topics

Business address and location
Computer equipment
Copiers
Environmental considerations
Equipment and furniture
Lighting

Office planning and decorating
Promoting your business
Regulations
Telephone equipment
Zoning

OFFICE PLANNING AND DECORATING

What you need to know   Home-based businesses need an identifiable and functional space for more reasons than satisfying tax regulations—living and working in the same space around the clock can be self-defeating. Achieving an office effect and separateness, even if it is just down the hall, can make the difference in focusing on business when you should and leaving it behind when office hours end. What you call an office is a highly individual matter, as is the equipment and furniture required. The economics of home office choices are not that different for a high-tech look whether it is built around the veneered fiberboard selections of a discount retailer or around functional antiques. What matters is that your choices satisfy you, your clients, and the tasks they have to support. Devices exist to make furniture move easily; sound, lighting, color, and texture manipulation lets you control mood; air conditioning, heating, and ventilation top the list of mechanical considerations. Professional help or the advice of a gifted acquaintance can help with the aesthetics. Function should be your domain—insist that it be the bedrock around which the rest of your office planning and decorating evolves.

Why you need to know it   Priorities are the key to successful home office planning and decorating. Focus on producing a survivable, functioning business first and an image-satisfying showcase second. Let the decorator home office wait for that first burst of discretionary income that arrives after cash flow has settled into a predictable pattern, debt service is comfortable, and an adequate reserve is in a liquid investment. With those goals in place and your business routine sufficiently shaken down through real-world operations, step up from survivably functional to very nice surroundings. Reversing those priorities can bring on the heartbreak of liquidating a very nice office that doesn't have a successful business to sustain it.

Where to learn more

▶ Libraries, bookstores, and working-at-home publications feature the latest approaches to planning and decorating a home office. Page through current editions. Here are several suggestions: a 160-page, heavily illustrated book called *Working at Home* by the editors of *Better Homes and Gardens; Home Offices and Workspaces,* a similar 96-page book by the editors of Sunset Books and Magazine (often seen in rack displays at building supply stores); and *Home Office Computing* magazine's periodic features on the subject.

▶ If you need professional help, look in the telephone yellow pages for a decorator. Office furniture dealers sometimes offer decorating and office layout advice as a part of your purchase.

▶ Used office furniture dealers are worth checking, as are furniture rental firms that sell their returns at off price.

▶ The National Association of Professional Organizers, 655 Alvernon, Suite 108, Tucson, AZ 85711 (602-322-9753), will help you locate someone to help organize your office.

▶ Software like Abracadata, Inc.'s *Design Your Own Home Interiors* (Mac or PC Connection: 800-800-2222 or 5555) and DesignWare, Inc.'s *myHouse* (Power Up: 800-851-2917) give you home office planning capabilities on your computer.

Related topics

Business address and location	Lighting
Business image	Mail and overnight delivery services
Computer equipment	**Managing growth**
Computer software	Merchandise buying services
Computer use	Noise
Copiers	Overhead expenses
Customer relations	Psychological factors
Disaster planning	Records
Employees	Reducing expenses
Environmental considerations	**Regulations**
Equipment and furniture	Security
Ergonomics	Separating business and personal
Franchises	**Telephone equipment**
Getting organized and	**Telephone services**
managing information	**Telephone use**
Information sources and research	Zoning

OVERHEAD EXPENSES

What you need to know   Overhead refers to all of the costs you experience that cannot be linked directly to producing the goods or services sold by your business. Among them are: insurance, heat, light, maintenance, and so on. Overhead is considered to be either fixed—the costs will stay the same no matter how good or poor business is, whether you are busy or not—or variable—the costs will rise or fall according to the level of activity. You have to be aware of your overhead expenses: (1) to be competitive with others doing the same thing—your overhead can't be too different from theirs unless you balance it with a unique level of productivity that leaves you making money at the industry average or higher, in spite of your higher overhead; and (2) to be able to pass them along accurately to your clients as part of the price of your services. Awareness of overhead expenses is essential for business planning. They represent a predictable obligation that you have to anticipate meeting regardless of how your business performs. As your business grows and you consider attracting investors, borrowing for expansion, or selling the business at a profit, anyone who analyzes your financials will be interested in your overhead. A consultant hired to help you improve profitability would take a hard look at overhead and advise you of possible savings that might be made without harming performance.

Why you need to know it   A danger for small business people is an overly simplistic look at the real costs of doing business. They base their fees intuitively, expecting that by charging a certain amount they must be making money. The real bottom line depends on what is left after accounting for everything that goes out versus everything that comes in. Especially in a home-based business, where the costs of operating the house were always considered personal expenses, it is necessary to adopt a new perspective. Prorating the overhead of the business use of your home is a necessary component of your cost of doing business, and you must deduct it before declaring yourself profitable.

Where to learn more

▶ Basic small business management books and courses can help you understand and manage overhead expenses. Depending on your learning style, consider books or tapes available in libraries, at bookstores, or in magazines and catalogs.

▶ College courses in small business management are another approach to developing an appreciation for overhead expenses. Auditing such a course for no credit is an alternative to traditional enrollment; another is just buying the text used for the course at the college, although networking with class members and the instructor makes enrollment worth considering.

▶ Entrepreneur, 2392 Morse Avenue, Irvine, CA 92714 (800-421-2300; 800-352-7449 in California), sells a small business management course.

♦ Robert Gehorsam's "Start-Up Diary," in the September 1993 issue of *Home Office Computing* magazine, is an excellent, realistic account of what you can expect to encounter in starting a serious business. Check your library or contact: Reprint Manager, *Home Office Computing*, 730 Broadway, New York, NY 10003; 212-505-3580.

Related topics

Accounting	License
Answering machines and voice mail	Lighting
Associations	Loans, credit, and venture capital
Banking services	Mail and overnight delivery services
Bidding	**Managing growth**
Bookkeeping	Marketing and market research
Budgeting	Newsletters
Business plan	Paper
Buying a business	Payroll
Cash flow	Presentations
Checking accounts	Printing
Computer equipment	Professional help
Conferences, seminars, shows, and workshops	**Profit**
	Projections
Copiers	Promoting your business
Direct mail and mailing lists	**Proposals**
Employees	Public relations
Equipment and furniture	Records
Evaluating your business	**Reducing expenses**
Expense sharing and joint ventures	Security
Fees and pricing	Supplies
Financial planning	Telephone equipment
Forms	Telephone services
Franchises	Telephone use
Insurance	Time-share offices
Leasing	Training

PAPER

What you need to know   Laser printers and page layout software are just the beginning when it comes to making your own professional-looking printed materials. It isn't just the font packages and clip art or even the sophisticated scanning of images that makes for an impressive final product, it's the paper the information is printed on. Paper presentation companies offer more than paper products. Many of them sell software templates and applications software that helps you achieve professional results on an ordinary laser printer. Paper is sold separately or in sets consisting of color- and design-coordinated brochures, mailers, letterheads, frames, envelopes, business cards, product and mailing labels, presentation folders, and presentation envelopes. You can print black type from your printer onto the multicolored paper products or make a master on white paper and run the colored papers through your copying machine. If you plan to do a large run, take the materials to a commercial printer. Exotic and accent papers are available in addition to the regular ones. Recycled products are among your choices, and special formats like announcements and invitations are available too.

Why you need to know it   Whether you are in the business of preparing printed materials for customers or for yourself, you would be wise to know about paper products that vastly expand your capabilities. This is an advantage even if you are dealing with a printer. Specialized paper products available from direct suppliers in small lots can put you in a league once reserved for major corporations. Order a catalog and then get samples of designs that complement your tastes. Granted, the information in your consulting reports or business proposals is what ultimately counts, but, other things being equal, an impressive presentation can give you a competitive edge.

Where to learn more

- Paper Access, 23 West 18th Street, New York, NY 10011 (212-463-7035 Monday through Friday 9:00 to 7:00, Saturday 11:00 to 6:00; Fax 212-463-7022, or 800-PAPER 01 for a catalog), has over 500 unique papers for your laser printer, copier, and printing needs. A kit sells for $25.
- Power Up! (800-851-2917) sells specialized computer printer papers and brochure stock.
- Paper Direct, P. O. Box 618, 205 Chubb Avenue, Lyndhurst, NJ 07071-0618 (201-507-1996, 800-272-7377, Fax 2010-507-0817), sells a complete line of specialty computer papers, brochures, business card stock, forms, certificates, color foils, and so on. Paper kit and selector unit price: about $20.
- The Drawing Board, P. O. Box 2944, Hartford, CT 06104-2944; 800-527-9530.

Related topics

Advertising	Fax
Business image	Forms
Camera-ready copy	Franchises
Computer use	Mail order
Contracts	Newsletters
Copiers	**Printing**
Customer relations	Promoting your business
Desktop publishing	Proposals
Direct mail and mailing lists	Public relations
Environmental considerations	Supplies
Evaluating your business	

PAYROLL

What you need to know   To determine what you should charge clients and to manage your business profitably, you must calculate the total costs of employing people or fully compensating yourself. The numbers in your payroll records provide the required information. The ultimate motivation for accurate and timely payroll records is the penalties that will be imposed by the government if you fail to meet your obligations. Processing payroll depends on whom you employ and your basis for paying them, but it probably includes calculating gross wages for the period (salary, hourly rate, bonuses, commissions, and so on), then figuring the taxes and withholding amounts (federal income tax, social security, and Medicare) and any additional deductions for employee benefits and state taxes. Quarterly, you have to make estimated payments to the government that are accompanied by the associated forms; at year-end, W-2 forms, W-3s, and other annual reports must be prepared and issued. These requirements make computer-based bookkeeping almost a necessity. With even simple checkbook programs like *Quicken,* you can figure out the basic parameters for each employee (including yourself) and rely on the program to accumulate the summaries required for payroll reporting.

Why you need to know it   Payroll is among your must-do business obligations, whether you are paying other employees or only yourself. Trouble lurks in satisfying the requirements for withholding, paying, and reporting taxes and other mandated government payments. Unless you plan to turn the whole responsibility over to your bookkeeper or accountant, computer software can make these tasks relatively painless. Take the trouble to understand the process, then let the computer carry the burden of the calculations and printing.

Where to learn more

▶ Consult IRS Publication 15, "Circular E, Employer's Tax Guide," Publication 505, "Tax Withholding and Estimated Tax," Publication 937, "Employment Taxes and Information Returns," and Publication 334, "Tax Guide for Small Business."

▶ Small business computer software either comes with a payroll calculating capability, or a function (*QuickPay,* in the case of *Quicken*) can be added inexpensively. *Quicken* products are available from Intuit (800-624-8742 or 415-322-0573). You can examine them, and competitive products like Best!Ware's *M.Y.O.B.,* at software resellers or in the catalogs mentioned in computer magazines and in Appendix C.

▶ Microrim's *In The Black* can help you manage payroll records and issue checks.

▶ The manuals that come with the computer software are excellent how-to guides for the mechanics of generating payroll documents and reports. However, they are not substitutes for a basic understanding of the process.

▶ Communicate with your accountant periodically, and be sure you are meeting your withholding and reporting requirements.

Related topics

Accountant

Accounting

Banking services

Bankruptcy

Bookkeeping

Budgeting

Cash flow

Computer software

Employees

Financial planning

Labor laws

Legal/illegal business operation

Managing growth

Money management

Overhead expenses

Personnel policies

Profit

Projections

Records

Reducing expenses

Regulations

Tax checklist

Temporary help

PERSONNEL POLICIES

What you need to know   When you employ people, you encounter legal liabilities and government regulations that must be satisfied. The basic approach to meeting your obligations and avoiding legal problems is a system of personnel policies and records designed to fulfill established requirements. Professional review by an attorney versed in labor law would be your best safeguard, but you can begin doing things right with guidance from published manuals and computer software that you can adapt to your own company. The advantage of working with such a program is that it leads you through the topics and considerations you need to face, asks the relevant questions, and translates your responses into acceptable policy statements. By keeping up with revisions to the software, you can remain current as new legislation emerges. As an example, how well versed are you in the provisions of the Americans with Disabilities Act or the Family and Medical Leave Act of 1993? Some topics are required only of employers who have some minimum number of employees, but there are issues that you should probably be considering even in your smaller organization. Among the programs you should address are: access to personnel records, AIDS policy, business travel reimbursement, conduct and work rules, drug and alcohol use and testing, equal opportunity, probationary period of employment, safety, sexual harassment, sick leave benefits, status during and after leave, termination, use of phone, vacation policy, and many more.

Why you need to know it   Among the possible growing pains your home-based business might face is the addition of employees. Although it is unlikely that you will ever employ enough people in your home to incur the obligations of some major government programs, many of the associated requirements have relevance for smaller actions individuals might bring against you. By being sensitive to the whole universe of modern workplace law, your policies may preclude suits that would otherwise be costly to defend against. Requirements of major employers may also highlight things you would like to do for your employees. When benefits are extended, it is prudent to do so within stated limits.

Where to learn more

▶ IRS Publication 334, "Tax Guide for Small Business," and Publication 583, "Taxpayers Starting a Business," are good starting points for information on the minimum records you need for tax reporting purposes.

▶ EZ Legal Books, 384 South Military Trail, Deerfield Beach, FL 33442 (305-480-8933; Fax 305-480-8906), markets a series of perforated forms books; one called *Personnel Director* contains over 240 ready-to-use personnel agreements, forms, letters, and documents. Price: about $25.

▶ Computer software like KnowledgePoint's *DescriptionsWrite Now!* and *PoliciesWrite Now!* offers a systematic and thorough way to craft a personnel policy manual and establish records. Both are available from Power Up! (800-851-2917), or check catalogs, magazines, and resellers for these and similar products. Palo Alto Software's *Employee Handbook Toolkit* will also be helpful.

Related topics

Accountant

Attorney

Business basics

Computer software

Contracts

Ethics

Forms

Getting organized and
    managing information

Independent contractor status

Insurance

Legal liability

Legal/illegal business operation

Payroll

Records

Regulations

Retirement

Security

Tax checklist

**Vacation, work styles, and
    schedules**

PRESENTATIONS

What you need to know   The term "presentations" has become synonymous with computer presentations graphics packages. Using software, you can do alone in an hour what once took days with the costly assistance of a graphic artist. If you can type your data into a spreadsheet and click the buttons that create a graph, you can prepare your own professional presentations. After graphics slides have been designed, it is easy to keep them up-to-date. Use software features that link your presentation back to the database or spreadsheet it is based on, and your slides will never be out of sync with their supporting documents. Change a number in the spreadsheet and it changes automatically in the linked slide. What you produce has become easier to use and more portable too. Whether you have a desktop computer or a notebook computer you can carry to a meeting, the software that created your slides displays them as a slide show on your computer's screen. If you make a group presentation, plug in an overhead projection peripheral that reads the computer output and turns it into an image that an overhead projector can put on a large screen. Alternatively, your output can always be printed and made into a conventional overhead slide transparency or 35-mm slide. Take the next step into multimedia and you can add sound and video to your presentations.

Why you need to know it Selling ideas and products, the primary task of the home-based business person, involves both preparing the materials and the field work of actually performing the presentation. The more you can cut your costs in terms of time and fees paid to third parties, the more profitable your business will be. Another important dimension is artistic control. You can achieve the effects you are most comfortable with and present your facts with maximum impact by crafting the presentation yourself.

Where to learn more

▶ To find software for your kind of equipment, read through Appendix C and check presentations listings in computer user magazines and catalogs. Several of the leading products are: *Freelance Graphics,* Lotus Development Corporation, Cambridge, MA (800-343-5414 or 617-577-8500); *Harvard Graphics,* Software Publishing Corporation, Santa Clara, CA (800-234-2500 or 408-986-8000); and *PowerPoint,* Microsoft Corporation, Redmond, WA (800-426-9400 or 206-882-8080).

▶ Conventional overhead projectors are available through local office equipment resellers and catalogs. A highly portable model is the Cobra from Apollo Audio Visual, 60 Trade Zone Court, Ronkonkoma, NY 11779 (800-777-3750 or 516-467-8033).

▶ Overhead projection attachments for your computer are available through office equipment and computer resellers.

Related topics

Business image
Camera-ready copy
Computer software
Conferences, seminars, shows, and workshops
Copyright, patent, trademark, and service mark
Customer relations
Desktop publishing
Equipment and furniture

Fax
Information sources and research
Marketing and market research
Media relations
Networking
Printing
Promoting your business
Proposals
Public relations
Sales representatives

PRINTING

What you need to know   Reading the reviews, you would think that laser printers, page preparation software, and the availability of fancy papers have eliminated the need for print shops. That is only true if you need a very limited number of copies. Once you cross the line into what qualifies as a production run, you need to speak the language of the print shop. The same is true for midsize runs where commercial-grade copying machines take the place of the printing press. If you are producing newsletters or promotional pieces regularly, you will quickly learn the few tricks of the trade that are necessary to know. Among the considerations you will need to explore with your print shop are: (1) whether to print the job or run it on a copy machine; (2) color, weight, and characteristics of the paper; (3) mailing considerations; (4) number of ink colors and whether separations are necessary; (5) treatment of photo ("continuous tone") and line images; (6) enlargements and reductions; and (7) cutting and folding. You can safely mark your camera-copy pages if you use a non-reproducing blue pencil (available at any office supplies store). Depending on the complexity of your project and your relationship with the printer, you will need to do some of the work of preparing "mechanicals"—the formal page layouts printers work from. Discuss the intended final product with your printer before delving heavily into trying to emulate professional mechanicals. Most printers settle for clean copy with enough instructions on margins and placement of graphics to know what you want the final product to look like. Printing your camera copy on high-quality laser paper and using crop marks and other page preparation options available in your software will go a long way toward satisfying the most demanding print shop.

Why you need to know it   It is easy enough to order envelopes and labels, but you should know your print shop's capability for doing custom work. The revolution in desktop publishing gives the home-based business person the ability to prepare high-quality copy, but if results are to meet expectations, communication is still needed with the person in charge of the press run. Unless your business *is* the professional preparation of printer's copy, don't spend an inordinate amount of time becoming a desktop publisher. Remember the highest and best use of your time rule. Going far beyond your printer's minimum requirements carries a risk of spending too much of your valuable time on ancillary things.

Where to learn more

▶ Business envelopes, labels, stationery, and supplies are available at reasonable prices from these mail-order firms: Business Envelope Manufacturers, Inc., 900 Grand Boulevard, Deer Park, NY 11729 (800-275-4400 or 516-667-8500); Quill, 100 Schelter Road, Lincolnshire, IL 60069-3621 (909-988-3200 far west; 708-634-4800 midwest and midsouth; 404-479-6100 southeast; 717-272-6100 northeast); and The Drawing Board, P. O. Box 2944, Hartford, CT 06104-2944 (800-527-9530).

▶ American Color Printing, Inc., 1731 NW 97 Avenue, Plantation, FL 33322 (305-473-4392; Fax 305-473-8621), prints four-color posters, catalogs, brochures, catalog sheets, postcards, calendars, manuals, media kits, newsletters, and so on.

▶ "Preparing Pages for a Print Shop," in the September 1992 issue of *Home Office Computing* magazine, gives the essentials of readying materials for an outside printer. Check your library or contact: Reprint Manager, *Home Office Computing,* 730 Broadway, New York, NY 10003; 212-505-3580.

▶ Rapidocolor, 705 E. Union Street, West Chester, PA 19382 (800-872-7436), offers a free 28-page handbook of printing information and fast color printing.

Related topics

Advertising
Bidding
Business address and location
Business cards
Business image
Business name
Camera-ready copy
Checking accounts
Computer equipment
Computer software
Copiers
Copyright, patent, trademark, and
   service mark
Customer relations
Desktop publishing
Direct mail and mailing lists
Direct selling and multilevel
   marketing
Environmental considerations
Equipment and furniture

Expense sharing and joint ventures
Fees and pricing
Forms
Franchises
Mail order
Marketing and market research
Media relations
Multimedia
Newsletters
Paper
Presentations
Promoting your business
Proposals
Public relations
Records
Reducing expenses
Sales representatives
Supplies
Training

PROFESSIONAL HELP

What you need to know   Bedrock professional help for the home-based business person consists of an accountant and an attorney. But, depending on your specialty, your need for professional help may not stop there. You will encounter people who are more expert than you in certain aspects of what you do. Initial research for a business plan or the adaptation of a thriving business to meet new demands will yield the names of people whose work you value—authors of books on the subject or of articles in magazines or professional journals; presenters at meetings and conventions; and other unexpected potential sources of professional help. You might need a designer or architect to assist in creating interesting office space, or a consultant who specializes in implementing the North American Free Trade Agreement (NAFTA) by smoothing a path to Mexican or Canadian markets for your services.

Why you need to know it   Even the most capable home-based business person needs the stimulation of outside thinking and periodic expert opinion. Although your circle of business associates and networking partners can supply much of what is needed, times come when professional consultation fees are money well spent. Every small business person struggles with do-it-myself decisions. Occasionally, challenges arise—sometimes legal, sometimes competitive—that call for insight from professionals of a unique stripe. When the need arises, engage the required professional help and consider it a cost of doing business.

Where to learn more

▶ There is no general list for all the kinds of professional help you might need. Engage in some detective work if you have no reference for the kind of person you seek. Begin by asking people who might have contact with experts in that specialty. Call companies that sell products or services relevant to your concern. Ask to speak with someone who deals with the topic, explain your requirements, and follow the leads of these informal referrals until you find the person you need.

▶ Don't overlook the telephone yellow pages for your own area or for a nearby large city. Automated searches of telephone book information can be done on CD-ROM disks that contain millions of listings.

▶ Use the business reference section of your library to find companies and individuals who might help.

▶ Consult Gale's *Directory of Associations* for groups that might refer you to consultants among their members.

Related topics

Accountant	**Expense sharing and joint ventures**
Agents and brokers	Expert witness
Associations	Foreign markets and languages
Attorney	**Information sources and research**
Banking services	Insurance
Bartering	Investing
Business associates	Legal liability
Buying a business	Legal/illegal business operation
Conferences, seminars, shows,	**License**
and workshops	Marketing and market research
Consulting	Media relations
Continuing education	Newsletters

Office planning and decorating	Stress and overworking
Promoting your business	Syndication
Public relations	Tax checklist
Sales representatives	Telephone use
Security	Training

PROFIT

What you need to know   You have to make a fair wage and a decent return on your investment if your business is to be viable. Use these four steps to determine whether your business meets the test of profitability: (1) calculate your indirect costs—what it costs to keep your doors open no matter how much business you do; (2) add your direct costs—what it costs to accomplish the service or make the product you sell; (3) determine your total revenues from all sources related to your business activity; (4) subtract the sum of your indirect and direct costs from your revenues (assuming they are greater). The amount that is left is your profit. With a little effort, the process can be refined to hone in precisely on the aspects of your business that are profitable and the ones that are not. The same procedure can reveal excessive costs that might be reduced to increase your profitability. Remember that your salary and the return on your investment are two separate things. Include your wages in your expenses; calculate your return on investment based on what is left—20 percent is a reasonable target. These are the concepts you need. A class on small business finance or a good text or self-help book on the subject can help you isolate the individual calculations.

Why you need to know it   Too many small business owners approach profit intuitively and end up generating more activity than profit. Make an honest, hard-nosed profit requirement an integral part of your business plan and review it regularly. Draw a line between emotional attachment to your business and the need to show honest profit. If it isn't there, raise your prices or lower your costs until you can. Anything short of that result is spinning your wheels, and you won't be in business for very long. Succeeding and surviving mean more than "doing lots of business." You must make enough profit to generate a competitive wage and a reasonable return on investment.

Where to learn more

▶ *Contracting Your Services,* by Robert L. Davidson III, contains several practical, applied chapters on small business financial management, including useful formulas for calculating profit.

▶ Your accountant is a logical source of advice for calculating and understanding the profitability of your enterprise.

▶ Financial software like Intuit's *Quicken* and Microrim's *In The Black* contain profit-and-loss statement generators and manuals that explain their use. Consult computer magazine reviews and catalogs for more information and similar products. (See Appendix C.)

Related topics

Accounting
Bidding
Billing
Bookkeeping
Budgeting
Business plan
Cash flow
Competition
Computer software
Contracts
Debt collection and creditworthiness
Direct mail and mailing lists
Direct selling and multilevel marketing

Evaluating your business
Expense sharing and joint ventures
Fees and pricing
Financial formulas
Financial planning
Money management
Negotiating
Overhead expenses
Projections
Proposals
Reducing expenses
Tax checklist

PROJECTIONS

What you need to know   You have to be able to foretell the financial future if you are to succeed in your own business. The process involves approximations, but you can come very close to actual results if you adapt past experiences to the ones you expect to encounter in the future. You can separate business and personal financial projections, but as a small business person you should calculate them side-by-side because one so intimately affects the other. Spreadsheet software or, more awkwardly, checkbook software—or even more awkwardly, a calculator, a pencil and some paper—will help you create an accurate summary of everything you spend now and are likely to spend in the next few years. Prepare your projections sequentially, month-by-month, just the way you will encounter them. Balance your expenses with projected income, and note where the red ink occurs. It signals, at best, a cash flow problem that has to be covered by rearranging the size and order of your income and expenditures, and, at worst, an unprofitable venture that needs to be changed or terminated and its debts paid by other means.

Why you need to know it   You are more capable of anticipating your financial condition in the months and years ahead than you might imagine. Many small business people just don't take the trouble or don't want to know. Unless you have an exceptional situation, your financial future as you operate your small business will be uneven. For that reason, you need to have an accurate prediction of the coming months so that you can make the needed adjustments rationally. If you have a cash flow problem this month, you borrow against delayed revenues that you know are coming next month, or the month after. Projections let you even out the financial peaks and valleys enough to keep your eye on long-range profitability.

Where to learn more

▶ Microrim's *In the Black* software includes financial planners (Appendix F).

▶ Spreadsheet software is the best financial planning device available. The accompanying manuals show you how to plan. Microsoft's *Excel* and Lotus's *Improv* are full-featured spreadsheets. Integrated software like *Microsoft Works* contains a spreadsheet along with other popular applications. The same capability is available from most software manufacturers. Review computer magazines and software catalogs for a product you like. (See Appendix C.)

▶ Business books and articles in financial and small business magazines can help you with financial projections. An example is Linda Stern's "Can You Quit Your Day Job?," in the March 1993 issue of *Home Office Computing* magazine, or *Smart Money's* November 1993 retirement planning issue. Look to business accounting software and books for strictly business financial projections.

Related topics

Accountant	Fees and pricing
Accounting	Financial formulas
Bidding	**Financial planning**
Billing	Information sources and research
Bookkeeping	Managing growth
Budgeting	Money management
Business plan	**Overhead expenses**
Buying a business	Payroll
Cash flow	Start-up
Competition	Tax checklist
Computer software	Telephone use
Contracts	Undercapitalization
Evaluating your business	

PROMOTING YOUR BUSINESS

What you need to know   Taking the initiative is the key to promoting your small business. There are dozens of things you can do, at relatively little cost, if you make promoting your business a priority. Begin by knowing and articulating what you do in a professional manner. Build your own "sound bite" and use it every time you get a chance to mention your business. If you run a business that fits well with telephone yellow pages or other community advertising, take advantage of those sources. Consider cooperative advertising where you split costs with others. Do the same with sales and services where cooperative efforts with others can bring you more business. Get into a referral network of complementary businesses that pass along each other's business cards to clients. Focus your business development on a specific client base and concentrate your efforts. Be cautious about breaking the junk-fax laws, but use the impact of fax notices to contact established clients and those who inquire about your business. Take advantage of being an expert in what you do: community organizations and small local broadcast outlets are always looking for interesting guests, and a guest spot constitutes free advertising for you. Postcards are an inexpensive and versatile form of advertising. Word-of-mouth promotion can be deliberately cultivated by asking your customers for referrals. Networking is the staple of promoting any small business. Do it your way and keep your relationships sincere and uncontrived, but stay connected with people who can use or tell others about your business. Surveys are multifaceted promotional devices. They yield (1) publicity during the surveys and (2) publications, appearances, and contacts to discuss the results afterward.

Why you need to know it   A small business that isn't generating new orders or new clients on a regular basis is soon going to be in trouble. You can't rely on established accounts being permanent or on unsolicited business coming to you. As a home-based business, you have no national marketing campaign or broader group of associates out there sending referrals back to you. If profitable activity is to be the hallmark of your home business environment, you are going to have to create and cultivate it by promoting your business at every opportunity.

Where to learn more

▶ Computer software that lends itself to business promotion includes a full range of graphics and publications programs plus specialty products like *Calendar Creator* (Power Up! 800-851-2917) and *Cards Now* (business cards) of Madison, WI (800-233-9767).

▶ Specialty paper sellers offer a variety of professional promotional options that you can personalize using your laser printer.

▶ The Drawing Board, P. O. Box 2944, Hartford, CT 06104-2944 (800-527-9530), sells promotional products, paper, and printed giveaways like key chains, pens, note pads, and similar reminders.

▶ For information and contacts, don't overlook local media promotion.

▶ Browse through current issues of small business magazines for the latest ideas on promotions. Examples are "Promoting for Pennies" and "Make Word-of-Mouth Work," in the April and November 1993 issues, respectively, of *Home Office Computing* magazine. Check your library or contact: Reprint Manager, *Home Office Computing*, 730 Broadway, New York, NY 10003; 212-505-3580.

▶ The Wharton School of the University of Pennsylvania sells a complete video seminar on marketing strategy through Kantola Productions, 55 Sunnyside Avenue, Mill Valley, CA 94941; 800-989-8272. Price: about $190.

Related topics

Advertising

Agents and brokers

Answering machines and voice
  mail

Associations

Better Business Bureau (BBB)

Bidding

Bulletin Board System (BBS)

Business address and location

Business associates

Business cards

Business image

Business name

Camera-ready copy

Chamber of Commerce

Computer software

Conferences, seminars, shows,
  and workshops

Customer relations

Desktop publishing

Direct mail and mailing lists

Direct selling and multilevel
  marketing

Expense sharing and joint ventures

Foreign markets and languages

Franchises

Mail and overnight delivery services

Mail order

Marketing and market research

Media relations

Multimedia

Negotiating

Networking

Newsletters

Paper

Presentations

Printing

Professional help

Proposals

Public relations

Regulations

Sales representatives

Syndication

Telephone equipment

Telephone services

Telephone use

PROPOSALS

What you need to know   Because your proposal is a solicitation, it needs
to be concise, orderly, persuasive, and able to keep the interest of the reader.
When you respond to requests for proposals from the government or other
sources, the format may be suggested or even mandated. More often, you will
be given the parameters of the project and asked to tell how you would approach it. Some jobs are small enough, or your relationship with the source is
sufficiently established that you can get the business with an expansive letter
on the subject—a letter proposal. In most instances, however, it will be necessary to develop a more formal proposal. In some orderly arrangement, your
package should provide the following: (1) a brief introduction that shows
you understand the problem, have an attractive approach to solving it, are
qualified to do so, and (ideally) can cite a successful example of doing similar
work for another impressive client; (2) a detailed discussion of the problem
and your way of solving it—an analytical, logical recitation that convinces
the reader that you would know what to do if you got the job; (3) an action
plan that details specifically how you would implement your approach—
organization, planning, management, staffing, schedules, and deliverables;
(4) an elaboration of your track record in similar projects—proof that you

have the training, contacts, and resources to do the job; and (5) supporting materials—a title page, an executive summary, a table of contents, appendices—anything that adds credibility and supports your claims. If the proposal calls for financial projections, look to business proposal approaches to flesh out your presentation. Special paper products and presentation or publication software can give your proposal a professional look.

Why you need to know it   To secure new accounts, you have to go after prospective business. It isn't always as simple as making a telephone call. The more likely approach is responding to a request for proposal (an RFP). Making yourself competitive in the proposal arena requires more than just dollars and sense. You have to respect the protocols, make your ideas easily read and understood, and engender respect for your professionalism through the bid you submit. Your proposal is a sample of the performance a client can expect if you are hired. Like a good resume, a good proposal can get you to the interview stage, where you can close the deal.

Where to learn more

▶ Herman Holtz's *The Consultant's Guide to Proposal Writing,* is a classic in its field. (See the Bibliography.)

▶ Business planning software also contains the basic components needed in proposal writing. *PFS: Business Plan* by Spinnaker, Palo Alto Software's *Business Plan Toolkit,* and Jian's *BizPlanBuilder* are examples. (See Appendix C for suppliers and sources of reviews.)

▶ Paper Access, 23 West 18th Street, New York, NY 10011 (212-463-7035 Monday through Friday 9:00 to 7:00, Saturday 11:00 to 6:00; Fax 212-463-7022 or 800-PAPER 01); Power Up! (800-851-2917) and Paper Direct, P. O. Box 618, 205 Chubb Avenue, Lyndhurst, NJ 07071-0618 (201-507-1996, 800-272-7377; Fax 2010-507-0817), sell special proposal presentation materials that you can customize with your printer.

Related topics

Agents and brokers
Bidding
Bonding
Budgeting
Business plan
Camera-ready copy
Cash flow
Competition
Computer equipment
Computer software
Computer use

Consulting
Contracts
Customer relations
Escrow
Ethics
Expense sharing and joint ventures
Fees and pricing
Financial formulas
Financial planning
Foreign markets and languages
Government customers

Independent contractor status
Information sources and research
Insurance
Legal liability
Legal/illegal business operation
License
Loans, credit, and venture capital
Negotiating
Networking

Overhead expenses
Paper
Presentations
Profit
Projections
Promoting your business
Reducing expenses
Regulations
Telephone use

PROPRIETARY INFORMATION

What you need to know   Proprietary information is knowledge or processes owned by a particular person or company. Such things can be patented, trademarked, or service marked, or copyrighted and formally protected by the government. More often, proprietary information refers to the less formal protection that stems from trade secrets law: any process, formula, tool, compound, or special approach to doing something of value that gives its owner competitive advantage, is protected. This is typically done by contract. Employees to whom the secret must be disclosed are bound not to reveal it or use it personally. Those who use proprietary information without the owner's permission can be stopped by injunctions, and damages can be recovered. The protection of proprietary information breaks down when the secret is legitimately discovered through analysis or independent invention, in which case the discoverer can use it freely.

Why you need to know it   As a small business person, you have two potential concerns with proprietary information: (1) protecting your own ideas, products, and processes, and (2) avoiding infringement on the rights of others who have a legal basis for interrupting your way of doing business or exacting costly penalties. The safest approach to protecting your own valuable property, intellectual and otherwise, is properly registering it under the appropriate federal copyright, patent, trademark, and service mark regulations.

Where to learn more

▸ Consult your attorney.

▸ Familiarize yourself with copyright, patent, trademark, and service mark regulations.

▸ Inquire about rights from companies whose products you might profitably incorporate into your business.

▸ Major companies make clear their proprietary positions. The licensing agreements on computer software products are an example; limitation on the generic use of words like Xerox to mean "copy" is another. Consult corporate legal departments if you want clarification of a use you are considering.

Related topics

Agents and brokers

Attorney

Bidding

Business associates

Business plan

Buying a business

Competition

Conferences, seminars, shows,
  and workshops

Consulting

**Copyright, patent, trademark,
  and service mark**

Desktop publishing

Diversification

Employees

Ethics

Evaluating your business

**Expense sharing and joint
  ventures**

Foreign markets and languages

Franchises

Government customers

Information sources and research

Legal liability

Legal/illegal business operation

License

Loans, credit, and venture capital

Managing growth

Marketing and market research

Negotiating

Networking

Newsletters

Personnel policies

Presentations

Promoting your business

Proposals

Records

Regulations

Sales representatives

Security

Temporary help

Training

PSYCHOLOGICAL FACTORS

What you need to know   Curing the psychological dislocations that can accompany the isolation of independent home office work begins with deliberately reestablishing some of the disciplines and routines that were imposed on you as an employee in an organization. This time it's your organization, even if it consists of only you and the world with which you interact. Set expectations for yourself that you would have welcomed in the corporate world: be fair but firm with yourself, and demand productivity and results. Working for yourself means dealing with the burden of unlimited freedom. You can overwork or underwork, be realistic or kid yourself, write your own role in your own scenario. Counter the temptation to ignore self-discipline; monitor your workload, schedule, compensation, benefits, perks, travel, vacation time, performance, and future prospects as though you had the power to make or break your career. (You do!) Every tangible problem you can articulate has a cure. The fix for loneliness or boredom is getting out and seeing other people in the course of your business-related activities; professional isolation is avoided by maintaining your professional memberships, commitments, and schedule of activities; concentration problems in a new environment require tweaking your work habits until you adjust; adapting to a new perspective means developing an appreciation and understanding of the pace, activities, and realities of noncommuters' lives. Your neighborhood did not become a tableau each day when you left for your office. Keep your identity and self-esteem by setting achievable goals and meeting them.

Why you need to know it   Independent people are attracted to the home-based business life-style, but it can pose unexpected mental challenges for even the most autonomous personalities. Those challenges will damage you and your business effort if you deny the reality of the dislocation when it hits you. Be prepared to cope in a manner that suits your values and your approach to life. Remember why you were motivated to leave the more structured workplace, if leaving was your choice. If you were declared redundant at your former employment, nothing is gained by clinging to the role of victim. The next act for you is titled "Opportunity." Make the necessary adjustments and go about your independent business.

Where to learn more

▶ Participate in a small business support group in your community. Some links include: The National Association of Women Business Owners (312-922-0465), which has local organizations to which it will refer you; The Network (800-825-8286 or 909-624-2227); LeTip (800-255-3847 or 619-275-0600); or Leads Club (800-783-3761 or 619-434-3761).

▶ Try an on-line computer bulletin board system where you can interact with others who share your interests.

▶ Read success literature—solid business magazine stories and books that describe people working hard and achieving success.

▶ Listen to motivational tapes and attend workshops that stress positive thought and goal-oriented behavior.

▶ If organized religion is important to you, be aware of its values in your business life and benefit from the psychological support it provides.

▶ Seek the advice of your professional associates and network members who may have faced similar psychological challenges in a change-of-work situation.

Related topics

Advertising
Attitude
Bankruptcy
Bidding
Bonding
Business image
Concerns about working from home
Conferences, seminars, shows, and workshops

Customer relations
Debt collection and creditworthiness
Direct mail and mailing lists
Direct selling and multilevel marketing
Disabilities
Disaster planning
Expense sharing and joint ventures

Family	Public relations
Lighting	Retirement
Loans, credit, and venture capital	**Role**
Managing growth	**Stress and overworking**
Negotiating	**Success and failure**
Networking	Telecommuting
Personnel policies	Telephone use
Presentations	Training
Professional help	Transitioning
Promoting your business	Vacation, work styles, and schedules

PUBLIC RELATIONS

What you need to know
Doing useful things for the community and having its residents associated with your business is the most common form of public relations. Speak before a community organization, and you gain recognition in return. Anytime you connect personally, future response to your business is apt to be more positive because people are receptive to dealing with someone they've met. Anything you can do to open the lines of communication between your business and the community is desirable public relations. Encourage input, receive questions and complaints graciously, actively seek opinions by conducting surveys, and use the survey results as a bridge to the community. Executive search firms are renowned for their executive compensation surveys, which bring them wonderful public relations with employers and prospects alike. Provide useful information by creating a newsletter, writing a relevant article for a local publication, or giving interviews to the media that connect with your public.

Why you need to know it
The public relations needs of the home-based business are broader than you might at first imagine. They are as obvious as the promotional activities that bring you clients and as subtle as the low profile you maintain in your residential setting to avoid the wrath of those who would resent a business operating in their midst.

Where to learn more

▶ Jian's *PublicityBuilder* is template software that supplements your computer word processor and helps you interact well with the media. You can attract reporters through sample press releases, press kit materials, telephone contact guidelines, and information on how to handle your publicity professionally. Purchase from a software reseller or call 800-346-5426. Price: about $130.

▶ Franchises and professional associations often have media kits and other materials they use nationally that can be adapted to local use. Call a few public relations coordinators and inquire.

Related topics

Advertising
Agents and brokers
Answering machines and voice mail
Associations
Attitude
Better Business Bureau (BBB)
Bulletin Board System (BBS)
Business associates
Business cards
Business image
Business name
Business use of home
Camera-ready copy
Chamber of Commerce
Computer software
Conferences, seminars, shows, and workshops
Customer relations
Desktop publishing

Direct mail and mailing lists
Direct selling and multilevel marketing
Environmental considerations
Ethics
Franchises
Homeowners' associations
Mail order
Managing growth
Marketing and market research
Media relations
Negotiating
Networking
Newsletters
Noise
Presentations
Professional help
Regulations
Sales representatives
Telephone use

RECORDS

What you need to know   There are two standards for small business record keeping: (1) what you need to manage your business and fend off erroneous claims for nonpayment, and (2) what the IRS says you need to complete your tax returns and substantiate the entries in case you are audited. The two standards overlap considerably. Set up a record-keeping system that satisfies the IRS, and supplement it with whatever additional management information you find useful. Oddly, the old shoebox method of record keeping adapts well to modern electronic filing. Whether you hire a bookkeeper or do the entries yourself, there is nothing wrong with pitching the receipts into the proverbial shoebox until: (1) your regular data entry time arrives or (2) you need a report that contains the shoebox data. File the hard-copy receipts in case they are needed for an audit or to prove payment. Practical guidelines for records include: (1) keep everything that supports your tax returns for seven years from the date of filing; (2) save copies of your actual tax returns indefinitely; (3) keep all records that establish your basis in any property you own (the tax consequences apply for at least as long as you own that property); (4) keep personnel records for seven years from the date an employee leaves; (5) keep loss records for the length of time stated in the carry-forward provisions of the tax law, plus seven years from the last return that involves them; and (6) keep the annual summaries of any pension or investment records for as long as you have assets committed. The IRS suggests that minimum small business records should probably include: a business checkbook, daily and monthly summaries of cash receipts, a check disbursements journal, a depreciation worksheet, and employee compensation records. The IRS dictates no specific record-keeping or accounting system, but its publications tell you what the IRS wants to know.

Why you need to know it   Without clerical support and staff, the home-based business can find itself disabled by too much or too little record keeping. You need a sense of what the essential minimums are and a disciplined, informed approach to weeding out the excess. Having a record-keeping system that fully supports your business almost certainly means electronic data management on a computer. Be aware of how easily that can be initiated and how wise it is to implement it early in the operation of your business.

Where to learn more

▸ IRS Publication 583, "Taxpayers Starting a Business," contains a full section on record keeping for income tax purposes. EZ Legal Books, 384 South Military Trail, Deerfield Beach, FL 33442 (305-480-8933/8906 Fax), sells *Records Organizer*, over 140 perforated personal, financial, and medical records that can completely organize your life. The format has been approved by the Consumer Law Foundation.

▸ Nolo Press's *Personal RecordKeeper* software keeps track of credit cards, insurance, medical history, and financial records, and readily produces detailed reports. Price: about $30 at your software reseller or from catalogs listed in Appendix C. Regular database and spreadsheet programs can be used to accomplish similar results.

▸ See Appendix A for information on using electronic forms software like *WordPerfect InForms* and Delrina's *PerForm Pro, PerForm Pro Plus* and *FormFlow* products. They will reduce the number of hard-copy records you need to maintain.

▸ Small Business Administration publications on record keeping are available from: SBA Publications, P. O. Box 1000, Fort Worth, TX 76119. Request the *Directory of Business Development Publications.*

▸ Order CPA Bernard Kamoroff's *Small-Time Operator: How to Start Your Own Small Business, Keep Your Books, Pay Your Taxes, and Stay Out of Trouble* (Bell Springs Publishing, Laytonville, CA 95454; 707-984-6746).

Related topics

Accounting	Business use of home
Attorney	Buying a business
Banking services	**Checking accounts**
Bartering	**Computer software**
Billing	Computer use
Bookkeeping	**Contracts**
Business use of car	Credit cards

Debt collection and creditworthiness
Disaster planning
Employees
Equipment and furniture
Evaluating your business
Expense sharing and joint ventures
Forms
Franchises
**Getting organized and
    managing information**
Independent contractor status
Insurance
Investing
Legal liability

Legal/illegal business operation
License
Loans, credit, and venture capital
Managing growth
Overhead expenses
Payroll
Personnel policies
Proposals
Proprietary information
Reducing expenses
Regulations
Retirement
Security
Tax checklist

REDUCING EXPENSES

What you need to know   Personnel is the largest expense for any company, government agency, or home-based business. The fewer people you employ, the more profit you make. Planned staff reductions ("downsizing") by major corporations has become a fundamental method of achieving future competitiveness for currently profitable firms. Your home-based business should make intelligent use of temporary services or employee sharing when a human being is essential for a task, and technology when a machine will do. Sophisticated telephone receptionist devices do an excellent job of answering and routing incoming calls. Batch fax and calling services will broadcast messages to any audience you designate. Mailing-related software and services efficiently prepare and send mailings at the lowest cost. Delivery services move tangible materials around the world at any speed you are willing to pay for. If delivery isn't too urgent, their fees are reasonable. Even the Environmental Protection Agency is reducing your electric bill by backing an Energy Star Rating system to encourage computer manufacturers to build-in a sleep mode that drops power consumption dramatically. The competitive office supplies and equipment market brings everything you need—including electronic equipment and computer software—to local discount stores or mail-order catalogs.

Why you need to know it   If you appreciate the basic formula for small business profitability—increase revenues and reduce expenses—you can see the importance of controlling spending. One of the great advantages of our free-wheeling capitalist system is the ever more competitive marketing of the things we buy. This is a particularly good time to be a home-based business person. You are as free as are major corporations to buy equipment at low prices.

Where to learn more

▸ Read product reviews in the magazines and catalogs mentioned in Appendix C. Look for products that can increase the efficiency of your home office. An example is *Friday, the Personal/Office Receptionist,* from Bogen Communications, 50 Spring Street, P. O. Box 575, Ramsey, NJ 07446; 201-934-8500. Price: about $400.

▸ Consult your telephone book for temporary help services, or ask the advice of business associates who have used them.

▸ Business envelopes, labels, stationery, and supplies are available at discount prices from these mail-order firms: Business Envelope Manufacturers, Inc., 900 Grand Boulevard, Deer Park, NY 11729 (800-275-4400 or 516-667-8500); Quill, 100 Schelter Road, Lincolnshire, IL 60069-3621 (909-988-3200 far west; 708-634-4800 midwest and midsouth; 404-479-6100 southeast; 717-272-6100 northeast).

Related topics

**Answering machines and
   voice mail**
Banking services
Bartering
Billing
Bookkeeping
Business address and location
Business use of car
Business use of home
Camera-ready copy
Cash flow
Computer use
Copiers
Credit cards
Debt collection and creditworthiness
Desktop publishing
Direct mail and mailing lists
Equipment and furniture
**Expense sharing and
   joint ventures**

Forms
Insurance
Leasing
Lighting
Loans, credit, and venture capital
Mail and overnight delivery services
Managing growth
Negotiating
Overhead expenses
Paper
Payroll
Printing
Profit
Records
Tax checklist
Telecommuting
Telephone use
Temporary help

REGULATIONS

What you need to know   Most of the superficial regulation requirements will come to your attention in sequence as you file the necessary applications to establish your business. If not, it won't be long before the interlocking bureaucracies invite you to sign up for anything you've missed in the regulatory maze. Actually, it isn't usually that complicated. When you sign up for a local business license, you will be referred to the zoning office for the necessary approvals, and to the fictitious name registry, unless your business and personal names are the same. If you sell something, you need to register to collect sales tax and file appropriate tax returns. You must comply with self-employment filing required by the state and federal tax authorities. There are copyright, patent, and trademark infringements to avoid (don't illegally copy or use software, for example) and the trade practices rules of the Federal Trade Commission (the 30-day shipping or notification rule for mail-order firms) to obey. The Federal Communications Commission's Telephone Consumer Protection Act (TCPA) of 1992 limits unsolicited fax and prerecorded telemarketing calls. Even the Federal Aviation Administration impacts the small business person who might use electronic devices while traveling in commercial aircraft.

Why you need to know it   Your seemingly innocuous home business can find itself facing complaints and penalties from regulators if you are not aware of their requirements. When organizing your business, seek an attorney's advice on compliance, and be sensitive to regulations that might affect your particular industry. Environmental laws might be important if you manufacture or dispose of any regulated products or materials.

Where to learn more

▶ Small Business Administration publications that help you address federal regulations are available from SBA Publications, P. O. Box 1000, Fort Worth, TX 76119. Request the *Directory of Business Development Publications.*

▶ Individual government agencies have regulatory compliance offices to assist small businesses. Find local offices in the government pages of your telephone book or use Washington (DC) telephone directories or library reference books to contact the relevant sources. Your local congressional office can also be helpful. (See Appendix B.)

▶ The Federal Communications Commission's information line for the Telephone Consumer Protection Act is 202-632-7554.

▶ The Federal Trade Commission's Washington number is 202-326-2222.

▶ The Environmental Protection Agency's Washington number is 202-260-7751.

Related topics

Accountant
Answering machines and
voice mail
Attorney
Banking services
Bankruptcy
Bartering
Bulletin Board System (BBS)
Business name

Business organization
Business use of car
Business use of home
Checking accounts
Computer on-line services
Computer use
Contracts
**Copyright, patent, trademark,
and service mark**

Credit cards
Debt collection and
creditworthiness
Desktop publishing
Direct mail and mailing lists
Direct selling and multilevel
marketing
Employees
Environmental considerations
Family
Fax
Foreign markets and languages
Franchises
Government customers
Homeowners' associations
Independent contractor status
Insurance

Investing
Labor laws
Legal liability
Legal/illegal business operation
License
Loans, credit, and venture capital
Mail and overnight delivery services
Mail order
Noise
Payroll
Personnel policies
Proprietary information
Records
Retirement
Tax checklist
Telephone use
Zoning

RETIREMENT

What you need to know   Different people need different levels of income to maintain what they consider to be reasonable life-styles. The respective income brackets cited by experts for luxury, comfortable, and basic retirement for a couple are $182,100, $70,970, and $32,860, respectively. If you earn $55,000 a year, you can count on social security providing about $20,000 a year when you retire. Add any pension you have coming, and the balance of the $55,000 will have to come from savings and investments. Calculation of the monthly savings needed to meet your retirement goal depends on your age now, your age at retirement, how long you will live in retirement, and interest and inflation rates. As complicated as it sounds, computer programs and even estimating tables published in books and magazines like *Smart Money* will reveal your requirements and let you set the proper course of investment. Here are some tax-advantaged types of investment plans to investigate with the help of your accountant: SEP IRA (Simplified Employee Pension Individual Retirement Account), profit-sharing Keogh, money purchase Keogh, paired Keoghs, and defined-benefit plans.

Why you need to know it   Unless you have the luxury of being a second-career home-based business person, you need to plan for retirement. The government will help you considerably if you make a disciplined commitment to investing regularly in a tax-sheltered plan designed to encourage retirement investment by the self-employed. It is never too late or too early to start retirement planning, but start now. Whether you do it yourself or rely on a third party, it is essential that you stay on top of changes affecting your retirement fund's adequacy. Falling interest rates, for example, have radically changed the choice of investments in recent years.

Where to learn more

◗ Software products that can help you with your retirement planning include these Macintosh and PC products: Nolo Press's *WillMaker, Living Trust and Personnel RecordKeeper* (800-800-2222 Mac/800-800-5555 PC); Reality Technologies, Inc.'s *WealthBuilder* (215-277-7600); and MECA Software's *Managing Your Money* (800-288-6322). For the PC only: *T. Rowe Price Retirement Planning Kit* (800-541-3036); Calypso Software Corporation's *Retire ASAP* (800-225-8246); Red Cat System's *Retire Easy* (800-374-9165); and DataTech Software's *Rich and Retired* (717-652-4344).

◗ Microrim's *In the Black* includes a retirement planner (Appendix F).

◗ Bookstores and libraries carry many titles on investments and retirement planning.

◗ Insurance companies, investment firms, and retirement plans offer publications that can familiarize you with options.

◗ Business and personal finance magazines publish current information on retirement planning. The November 1993 issue of *Smart Money* carried a very useful series of articles titled "Invest for Retirement," "Calculate Your Retirement Gap" (complete with worksheets), and "Make the Most of Your Money." Check your library or purchase a reprint by calling 212-492-1300.

◗ Linda Stern's "The Best Ways to Sock Away Money," is a useful retirement planning article, as is Stephen L. Nelson's "Solve 13 Common Money Problems," which contains spreadsheet retirement formulas. They appeared in the September 1993 and October 1992 issues, respectively, of *Home Office Computing*. Check your library or contact: Reprint Manager, *Home Office Computing*, 730 Broadway, New York, NY 10003; 212-505-3580.

Related topics

Accountant	Goal setting
Attorney	Independent contractor status
Banking services	Insurance
Budgeting	**Investing**
Business organization	Legal liability
Computer software	Legal/illegal business operation
Concerns about working from home	Managing growth
Conferences, seminars, shows, and workshops	Money management
Employees	Negotiating
Evaluating your business	**Personnel policies**
Financial formulas	Professional help
Financial planning	**Projections**
	Psychological factors

ROLE

What you need to know   Identity has a lot to do with competent performance. This is particularly true of the home-based business person, who must wear many hats with grace and do many jobs effectively. Consider these roles: (1) executive—essential vision and planning; (2) purchasing officer—the cost control that is vital to profitability and survival; (3) office manager/supervisor—the responsibility for overseeing the process of getting things done; (4) security—protection of proprietary information and the physical safety of a combined home and business; and (5) marketing and sales management—the lifeblood of any business. Blend these all together and there are potential conflicts of style and personality that are typically spread over several people in an organization. As a one- or two-person shop, you have to struggle with being many somewhat conflicting role models at once, every day. It can be fatal to the success and survival of your business to let any one role take on disproportionate importance relative to the others. The small business manager's juggling act isn't limited to just time and money; it goes to the soul of the man or woman operating the enterprise. Succeeding as an effective self-manager is as critical to achieving your entrepreneurial goals as is your business plan.

Why you need to know it   Your satisfaction as a small business person often comes from the same source as your greatest frustrations—the required versatility. A realistic expectation that you will be a jack-of-all-trades in the broadest sense of the term is essential to persisting in a home-based business. If you understand that you are your own support system in so many ways, you'll be better able to accept your down times, when the role you occupy is not satisfying, along with your up times, when you know a role is too lofty to last. A sense of balance relative to your roles in your own enterprise is a mental health necessity, especially when most of your operation takes place in the relative isolation of your home office.

Where to learn more

▶ Your business associates and network can help you maintain a balanced perspective.

▶ Participate in a small business support group in your community. Some links include: The National Association of Women Business Owners (312-922-0465), which has local organizations to which it will refer you; The Network (800-825-

8286 or 909-624-2227); LeTip (800-255-3847 or 619-275-0600); or Leads Club (800-783-3761 or 619-434-3761).

▶ Try an on-line computer bulletin board system where you can interact with others who share your interests.

Related topics

Attitude	Expense sharing and joint ventures
Business associates	Family
Business organization	Foreign markets and languages
Business plan	Franchises
Concerns about working from home	**Independent contractor status**
	Managing growth
Conferences, seminars, shows, and workshops	Negotiating
	Networking
Customer relations	**Personnel policies**
Diversification	Promoting your business
Employees	Public relations
Evaluating your business	Stress and overworking

SALES REPRESENTATIVES

What you need to know Multipliers can be added to your home-based business, and they don't always come in the form of temporary help or technology. A traditional multiplier is an independent sales representative who works individually or in a group and sells a line of related products from a variety of sources. You can find sales representatives through advertisements in trade publications that serve your industry, by attending trade shows and conferences, and by word-of-mouth recommendations. The latter can be solicited. Expect to pay for the service—typical commissions run around 15 percent and sometimes as high as 20 percent. Most sales representatives are product-oriented, but there are similar individuals (and organizations) who sell expert opinion and intellectual property. As is true with all services, quality and professionalism vary widely. Be selective about the person who will represent you; his or her image will be related to your business. Expect to assume a certain amount of sales management responsibility by keeping your representatives informed, motivated, and in check. Sales representatives provide excellent feedback that should be encouraged and incorporated into your operations.

Why you need to know it Selling is a dual-interest item for the home-based business person. Selling represents one of the oldest and most versatile at-home businesses, and it provides the non-sales-oriented home business person with the means to reach broader markets for the price of a sales commission. Selling, like desktop publishing and other activities you might do yourself, requires a judgment call on whether it represents the best use of your limited time or whether someone else should be paid to do it. Geographic reach alone often favors hiring sales representatives who will cover key territories.

Where to learn more

▶ Manufacturers' Agents National Association (MANA) in Laguna Hills, CA (714-859-4040), is the national professional association for people who sell independently for other companies. Examine its journal and publications, which set the standards for the industry.

▶ *Business Organizations, Agencies, and Publications Directory,* Gale Research, 835 Penobscot Building, Detroit, MI 48226 (313-961-2242 or 800-877-4253), is a 1,400-page authority on business contacts and information; it can lead you to appropriate sources of sales representatives.

▶ Gale's *Directory of Associations* lists dates and locations of organizations' upcoming meetings. Review the publication at a library; trade shows representing your type of products will be listed. Plan to attend and network with representatives seeking to add new items to the lines they now market.

▶ Business magazines advertise specialized meetings that cross individual product and professional lines. Request detailed information, talk with others who have attended previous sessions, and evaluate the potential value versus the expense before deciding whether to attend.

▶ Ask for a calendar of upcoming events at conference centers and hotels within your geographic area that cater to the kinds of meetings that interest you. Chambers of Commerce and economic development councils are also worth checking.

▶ Ask retailers with whom you already deal about sales representatives whom they regard as competent professionals and would recommend. Do the same by calling buyers at outlets you are familiar with.

Related topics

Advertising
Agents and brokers
Bonding
Business associates
Business image
Conferences, seminars, shows, and workshops
Contracts
Customer relations
Direct selling and multilevel marketing
Diversification
Expense sharing and joint ventures
Fees and pricing
Independent contractor status

Legal liability
Managing growth
Marketing and market research
Negotiating
Newsletters
Presentations
Printing
Proprietary information
Records
Tax checklist
Telephone equipment
Telephone services
Telephone use
Training

SECURITY

What you need to know   Home security is a desirable extension of a business located in your residence. Split the cost of installing a system between your personal and business expenses, and consider allocating the greater share to the business because of the increased exposure it has introduced. On the positive side, your presence in the home for more hours may reduce the risk of burglary. A negative factor is your increased vulnerability in being home alone. Be alert to the relatively remote, but nonetheless real, potential for you to be accosted in your home business, and take sensible precautions. Have a speed dialer set to call help at the touch of a button, lock your doors, be vigilant for danger, and try not to exhibit patterns of behavior that might telegraph your vulnerability to criminals. Additional security measures might include the installation of motion detection devices and an intercom to announce visitors. Inexpensive sensors can sound when anyone enters your driveway or when windows or doors are jarred or opened. Similar equipment is available for your automobile. Timers and lights add a lived-in look to your home when you are away. A more specific kind of security applies to your computer information. In addition to protection against theft, you need to secure your data by having backup copies stored properly. To avoid introducing viruses into your system, limit the use of outside disks, screen input, and check your system regularly with antivirus software. Be aware of the potential for compromising client information, or your own, via your trash and improperly discarded computer disks. If you deal in proprietary information, consider the use of a paper shredder and software that totally voids electronic disks.

Why you need to know it   When you add a home-based business to your residence, you increase your need for security by adding valuable equipment, information, and, sometimes, merchandise. If your automobile is used in your business, be concerned about its security. Being alone in your home presents a risk not found in busy office settings. Residential neighborhoods empty out during business hours and are the targets of crime during that period. Recognize that a residential fire or other disaster would be catastrophic for your business records. Store backup computer disks and vital information safely offsite. If you are a consultant privy to valuable trade information, take the necessary steps to protect client information.

Where to learn more

▸ CMG Data Security Products, 1001 Capital of Texas Highway South, Austin, TX 78746 (800-880-9980 or 512-329-8220), sells a floppy disk-drive slot lock that keeps others from using your drives to remove data or introduce a virus.

▸ Fire-Safe Media Chest is designed to protect computer disks from fire. Sold by Sentry Group, 900 Linden Avenue, Rochester, NY 14625; 800-828-1438 or 716-381-4900.

▶ Radio Shack stocks a complete line of home security products.

▶ Crutchfield, 1 Crutchfield Park, P. O. Box 9042, Charlottesville, VA 22906-9042 ·(800-955-3000), markets home and vehicle security devices. The Crutchfield catalog is an excellent source of information, as are its telephone representatives.

▶ Office supply and computer catalogs listed in Appendix C offer security-related items.

Related topics

Banking services

Bonding

Business address and location

Business image

Business use of home

Computer equipment

Computer software

Computer use

Concerns about working from home

Disaster planning

Diversification

Electronic banking

Employees

Escrow

Evaluating your business

Foreign markets and languages

Insurance

Legal liability

Lighting

Money management

Networking

Office planning and decorating

Personnel policies

Proprietary information

Telephone equipment

Telephone services

Telephone use

Temporary help

SEPARATING BUSINESS AND PERSONAL

What you need to know   An attraction of the home-based business lifestyle is the blending of business and personal. You live and work under the same roof and enjoy the convenience and economies of doing so. Home working environments have their own version of the "economies of scale" principle. Purchases you couldn't justify personally can be shared with the business, which makes the expense acceptable—cleaning services, for example. At some point, the advantages of sharing end and an axiom of the home-based business applies: business and personal must be kept separate. It is an essential practice for a number of reasons: (1) tax law requires distinct allocation of business and personal expenses and property; (2) insurance coverage is limited to an insurable that it was designated to protect, and if business or personal is not an understood part of the equation, you can find yourself with residual risks; (3) productivity generally requires a focused effort that demands separation of business and personal life-styles; (4) business services like checking accounts and telephone services generally require you to register as a personal or commercial customer and pay the fees appropriate to the service you receive; and

(5) business image is rarely supported by personal-life intrusions like a child's answering a client's call.

Why you need to know it   The discipline of home business management falls to you, except in those cases where the lack of it brings in outsiders like IRS auditors to help. As you begin your business, establish a mindset that focuses on the conscious separation of your business and personal activities. Take advantage of the overlapping that occurs, but remain attentive to the requirement that the two must be separate for accounting purposes.

Where to learn more

▶ IRS Publication 587, "Business Use of Your Home," and Publication 334, "Tax Guide for Small Business," help you define business and personal use. For information and assistance, call 800-829-1040; for forms and other publications, call 800-829-FORM.

▶ Your telephone book and company representative can assist in upgrading service to the proper business status if you are doing more than a limited amount of company calling on your personal line. In some areas, you can be fined and made to pay retroactive adjustments for the improper use of your personal line. A more costly business line is inappropriate, however, for an emerging home-based business that is still testing the waters.

▶ As soon as commercial services are needed from your bank, you will be asked to open an appropriate account. Bank representatives can describe the options and costs.

Related topics

Accountant

Accounting

Advertising

**Answering machines and
  voice mail**

Banking services

Bankruptcy

Business address and location

Business image

Business name

Business use of car

Business use of home

Cash flow

Checking accounts

Computer equipment

Computer use

**Concerns about working
  from home**

Credit cards

Ethics

Evaluating your business

Family

Financial planning

Homeowners' associations

Insurance

Investing

Legal liability

Loans, credit, and venture capital

Managing growth

Office planning and decorating

Tax checklist

Telephone equipment

Telephone services

Telephone use

Vacation, work styles, and schedules

SERVICE CORPS OF RETIRED EXECUTIVES (SCORE)

What you need to know   Service Corps of Retired Executives (SCORE) is affiliated with the Small Business Administration of the federal government. At hundreds of locations throughout the country, thousands of volunteer retired executives provide free business counseling to people who request it. SCORE is linked to local Chambers of Commerce, and referrals often come from them. As with any volunteer organization, the quality of advice is uneven. Be selective in your use of SCORE advisers, and do not hesitate to screen them for knowledge and experience that are relevant to your business situation and requirements. The advice of a large corporate executive might be quite useful to a home-based business person in some instances, but it could be misleading in others. The same is true of retired public-sector managers who give advice to small for-profit organizations and individuals. The range of volunteers is broad, and their usefulness will be in direct proportion to your ability to choose among them.

Why you need to know it   SCORE is a valuable service that provides its share of assistance to small businesses. It is your job to be an intelligent consumer of its free advice. Just because it carries the imprimatur of the Small Business Administration doesn't necessarily make SCORE's counsel appropriate in your particular case. The outcome will depend on the right match of a SCORE counselor's background, attitude, and capabilities to your business needs. By all means avail yourself of this useful service, but be selective.

Where to learn more

▶ Service Corps of Retired Executives (SCORE), 1030 15th Street, NW, Washington, DC 20005; 800-827-5722 or 202-653-6958/6279. SBA-sponsored retired executives offer free counseling throughout the country. Inquire first at your local Chamber of Commerce.

Related topics

Budgeting
Business organization
Business plan
Buying a business
Chamber of Commerce
Competition
Computer use
Consulting
Customer relations
Debt collection and creditworthiness
Diversification
Evaluating your business
Expense sharing and joint ventures

Fees and pricing
Financial planning
Foreign markets and languages
**Getting organized and
    managing information**
Government customers
Information sources and research
Insurance
Legal/illegal business operation
Loans, credit, and venture capital
Managing growth
Marketing and market research
Negotiating

Networking
Personnel policies
Professional help
Profit
Projections
Promoting your business
Proposals
Proprietary information

Public relations
Reducing expenses
Regulations
Retirement
Start-up
Time management
Undercapitalization

SMALL BUSINESS ADMINISTRATION (SBA)

What you need to know   The Small Business Administration is the government agency formed and maintained to help people start and successfully operate small businesses. Traditionally, SBA services have taken the form of publications and lending programs. The Small Business Administration's *Directory of Business Development Publications* includes titles like *How to Buy or Sell a Business, Research Your Market, Starting and Managing a Small Business of Your Own,* and *Starting and Managing a Small Service Business.* The best known and longest running loans are bank-administered programs underwritten by government guarantees. The American Bankers Association (ABA) provides to its members lending guideline books that can also be helpful to applicants for SBA loans (*SBA Lending Made Easy* is an example; to order, call 800-338-0626). In recent years, the lending system has been energized by what are being referred to as "microloans" in the $25,000 range (as high as $50,000, but averaging $7,500) made by 96 nonprofit community development agencies. The SBA works in conjunction with industry. Corporations fund programs like the Pratt & Whitney-sponsored Transition '93, an SBA program designed to assist workers laid off from industry who want to start their own businesses. Among this group, 40 percent claim they want to be entrepreneurs, but only 15 percent achieve the goal.

Why you need to know it   Free advice is always worth investigating. You have to sort through the SBA bureaucracy, but the SBA has its heart in the right place and is a force for good in the small business community. It can be your source for many useful services within the federal system.

Where to learn more

‣ The public information number for the Small Business Administration in Washington (DC) is 800-827-5722. Field offices are located throughout the country. Check the federal government listing in your local telephone book.

‣ SBA Online is an electronic bulletin board of information on SBA and general business information. It can be accessed directly by computer users with modems: 2400 bps, call 800-859-4636 or 202-205-7265; 9600 bps, call 800-697-4636 or 202-401-9600.

◗ The Small Business Administration's *Directory of Business Development Publications* is available from: SBA Publications, P. O. Box 1000, Fort Worth, TX 76119.

◗ Small Business Administration, Office of Small Business Loans, 1441 L Street, NW, Washington, DC 20416; 202-653-6570.

◗ Service Corps of Retired Executives (SCORE), 1030 15th Street, NW, Washington, DC 20005; 800-827-5722 or 202-653-6958/6279. SBA-sponsored retired executives offer free counseling at locations nationwide.

◗ Federal government directories like Matthew Lesko's *Information USA* are found in the reference section of libraries and can guide you to specific points of contact within the SBA.

Related topics

Business basics	**Government customers**
Business organization	**Information sources and research**
Buying a business	**Loans, credit, and venture capital**
Conferences, seminars, shows, and workshops	Managing growth
Continuing education	Money management
Evaluating your business	Promoting your business
Financial planning	**Regulations**
Foreign markets and languages	**Training**
Franchises	**Women's programs**
Getting organized and managing information	

START-UP

What you need to know   The basic necessities of starting a home-based business include: (1) selecting a name and registering it, if it differs from your own; (2) choosing a form of legal organization for your company—most likely a sole proprietorship, but possibly a partnership or corporation of some sort; (3) getting a local business license from the municipal office that controls such things (a related requirement is the possibility of a zoning variance or "franchise" that lets you operate in a residential setting); (4) checking your homeowner's and automobile insurance policies to be sure your business activities are adequately covered, but avoiding a conversion to full-blown business coverage (especially for your automobile) before you need it; and (5) securing the necessary taxpayer numbers and forms for estimated payments, withholding, and sales tax (if applicable). Another category of preparation for a small business start-up is planning. Develop and refine a business plan that analyzes what you plan to do, who your competitors are and how you can prevail, what your financial requirements and resources are and how lending will supplement them, and how your debt will be serviced. Don't forget to factor-in the necessities of normal life—financial, personal, and psychological. Consider the moonlighting/part-time approach if you have doubts about being ready for a total commitment to your small business.

Why you need to know it   Starting a business is demanding and risky in many respects. Failure can alter your life for years to come. Depending on how thoroughly you burn your bridges behind you, starting a small business can leave you with few options but to succeed. The success literature correctly tells you that success can be very motivating, but writers tend to gloss over the fact that a failed start-up can be devastating. Approach your small business start-up as the deadly serious opportunity it is. Do your planning realistically, have the contingencies covered, take the plunge, and enjoy your success. But be ready for the bumps in the road.

Where to learn more

▶ Robert Gehorsam's "Start-Up Diary," in the September 1993 issue of *Home Office Computing* magazine, is an excellent and realistic account of what you can expect to encounter in starting a serious business. Check your library or contact: Reprint Manager, *Home Office Computing*, 730 Broadway, New York, NY 10003; 212-505-3580.

▶ Bookstores and libraries offer a variety of approaches to small business start-up. Here are several suggestions: CPA Bernard Kamoroff's *Small-Time Operator: How to Start Your Own Small Business, Keep Your Books, Pay Your Taxes, and Stay Out of Trouble* (Bell Springs Publishing, Laytonville, CA 95454; 707-984-6746); David Eyler's *Starting and Operating a Home-Based Business* (John Wiley & Sons); and Harvey Mackay's *Sharkproof: Get the Job You Want, Keep the Job You Love* (HarperCollins).

▶ The Small Business Administration's *Directory of Business Development Publications* is available from: SBA Publications, P. O. Box 1000, Fort Worth, TX 76119. Titles like *Starting and Managing a Small Business of Your Own*, and *Starting and Managing a Small Service Business* are worth examining.

Related topics

Accountant	**Business use of home**
Attorney	**Cash flow**
Banking services	Chamber of Commerce
Better Business Bureau (BBB)	Checking accounts
Business basics	Computer use
Business cards	Concerns about working from home
Business image	Conferences, seminars, shows,
Business incubator	and workshops
Business name	Equipment and furniture
Business organization	**Fees and pricing**
Business plan	**Financial planning**
Business use of car	Forms

STRESS AND OVERWORKING

What you need to know   Working hard doesn't necessarily increase stress, and having control over your life and work actually reduces stress. Home-based business people experience stress, but they have distinct advantages in managing it. Assuming that your business is financially sound and you are doing something you want to do, the rest of the stress formula is manageable and potentially stimulating. Deadlines can be viewed as demanding goals to be met. Changes in client specifications produce new challenges, create new ways of solving problems, and break a repetitive routine. Overworking is an individually defined phenomenon. If your work is also your pleasure, long hours need not be stressful. The challenge is maintaining balance in your total life, to prevent an obsession with business that damages other important relationships and creates broader stress. A measure by which stress can be judged good or bad is the degree of control involved. For that reason, financial difficulties are extremely stressful for the small business person: loss of control is directly threatened. The mechanisms for managing stress that you have at your disposal as a home-based business person include: (1) choice of what to do and how to do it; (2) ability to make plans and amend them; (3) arrangement of priorities to complement your instincts; (4) allocation of time and resources; and (5) scheduling of business and personal activities. With this mix of life forces within your control, there is no excuse for letting stress be a protracted problem in a financially sound business.

Why you need to know it   Stress is largely a matter of perception, and there are few sources of it in your own business that you cannot adequately control. Plan rationally, and minimize the risk of financial stress, the one kind of stress that you cannot cope with indefinitely. Stress should not be a relentless and significant problem in a successful business.

Where to learn more

▶ Stress management tapes and books are available in bookstores, libraries, and catalogs.

▶ SMI International, 5000 Lakewood Drive, Waco, TX 76710, offers a catalog of tapes that include stress reduction.

▶ *Successories* is a catalog of quality motivational and stress management art in the form of posters, cards, desk accessories, clothing, and books; available via High Street Emporium (800-362-5500). *Executive Gallery* (800-848-2618) offers similar products.

Related topics

Attitude	**Managing growth**
Bidding	Motivation
Business basics	Office planning and decorating
Business plan	Professional help
Cash flow	**Psychological factors**
Competition	Reducing expenses
Computer use	Role
Concerns about working from home	Sales representatives
Equipment and furniture	Separating business and personal
Ergonomics	Success and failure
Evaluating your business	**Telephone equipment**
Expense sharing and joint ventures	**Telephone services**
Financial planning	**Telephone use**
Franchises	Temporary help
Getting organized and managing information	Time-share offices
	Undercapitalization
Goal setting	**Vacation, work styles, and**
Loans, credit, and venture capital	**schedules**

SUCCESS AND FAILURE

What you need to know   The home-based business movement hasn't radically altered the formula for succeeding or failing in a small business venture. Don't put too much credence in advocates who make it sound like a guaranteed success formula. The accurate part of what they say is that it has reduced the capitalization needed and increased the entrepreneur's convenience, and, to that extent, made it easier to get started and stay afloat. The basic business realities still have to be satisfied: (1) a sound business idea; (2) adequate initial capitalization to give the start-up a chance to reach profitability; (3) a market that hasn't been oversold; (4) a marketing orientation that constantly generates new business; (5) a competitive fee structure; (6) a ratio of revenues to expenditures that yields a profit and return on investment after the costs of doing business are paid; and (7) a satisfying enough life-style to persist beyond the boundaries of salaried employment. To these realities, add: good ethical practices, respecting confidences, doing more than is expected, realizing you can be replaced, a positive attitude toward everyone with whom you deal, and awareness of your limitations. Approach the whole business experience as a learning process that never ends, apply the principles just listed, and small business success can be yours.

Why you need to know it   Striking the right balance between your expectations for success and your fears of failure is vitally important in making your home business experience work. When you muster the confidence to assume the risks of launching a business, don't adopt unhealthy measures of positive thinking "advice." Understand that the qualities of positive thought are indeed necessary and productive, but remember that they constitute the bread and butter of the many people who advocate particular approaches to success. Keep motivational materials and prepackaged success routes in perspective. Examine them for what they might add to your own sound ideas and planning, but measure them against a keen sense of reality.

Where to learn more

▶ Success tapes and books are available in bookstores, libraries, and catalogs.

▶ SMI International, 5000 Lakewood Drive, Waco, TX 76710, offers a catalog of tapes.

▶ *Successories* is a catalog of quality motivational art in the form of posters, cards, desk accessories, clothing and books; available via High Street Emporium (800-362-5500). *Executive Gallery* (800-848-2618) offers similar products.

Related topics

Accountant
Agents and brokers
Attorney
Banking services
Bankruptcy
Bidding
Billing
Bookkeeping
Budgeting
Business associates
Business basics
Business plan
Cash flow

Competition
Computer use
Conferences, seminars, shows,
    and workshops
Continuing education
Fees and pricing
Financial planning
Franchises
Getting organized and
    managing information
Goal setting
Loans, credit, and venture capital
Managing growth

Marketing and market research
Networking
Overhead expenses
Projections
Promoting your business
Reducing expenses
Separating business and personal
Stress and overworking

Tax checklist
Telephone use
Time management
Training
Transitioning
Undercapitalization
Vacation, work styles, and schedules

SUPPLIES

What you need to know   Literally everything you buy to support the operation of your home-based business is available from many sources, locally or by mail order. Their astonishing selection is not limited by where you establish your business. Combined with overnight delivery services, the mail-order marketplace brings the finest technology and most cost-competitive office and specialty supplies to your door with the convenience of a toll-free telephone call and a credit card. In urban areas, similar services are available from discount resellers that present everything you could possibly need, at mass purchasing prices and in settings where you can examine the products. Service and advice are not necessarily lost in mass marketing; many companies offer purchasing advice and technical assistance by telephone or in specialized walk-in departments of the retail operation. It is wise to identify more than one supplier for things that are essential to your business, in case an outlet goes out of business, changes its orientation significantly, or is temporarily out of stock of the desired item. Use your network and the Better Business Bureau to verify the quality of service you might expect from the resellers. Among your concerns are: (1) prompt delivery; (2) quality merchandise; (3) current merchandise (especially important for software and perishable supplies like printer cartridges); (4) replacement policy for defective merchandise or dissatisfaction; (5) supplier credit; and (6) adequate inventory for current delivery.

Why you need to know it   Controlling expenses is a major factor in small business success. Another important consideration is rapid, convenient access to the kinds of supplies your clients expect you to work with to be competitive. Identifying suppliers that offer the combination of price, quality, and convenience your business requires is a major factor in success. Suppliers that also serve as de facto consultants keep you informed of changes that might benefit your business—for example, intelligently prepared catalogs that describe the latest products and how they relate to your business success.

Where to learn more

▶ Local business supply outlets like Staples, Office Depot, and others, offer everything from office supplies to computers, at off-price.

- Business Envelope Manufacturers, Inc., 900 Grand Boulevard, Deer Park, NY 11729 (800-275-4400 or 516-667-8500; Fax 516-586-5988), sells envelopes, labels, and stationery inexpensively.

- MacConnection, 14 Mill Street, Marlow, NH 03456 (800-800-2222), is a direct supplier of computer software and peripherals for the Macintosh.

- Paper Direct, 205 Chubb Avenue, Lyndhurst, NJ 07071 (800-A-PAPERS), and Power Up!, P. O. Box 7600, San Mateo, CA 94403-7600 (800-851-2917), are direct suppliers of specialty papers for printing letterhead, business cards, brochures, presentation products, and similar output, on your laser printer.

- PC Connection, 6 Mill Street, Marlow, NH 03456 (800-800-5555), is a direct supplier of computers, software, and peripherals for PCs and clones.

- Quill, 100 Schelter Road, Lincolnshire, IL 60069-3621 (909-988-3200 far west; 708-634-4800 midwest and midsouth; 404-479-6100 southeast; 717-272-6100 northeast), is a direct supplier of office supplies, equipment, and printed materials for the office.

- Reliable Home Office, P. O. Box 1501, Ottawa, IL 61350-9916 (800-869-6000), is a direct supplier of quality home office furnishings and equipment.

- The Drawing Board, P. O. Box 2944, Hartford, CT 06104-2944 (800-527-9530), is a direct supplier of printed materials for the home office.

Related topics

Bartering	**Financial planning**
Budgeting	Forms
Cash flow	**Managing growth**
Computer use	**Negotiating**
Copiers	**Overhead expenses**
Disaster planning	Paper
Diversification	Printing
Environmental considerations	Profit
Evaluating your business	**Reducing expenses**
Expense sharing and joint ventures	Separating business and personal

SYNDICATION

What you need to know   Syndication is an approach to launching an ambitious business with the help of a limited group of investors. To syndicate, you have to have a business idea that promises to pay better dividends than competitive investments do, and you have to convince investors that you are the person who can successfully organize and implement the concept. Syndication works as a home-based business because your role is that of planner, consultant, manager, and marketing person—all tasks that can be run from home. The business itself is to be external to your home—quite likely, a proven franchise, a real estate investment, or a turnaround situation of some kind. Here are the steps involved in a syndication: (1) choose a business idea worthy of developing; (2) research it thoroughly and prove its viability and profit potential; (3) write a business plan that is accurate and convincing; (4) enlist the help of experts in the business specialty; (5) get sound legal and financial advice on forming, marketing, and operating the syndicate; (6) comply with state and federal securities laws; (7) act as the general partner for implementing the plan; (8) manage the business or hire someone who can; (9) inform and involve the syndicate members; (10) meet the legal, accounting, and tax obligations of the syndicate; and (11) collect an agreed fee for your efforts in forming the syndicate and managing the business. Then enjoy your equity position in a successful enterprise. As one syndicate comes on line, repeat the cycle with another business idea and group of investors.

Why you need to know it   You don't always have the cash or personal borrowing power to launch a business that requires substantial capital. An alternative is attracting a group of people who will take shares in the start-up for a stake in the increased value of the successful business. By lifting your sights above what your borrowing power will support, you can enter the business world on a loftier level with less traditional financial anxiety—if you have the qualities necessary to package and implement a successful enterprise and are willing to share the proceeds with investors.

Where to learn more

▶ Richard H. Beguelin's *The Secrets of Syndication* is an excellent book on syndicating a business. Consult your librarian.

▶ David R. Eyler's *The Executive Moonlighter* (John Wiley, NY) includes a chapter on syndication as an approach to forming a business. Published in 1989, it is out of print but may be available at the library. The ISBN number is 0-471-50070-4.

Related topics

Accountant
Attorney
Banking services
Bookkeeping
Budgeting
Business associates
Business ideas
Business organization
Business plan
Buying a business
Cash flow
Consulting
Contracts

Environmental considerations
Ethics
Expense sharing and joint ventures
Fees and pricing
Financial formulas
Financial planning
Franchises
Getting organized and managing information
Goal setting
Information sources and research

Insurance
Investing
Legal liability
Legal/illegal business operation
Loans, credit, and venture capital
Managing growth
Marketing and market research
Money management
Negotiating
Networking
Overhead expenses
Presentations

Professional help
Profit
Projections
Promoting your business
Proposals
Records
Regulations
Separating business and personal
Tax checklist
Telephone use
Time-share offices
Undercapitalization

TAX CHECKLIST

What you need to know   Keeping up with tax obligations goes beyond the April 15th deadline for filing and is a year-round activity. Be alert to quarterly estimated income tax payments to the federal and state governments, and business license and property taxes to your local taxing authority. To avoid penalties, make your quarterly payments total at least what you owed in taxes the year before. The home office tax deduction is based on the part of your home that is devoted to business use. The tests and means for calculating your deductions are detailed in IRS Publication 587, "Business Use of Your Home." (See Appendix E.) Calculate them on Form 8829, "Expenses for Business Use of Your Home," and use the accompanying worksheet. (Both are in Publication 587.) In addition to claiming your home office expenses, take regular business expenses on Schedule C. As allowed under Section 179 of the Internal Revenue Code, use direct expensing (rather than depreciating) of up to $17,500 worth of equipment, and remember to deduct business wear and tear on your car, and health insurance premiums (25 percent if you are unincorporated/100 percent if you are incorporated). Watch for changes; the deductible portion of business meals and entertainment dropped from 80 percent to 50 percent in 1993. Take advantage of tax-sheltered retirement investment plans like Keoghs and SEPs (Simplified Employee Pensions). Time the taking of income and making of payments to cope most effectively with other levies, like the alternative minimum tax.

Why you need to know it   Business taxes are too complex and change too frequently for most individuals to maintain an authoritative knowledge of them. Computer software helps to estimate taxes, but it is essentially a spreadsheet and forms generator, and cannot be substituted for professional advice. If your taxes are at all complex, read the popular business and personal finance literature to keep abreast of the changing issues, and use that limited knowledge to work intelligently with your accountant. Checkbook and accounting software can ease your preparation of data for your tax professional, but leave the strategy and options selection to someone who knows the law intimately.

Where to learn more

▶ IRS publications can be obtained at banks, post offices, and libraries, or by calling 800-829-FORM (for forms and publications) or 800-829-1040 (for information and assistance). Publications of particular interest are: Publication 587, "Business Use of Your Home" (see Appendix E); Publication 583, "Taxpayers Starting a Business"; and Publication 334, "Tax Guide for Small Business." (An extensive list of IRS publications and forms is included at the end of Appendix E.)

▶ *TurboTax*, for the PC, and *MacInTax*, for the Macintosh, are among the computer software programs that prepare taxes. They and competing products are available at software resellers, including the catalog companies listed in Appendix C. Microrim's *In The Black* accounting software exports data to popular PC tax programs.

▶ Bookstores and libraries have extensive collections on tax subjects. Among the most helpful are commercial interpretations of the actual tax codes, which can be found in libraries. Business and personal finance periodicals publish end-of-year articles alerting you to potential deductions and ways to save on taxes. A few of the perennial favorites are: *The Ernst & Young Tax Guide* (Wiley), *J. K. Lasser's Year-Round Tax Strategies* (Prentice-Hall), *Guide to Income Tax Preparation* (Consumer Reports Books), and CPA Bernard Kamoroff's *Small-Time Operator: How to Start Your Own Small Business, Keep Your Books, Pay Your Taxes, and Stay Out of Trouble* (Bell Springs Publishing, Laytonville, CA 95454; 707-984-6746).

Related topics

Accountant
Accounting
Attorney
Banking services
Bartering
Bookkeeping
Business organization
Business travel
Business use of car
Business use of home
Checking accounts
Computer equipment
Computer software
Computer use
Employees
Equipment and furniture
Ethics

Evaluating your business
Financial planning
Foreign markets and languages
Forms
Getting organized and managing
    information
Independent contractor status
Insurance
Investing
Legal liability
Legal/illegal business operation
**Loans, credit, and venture
    capital**
Managing growth
Money management
Negotiating
Overhead expenses

TELECOMMUTING

What you need to know   Telecommuting is going to work via the telephone line. You are still the employee of a traditional organization, but your office is off-site in your home. The telecommuter is distinguished from other home-based workers by the company paycheck and benefits package he or she receives. It is not an independent contractor arrangement; the work is not done independently. The employer dictates how and when the work is to be done and supplies the equipment with which to do it. Telecommuting is an established pattern with a number of large companies and with state and federal government agencies, but the number of telecommuters is relatively small. Opportunities to seek out a telecommuting arrangement are few. Those that are most successful are negotiated by valued employees who are already known to their companies. At its best, telecommuting offers these advantages to the employer: increased productivity and satisfaction, recruiting advantages, staffing flexibility, and reduced office space requirements. The telecommuting employee gains: fewer work interruptions, increased sense of control over work, scheduling flexibility, and savings on meals, clothing, and transportation. Concerns include losing touch with office politics, the intangible value of hourly interaction with staff, and less direct supervision.

Why you need to know it   Realistically, employers would rather retain you as an independent contractor than as a telecommuting employee. That is not universally true, however, and you should inquire. Your chances of securing telecommuter status are best before leaving your present job. Explore the possibilities while there is still funding for your position and benefits and all the company has to do is allow you the flexibility to work at home.

Where to learn more

▶ Begin by making a telecommuting proposal to your present organization—before leaving or offering the organization the opportunity to hire you sans benefits as an independent contractor.

▶ Broadcast your proposal to other organizations that are known users of the service you provide. Use business references found at the library, or contact trade and professional associations for directories and referrals.

▶ Ask your librarian if you might review a copy of Gale's catalog of research publications, or order a copy from the publisher by calling 800-877-GALE.

▶ Monitor Leadership Directories, Inc., 104 Fifth Avenue, 2nd Floor, New York, NY 10011 (212-627-4140), is a source of business and government directories. Emphasis is on the top leadership of organizations.

▶ GTE leases employee work space at its Telebusiness Centers to companies with telecommuters in the states of California, Kentucky, and Washington. Contact local offices in these states for further information.

Related topics

Answering machines and voice mail
Attitude
Business address and location
Business associates
Business use of home
Computer equipment
Computer on-line services
Computer software
Direct selling and multilevel marketing
Diversification
Family
Fax
Getting organized and managing information

Labor laws
Mail and overnight delivery services
Personnel policies
Presentations
Proposals
Psychological factors
Reducing expenses
Regulations
Role
Tax checklist
Telephone equipment
Telephone services
Telephone use
Time management

TELEPHONE EQUIPMENT

What you need to know   Telephone equipment includes not only telephone sets, but answering machines, call routing devices, and other hardware features to match your communications needs. The basic telephone comes in one-, two-, three-, and multiline models. Here are the features to select from in a telephone: cordless, multiline capacity, built-in answering machine, number of one-touch dialing buttons, speed dialing memory capacity, on-hook dialing, last number redial, automatic busy number redial, programmable pulse dialing, flash key (to ease use of telephone company services like call waiting), electronic hold, mute, ringer off, conference calling, and speaker. For answering machines, consider: built-in phone, voice activated recording (saves messages space), cassette/microcassette or memory chip, incoming and outgoing message lengths, remote security code, remote on/off, message forwarding, toll saver, call screening, automatic disconnect, time/date stamp, conversation recording, and message counter. Cellular telephones—car phones, transportables, and handhelds—use radio frequencies to broadcast conversations over hundreds of grids called cells. The next step up from an answering machine is an electronic receptionist that can ask who is calling, page you, forward calls, deliver messages, use musical hold, take messages, and more. Small, inexpensive devices can also use a single line and route calls to voice, fax, and answering machine.

Some answering machines receive faxes that you can retrieve remotely. Pagers give you the ability to receive messages and return calls anywhere, anytime.

Why you need to know it   Technology is a great multiplier for the home-based business. Telecommunications equipment that keeps you in touch with clients and suppliers without the expense of a receptionist is on a par with your computer for projecting productivity and professional image.

Where to learn more

▶ Crutchfield, 1 Crutchfield Park, P. O. Box 9045, Charlottesville, VA 22906-9045 (800-955-3000), publishes an excellent catalog with features compared in easy-to-comprehend tables.

▶ Check local office supply and electronics resellers and catalogs listed in Appendix C. Also look under the many topics and cross-references that begin with "Telephone" in the telephone yellow pages.

▶ Bogen Communications, 50 Spring Street, P. O. Box 575, Ramsey, NJ 07446 (201-934-8500), sells voice mail devices.

▶ Call Management Products, 2150 W. Sixth Avenue, N. Broomfield, CO 80020 (303-465-0651 or 800-245-9933), and Command Communications, Inc., 10800 E Bethany Drive, Aurora, CO 80014 (303-751-7000 or 800-288-3491), sell call-routing devices.

▶ Remote access answering machines for your fax include EMI's SmarterFAX Mailbox Manager (about $700; call 214-340-6789), and Macronix's Vomax 2000 (about $500; call 408-453-8088).

▶ Panasonic Company, One Panasonic Way, Secaucus, NJ 07094; 201-348-9090.

▶ Southwestern Bell, 7442 Shadeland Station Way, Indianapolis, IN 46256; 317-841-8006 or 800-255-8480.

▶ AT&T, 5 Wood Hollow Road, Parsippany, NJ 07054; 800-222-3111.

▶ *Teleconnect Magazine: The Independent Guide to Choosing, Using and Installing Telecommunications Equipment and Services*, 12 West 21st Street, New York, NY 10010 (212-691-8215), is a journal of the commercial telecommunications industry.

Related topics

Advertising
**Answering machines and
  voice mail**
Business plan
Business travel
Business use of car
Business use of home
Buying a business

Computer equipment
Computer on-line services
Computer software
Computer use
Conferences, seminars, shows,
  and workshops
Consulting
Customer relations

Direct selling and multilevel
  marketing
Electronic banking
Equipment and furniture
Ergonomics
Evaluating your business
Fax
Information sources and research
Insurance
Leasing
Legal/illegal business operation
Mail order
Managing growth

Marketing and market research
Media relations
Merchandise buying services
Noise
Office planning and decorating
Reducing expenses
Regulations
Security
Start-up
Tax checklist
Telecommuting
Telephone services
Telephone use

TELEPHONE SERVICES

What you need to know   A variety of services are available from local telephone companies. The options might include: call forwarding, answering, message storage and retrieval, blocking calls from numbers of your choosing, blocking calls from numbers not identified by your caller ID, call tracing, call waiting that lets you know another person is trying to reach you while taking another call, distinctive rings for different lines, distinctive rings for calls from designated numbers, home intercom, repeat calling, return calling, selective forwarding of designated numbers, speed calling, three-way calling, and voice mail. Long-distance telephone carriers offer services like call accounting, which lets you assign codes to clients, and they sort your monthly charges by client. You can arrange 700, 800, and 900 number service with your local telephone company or long-distance carrier. The 700 number service arranges for calls to your number to ring in at any number you have programmed from a touch-tone telephone. Different 800 number options let callers reach you toll-free from a calling area you designate. For the 900 number services, the telephone company collects a fee from callers for time spent connected to your number. Other services receive and store faxes while you are traveling. You can retrieve them remotely—they operate like voice mail for fax.

Why you need to know it   By making smart use of services available from your telephone company, you can increase the efficiency and improve the image of your home business. For example, for a small monthly charge, you can have three or four different telephone numbers, each with a distinctive ring, serving your single-line home office telephone. When voice mail and answering services are based on a monthly charge, they are less costly to try. You can always purchase them later if they prove desirable. Services like these also solve unique problems; for example, they eliminate the risk of theft or lightning damage to expensive equipment. You also save valuable space and can forget about maintenance and obsolescence.

Where to learn more

▶ Read the description of available services in your telephone book, or call the number listed for business services information.

▶ Call accounting can be arranged by calling: AT&T Small-Business Services (800-222-0400); MCI Prism Plus (800-444-2222) or MCI Preferred (800-727-5555); or Sprint (800-800-2568).

▶ Fax mail is a service for receiving your faxes remotely. Subscribe to the service through your regional telephone company or long-distance carrier. Call AT&T (800-446-2452); Ameritech (800-343-8200); US West (612-944-0655); or Envoy Global (503-224-6505).

▶ Toni Moore's *Dialing for Dollars: An Entrepreneur's Guide to Getting Started in the 900 Industry* costs about $30. To order, call 800-366-5596.

▶ National Media Communications, 30 N. Second Street, P. O. Box 115, Crompond, NY 10517, will give you details of its system for renting 900 number service. Send a self-addressed, stamped, business-size envelope, and include your telephone number.

Related topics

Advertising
Answering machines and voice mail
Banking services
Bulletin Board System (BBS)
Business image
Business use of car
Business use of home
Buying a business
Computer on-line services
Computer software
Computer use
Conferences, seminars, shows, and workshops
Consulting
Copyright, patent, trademark, and service mark
Credit cards
Customer relations
Debt collection and creditworthiness
Direct selling and multilevel marketing
Disabilities

Disaster planning
Diversification
Electronic banking
Equipment and furniture
Foreign markets and languages
Information sources and research
Legal liability
Legal/illegal business operation
Managing growth
Marketing and market research
Merchandise buying services
Networking
Presentations
Promoting your business
Reducing expenses
Regulations
Security
Start-up
Tax checklist
Telecommuting
Telephone equipment
Telephone use
Time-share offices

TELEPHONE USE

What you need to know   Distinctions are made between commercial and home use of telephone services. Although it is common to begin a home-based business with residential telephone service, plan to convert to commercial service when business calling constitutes more than occasional use. Requesting services like a yellow pages listing, using a number in published advertising, and adding multiple lines will indicate potential business use and invite inquiries from the telephone company. In most cases, you are requested to change to business service, although retroactive adjustments are a possibility. Telephone companies are generally anxious to encourage business use and many, like Pacific Bell, assign service representatives to assist small businesses. The approaches to using your telephone service and equipment to enhance, or even create, a home-based business are nearly limitless. Combined with your computer and specialized software and equipment, your home office can support sophisticated telemarketing. Combined with caller ID, software can tell you who is calling and bring up an information file on the caller as you answer the phone. Specialized applications, ranging from the bizarre to professional services like legal advising, can use 900 number service where callers pay directly (no billing). Computer software like *ACT!* and other contact managers can support your outbound calls with direct dialing and customer information.

Why you need to know it   The home-based business person faces ethical questions along with business considerations in making the best use of rapidly evolving telephone technology. The starting point for exploiting the full potential of your telephone is an appropriate commercial listing. There is little contest between technological versus human services solutions to such common problems as answering telephones and handling messages—technology wins hands down for the lightly staffed office. The choices are between owning equipment or purchasing services from telephone and other technology companies.

Where to learn more

▶ Pacific Bell's home-office telephone service advisers are located in: Metro/South LA (800-281-1258), San Fernando Valley (800-498-0419), San Gabriel Valley (800-371-0327), and Orange, Riverside, and San Bernadino counties (800-281-8811).

▶ Regional telephone companies provide business service numbers. Inquire about specific small business advisory services.

▶ *ACT!* and other contact manager software is available from software resellers and the catalogs listed in Appendix C.

▶ Toni Moore's *Dialing for Dollars: An Entrepreneur's Guide to Getting Started in the 900 Industry* costs about $30 plus shipping and handling. Call 800-366-5596.

Related topics

Advertising

**Answering machines and
  voice mail**

Banking services

Bulletin Board System (BBS)

Business image

Business use of car

Business use of home

Buying a business

Computer on-line services

Computer software

Computer use

Conferences, seminars, shows,
  and workshops

Consulting

Credit cards

Customer relations

Debt collection and creditworthiness

Direct selling and multilevel
  marketing

Disabilities

Disaster planning

Diversification

Electronic banking

Equipment and furniture

Foreign markets and languages

Information sources and research

Legal liability

Legal/illegal business operation

Managing growth

Marketing and market research

Merchandise buying services

Networking

Presentations

Promoting your business

Reducing expenses

Regulations

Security

Start-up

Tax checklist

Telecommuting

Telephone equipment

Telephone services

Time-share offices

TEMPORARY HELP

What you need to know   Temporary help is preferable to full-time employees for most home business personnel needs. The advantages include not having to advertise for and screen applicants, bonding, company training and benefits, and a sense of professionalism often lacking in unaffiliated short-term employees. Specialization is available, and you can target the category of employee you need. By examining the telephone yellow pages in a large city, you can find temporary workers who have technical, marketing, light industrial, word processing, records management, legal, accounting, data entry, travel, health care, and other specialties. If you are less concerned about hiring a professionally prepared temporary, the hourly rate for college students can be more reasonable. If you are planning to add an employee, consider temporary hires as an excellent way to find the right person with minimal risk. Open advertising can be quite time-consuming, and you face complying with equal opportunity and other regulations. For an agreed fee, most temporary services will let you hire a person whom you've used in a temporary capacity.

Why you need to know it   In addition to the convenience and long-term economies of hiring temporary employees, there is a security factor to consider. Introducing an unknown person into the intimacy of your home office environment should be done with caution. Use a reliable service or screen your candidates carefully with references you believe to be reliable.

Where to learn more

▶ Yellow pages listings can be found under "Employment Agencies" and "Employment Contractors—Temporary Help."

▶ College placement offices.

▶ Community newspapers and bulletin boards.

▶ Referrals from your professional associates and network.

Related topics

Bonding	Legal/illegal business operation
Bookkeeping	**Managing growth**
Computer use	Professional help
Customer relations	Proprietary information
Desktop publishing	**Reducing expenses**
Foreign markets and languages	Security
Getting organized and	Stress and overworking
managing information	**Time-share offices**
Independent contractor status	Vacation, work styles, and schedules
Legal liability	

TIME MANAGEMENT

What you need to know   Being self-employed presumes large measures of discipline and purpose. If you have problems getting started or focusing on your work, no amount of self-management gimmickry is going to make you a productive home-based business person. There are sensible ways to approach the tasks before you. Planning with the benefit of calendars, to-do lists, computerized contact managers, or whatever devices you find useful can help, but the primary motivators for the work-alone professional are affinity for the work being done (you love your work) and economics (if you are not effective, you won't have the privilege of working for yourself for long). The flexibility of working from home lets you make the most of your natural tendencies to work better in certain settings or at particular times of the day or night. But the fundamentals that applied at the office pertain to work at home as well. The golden rule of a franchise firm is "Dollars now!" That is, pick the thing that is most apt to make money in the shortest time possible, and act on it immediately. If circumstances change with the next telephone call and a higher priority clearly presents itself, shuffle the deck and do it now.

Why you need to know it   Avoid turning your home-based business into the same kind of organizational nightmare you left behind in industry, where rules dictated how to do the obvious. Be intuitive. Act on impulse. Keep your eye on the most profitable business opportunities you can unearth, and work them diligently, attending to the most promising first. If you need advice on how to run errands efficiently or stay away from the TV and refrigerator, get a job; you need close supervision.

Where to learn more

▶ Bookstores and libraries carry personal time management products like Kenneth Blanchard and Spencer Johnson's best-selling *One-Minute Manager* and the classic *How to Get Control of Your Time and Your Life* by Alan Lakein.

▶ Day-Timers, Inc., One Day-Timer Plaza, Allentown, PA 18195-1551 (215-395-5884), publishes a catalog of useful calendars, tapes, and other time management materials.

▶ Tapes on time management are easily found in bookstores. An example is Brian Tracy's *How to Master Your Time*. You can order it directly from the producer, Nightingale Conant, at 800-323-5552.

Related topics

Answering machines and voice mail
Business associates
Business use of home
Computer on-line service
Computer software
Computer use
Concerns about working from home
Employees
Evaluating your business
Getting organized and managing information

Managing growth
Separating business and personal
Stress and overworking
Success and failure
Telephone equipment
Telephone services
Telephone use
Temporary help
Time-share offices
Vacation, work styles, and schedules

TIME-SHARE OFFICES

What you need to know   If your business activity includes occasions when your home office is not conducive to the kind of meeting you need to have, consider the option of time-share offices. These facilities can also be the answer to zoning and homeowners' association challenges that make it necessary to have a primary business address outside your home. Time-share business centers offer flexible lease terms, single and multiple office suites, use of sister properties in other cities, and proximity to airports, transportation routes, commercial districts, and hotels. They feature elegantly furnished offices and conference rooms, first-class amenities, personalized telephone answering, audiovisual equipment, word processing, desktop publishing, and copying and binding services, in addition to receptionists, voice mail, fax, and telex. The services are not inexpensive, but compared to establishing permanent traditional offices in your city or at other locations around the country, they offer an economical and sophisticated option.

Why you need to know it   By being aware of what supporting services are available, your business can host client meetings in first-class business facilities around the country, while maintaining your home office in your residence.

Where to learn more

▶ Alliance Business Centers, locations nationwide: 800-869-9595.

▶ InterOffice, staffed and equipped offices nationwide: 800-776-8330.

▶ Airline in-flight and national business magazines advertise other properties, as do your local telephone yellow pages.

▶ Inquire at hotels in the area where you do business; meeting space is often available for rental.

Related topics

Answering machines and voice mail
Associations
Business address and location
Business associates
Business image
Business incubator
Competition
Computer equipment
Computer use
Concerns about working from home
Conferences, seminars, shows, and workshops
Contracts
Copiers
Customer relations
Disaster planning
Diversification

Equipment and furniture
Expense sharing and joint ventures
Fax
Leasing
Managing growth
Networking
Office planning and decorating
Presentations
Promoting your business
Separating business and personal
Start-up
Telephone equipment
Telephone services
Telephone use
Zoning

TRAINING

What you need to know   The lines between education—the formal pursuit of knowledge toward some traditional competency like an academic degree—and training—the more applied, skill-imparting exercises the military services refined so well—have blurred. Today, people who have been educated find it necessary to be trained, and retrained, over the course of their lives and careers. Home-based workers are not immune from this need; in fact, they are sometimes refugees from industry who retreat to their home offices in order to adapt their education to new commercial applications. Education is seldom wasted, but it becomes obsolete and needs enhancing with practical, up-to-the-minute training. Home-based business people do for themselves, on a more sophisticated and self-controlled basis, what occupational training programs do for the broader working population in changing economic times: they learn new skills and ways to market them successfully. The training you need depends on your goals and circumstances. The choices run the gamut from college courses to correspondence study, from a book on a technical subject to a motivational seminar. If you know what you want to do, call people who are doing it successfully and ask for their suggestions on worthwhile training experiences you might attend. If you are still determining your interests, a course or seminar is an excellent way to get a feel for a specialized field—and to meet people who can network you into the middle of it if you decide to pursue it.

Why you need to know it   Training is more than an opportunity to gain knowledge. The in-person variety is a vital link in developing and maintaining your network. Similar kinds of people gravitate to the same kinds of training sessions. Even if you are an expert in your field, it pays to respect the value of hearing new ideas and meeting new people.

Where to learn more

▸ Contact the adult continuing education departments of your local colleges for traditional classroom learning experiences in the field of your choice.

▸ Use national association directories in your library to contact organizations in your field of interest regarding training programs and seminars.

▸ Specialized commercial groups like The Computer Book Club, Blue Ridge Summit, PA 17294-0820, sell publications that inform their members on how-to subjects. They exist in almost any specialty and can be found by reading the periodicals that cater to your interests.

▸ Specific training products are advertised in publications whose readership might purchase their products. Check periodicals in your field. Examples include M-USA (800-933-6872), a company that sells video training materials for computer software, and NRI Schools, McGraw-Hill Continuing Education Center, 4401 Connecticut Avenue, NW, Washington, DC 20008, a firm that markets computer training correspondence programs.

▸ Anthony Robbins' "Mastery University" (800-445-8183) conducts pricey seminars at resort locations, featuring speakers like General Norman Schwarzkopf and Sir John Templeton.

▸ Seminars with speakers such as Mario Cuomo, Job Gibbs (former NFL coach), Larry King, Debbi Fields (Mrs. Fields' cookies), and motivational speakers Zig Ziglar and Peter Lowe are held in Washington and other major cities. Call 800-444-9159 for scheduling information.

Related topics

Associations

Computer use

Conferences, seminars, shows, and workshops

Continuing education

Franchises

Mail order

Service Corps of Retired Executives (SCORE)

Small Business Administration (SBA)

TRANSITIONING

What you need to know   Most people come to their home-based business status from traditional employment and conventional business settings. When recession threatens the survival of a fully staffed business that is renting commercial space, it is not uncommon for owners to take their accounts home with them and eliminate the overhead that threatens their solvency. People who receive termination notices or read the handwriting on the wall decide their skills are salable and choose home as their most cost-effective base for starting a business. Depending on the circumstances, that move need not be abrupt. There is often time for a deliberate, planned, rational transition from traditional employment to self-employment. Where available, severance packages provide cash flow for the initial months while a business can be brought to profitability. Other situations call for after-hours effort as a moonlighter while phasing out of a salaried position and into independent business. Still others take part of the job with them into transition by bringing along existing clients or turning the former employer into an instant account. Transitions can be eased by planned life-style adjustments that make a single income, in a previously dual-income family, sufficient until the business comes on line. In a worst-case scenario, unemployment checks and government mandated rights to continue health insurance plans (COBRA) at your own expense can help.

Why you need to know it   The more you can anticipate change, the less traumatic it is when it comes. Many people voluntarily choose to start home businesses, but increasing numbers of employees with excellent positions do it in response to perceived threats to their future security. Avoid freezing up and wasting any valuable transition time. Begin your transition while you have as much of your financial infrastructure intact as possible. Even if you are not threatened, a year or two of easing your way into an independent business after hours will put you in a much stronger position when it comes time to take the plunge.

Where to learn more

▶ Read Robert Gehorsam's "Start-Up Diary" in the September 1993 issue of *Home Office Computing* magazine. It is an excellent, realistic account of what you can expect to encounter in starting a serious business. Check your library or contact:

Reprint Manager, *Home Office Computing,* 730 Broadway, New York, NY 10003; 212-505-3580.

▶ The definitive work on the moonlighting approach to starting a business is David R. Eyler's *The Executive Moonlighter: Building Your Next Career Without Leaving Your Present Job.* Published in 1989; it is out of print but may be available at the library. The ISBN number is 0-471-50070-4.

▶ Consolidated Omnibus Budget Reconciliation Act (COBRA) guarantees employees the right to continue health coverage at their own expense for a period of 18 to 36 months. Private-sector employees can get information by writing to Division of Technical Assistance and Inquiries, Room N-5658, Pension and Welfare Benefits Administration, U.S. Department of Labor, 200 Constitution Avenue, NW, Washington, DC 20210. State and local government employees can write: Grants Policy Branch (COBRA), Room 17A-45, Office of the Assistant Secretary for Health, U.S. Public Health Service, 5600 Fishers Lane, Rockville, MD 20857. Federal employees should contact their agency personnel office.

▶ David R. Eyler's *Resumes That Mean Business,* 2nd edition (Random House, 1993) contains a chapter entitled "Protecting Your Employee Benefits When You Change Jobs." Its content is relevant to employees transitioning to self-employment.

Related topics

Buying a business
Computer use
Expense sharing and
    joint ventures

Moonlighting
Reducing expenses
Telephone use

UNDERCAPITALIZATION

What you need to know   There is no substitute for meeting your financial obligations when you start a business. Life goes on, and the bills continue to arrive for the operation of both your business and your personal life. A good business plan that includes realistic cash flow projections will illustrate this dramatically. Before you cut your ties to a regular income, be certain that you have the resources to pay the bills during the perfectly normal period of time it takes for your business to attract clients, compete for projects, complete them, send invoices, wait to receive payment, and wait for the checks to clear. Chart month-by-month cash flows for what you know you will have to pay out, match them with conservative estimates of revenues you expect to receive, and note the differences. If you plan to borrow to meet the shortfalls, have the lines of credit in place and add the debt service to your cash flow projections. If you do not have an honest plan to run the business and pay your bills for at least a year, you are probably undercapitalized and courting failure before you begin.

Why you need to know it   It is naive and asking far too much to expect your new business to carry its obligations *and* pay you a dependable salary during its first year or two. That is true even if the idea is good, the business plan is sound, and you encounter no serious problems. Business is a cycle of spending resources and being rewarded with profits for doing it intelligently. The beginning of that cycle almost certainly consists of more outgo than income. You need enough financial resources to carry the operation and your personal obligations until the cycle turns, the initial operating funds return, and you can take a profit.

Where to learn more

▶ Bookstores and libraries carry small business start-up books that can be helpful in judging undercapitalization situations. Examples include David R. Eyler's *Starting and Operating a Home-Based Business* (John Wiley & Sons) and Harvey Mackay's *Sharkproof: Get the Job You Want, Keep the Job You Love* (Harper-Collins).

▶ The Small Business Administration's *Directory of Business Development Publications* is available from SBA Publications, P. O. Box 1000, Fort Worth, TX 76119. Titles like *Starting and Managing a Small Business of Your Own* and *Starting and Managing a Small Service Business* are worth examining.

▶ Small business financial software packages have manuals that describe how their products can assist you with managing cash flow. One program that addresses cash flow directly is *Up Your Cash Flow* by Granville Publications Software. It includes CPA Harvey A. Goldstein's best-selling book by the same name. You can order it from *Power Up Direct* (800-851-2917) for about $80. Most checkbook and small business accounting software like *Quicken* and *M.Y.O.B.* include budget and cash flow analysis features. They are available at software resellers or through catalogs listed in Appendix C.

▶ Robert Gehorsam's "Start-Up Diary," in the September 1993 issue of *Home Office Computing* magazine, is an excellent and realistic account of what you can expect to encounter in starting a serious business. Check your library or contact: Reprint Manager, *Home Office Computing*, 730 Broadway, New York, NY 10003; 212-505-3580.

Related topics

Bankruptcy	**Managing growth**
Budgeting	Projections
Cash flow	Reducing expenses
Financial planning	**Start-up**
Loans, credit, and venture capital	**Success and failure**

VACATION, WORK STYLES, AND SCHEDULES

What you need to know   The purpose of starting a business is making a living, but there is more to consider. Home-based entrepreneurs in particular value independence and work styles that suit their preferences. A business of your own can be all-consuming unless you deliberately take steps to make it otherwise, and this is doubly true when the office is at home. The temptation to work all the time is tremendous, and it can ruin an otherwise desirable way to live and work. In a business plan, it is essential to calculate an honest profit, pay yourself a fair salary, and provide a decent return on your investment. Carry that logic another step, and take into account the life-style necessities like a reasonable amount of time away from work. A real vacation should be built into your planning from the beginning. Extravagance isn't necessary, but a valid break from the working routine and the money to pay for it are important parts of your broader success plan. Having your own business brings with it the curse of freedom to work the way you want, for as long as you'd like. The expected problem is that you will not work diligently enough in the face of all this freedom, but the reality is that overwork is the greater threat. Do conscious reviews of the balance you maintain between your work and leisure as your business grows. Don't ignore the necessity to stop and smell the roses.

Why you need to know it   Passion for your work, fear of failure, and the absence of anyone setting a better example in your immediate proximity can lead to overwork in a home-based business. Work hard, keep long hours, meet your obligations and then some, but be attentive to factoring in some down time and a scheduled vacation that is considered part of the cost of doing business.

Where to learn more

▶ Marilyn and Tom Ross's book, *Country Bound,* published by Communications Creativity, P. O. Box 909, 425 Cedar Street, Buena Vista, CO 81211 (719-395-8659 or 800-331-8355), is full of advice on rationally choosing a rural life and work style.

▶ David R. Eyler's *The Executive Moonlighter: Building Your Next Career Without Leaving Your Present Job.* Tells you how to build a business and move it to where you'd like to be. Published in 1989, it is out of print but may be available at the library. The ISBN number is 0-471-50070-4.

Related topics

Attitude

Business address and location

Concerns about working from home

Customer relations

Evaluating your business

Managing growth

Psychological factors

Separating business and personal

Stress and overworking

Time management

VALUES

What you need to know   One in five home-based workers are there because they lost their corporate jobs, according to surveys. But there is more to the choice to work from home than not finding employment elsewhere. Turmoil in the economy, at the management levels in particular, have people reevaluating why they work and what they would do differently if forced to change positions or if they were to choose to do so voluntarily. Nearly three out of four people surveyed expressed the desire to be their own boss, and more than half of them wanted to break the routine that governs how they live and work. Most aren't unhappy with the work itself, or their colleagues, or even the corporate world, but they want more control. More time with families is a goal for about one third of those who start home-based businesses. A strong work ethic, an independent spirit, and the willingness to experience risk are among the primary traits in work-at-home entrepreneurs' values.

Why you need to know it   Entrepreneurship in general, and working at home in particular, demands pursuits that require certain psychological underpinnings for success. To tolerate the ambiguities of self-employment and the relatively isolated life-style of the home-based business, your values must be complementary to the challenges you face.

Where to learn more

▶ Robert Gehorsam's "Start-Up Diary," in the September 1993 issue of *Home Office Computing* magazine, is an excellent and realistic account of what you can expect to encounter in starting a serious business. Check your library or contact: Reprint Manager, *Home Office Computing*, 730 Broadway, New York, NY 10003; 212-505-3580.

▶ Paul and Sarah Edwards' *Working From Home*, published by Jeremy Tarcher, Inc., is heavily interlaced with discussions of values the authors find important in home business success.

Related topics

Advertising	Personnel policies
Business associates	Promoting your business
Business image	Public relations
Customer relations	Role
Ethics	Separating business and personal
Family	Stress and overworking
Legal/illegal business	Telecommuting
operation	**Vacation, work styles, and**
Negotiating	**schedules**

WOMEN'S PROGRAMS

What you need to know   Women face the same entrepreneurial challenges that men do, but our society has placed a priority on making opportunities available to women, including entry to the free enterprise system and business ownership. The Small Business Administration is the national point of contact for federal programs. SBA regional offices are also engaged in supporting women's efforts to start and operate their own businesses. These programs consist of the expected emphasis on learning basic business planning and management skills, plus assistance with financing. Entrepreneurship has also become a significant outlet for women who encounter the "glass ceiling" in corporations. Regardless of your feelings about being defined as a group to receive special assistance, you are well advised to be rational about pursuing the possibilities of more favorable lending opportunities if your application is tendered as a woman's initiative. The same is true for securing corporate and government contracts. Special initiatives exist in both sectors to channel business toward companies owned by women.

Why you need to know it   The home-based business approach offers women a relatively low-risk avenue to starting their own businesses. Assistance available specifically to help women get started in business is a definite advantage in locating financing and securing business from companies and government agencies anxious to support the movement. This may be a factor in a husband-and-wife business where it is beneficial to structure the company's ownership in such a way as to benefit from women's programs.

Where to learn more

▶ The SBA's Office of Women's Business Ownership (202-205-6673) can help you identify special programs backing women entrepreneurs.

▶ National Association of Female Executives (212-645-0770) makes loans and otherwise assists women starting businesses.

▶ *National Directory of Women-Owned Business Firms,* published by Business Research Services in 1992, sells for $225. Check your library or call 800-877-GALE.

▶ *Women's Information Directory* is a guide to organizations, agencies, institutions, programs, publications, services, and other resources concerned with women in the United States. Shawn Brenna is the editor. To order, call 800-877-GALE.

▶ State and local economic development programs exist for women in many states. Send inquiries to your state's elected representatives or ask about women's programs through the state government's public information number in your state capital.

▶ Contact purchasing and contracting officers in business and government to inquire about opportunities for companies owned by women.

▶ Microloan programs backed by the SBA and other sources often emphasize financing for women's enterprises. *Home Office Computing*'s BizFAX service (800-227-5638, ext. 730) will fax a directory to you for $6.95.

Related topics

Associations

Banking services

Business associates

Business basics

Buying a business

Conferences, seminars, shows, and workshops

Continuing education

Debt collection and
  creditworthiness
Expense sharing and joint ventures
Financial planning
Government customers
Legal/illegal business operation

Loans, credit, and venture capital
Marketing and market research
Regulations
Small Business Administration
  (SBA)
Transitioning

ZONING

What you need to know The key to operating a home-based business without inviting the strict interpretation of zoning laws is keeping a low profile. As long as the setting is residential, avoid doing anything that alters the appearance or character of the neighborhood. If your home-based business takes on a commercial appearance or level of activity, expect objections followed by a cease-and-desist order closing your business. Fortunately, modern home-based businesses are mostly administrative in nature and rely on quiet, clean, unobtrusive equipment like computers and telephones. Zoning restrictions are not usually invoked unless there is a complaint. Avoid objections by not operating a prohibited business or drawing attention with signs, with advertising that includes the residential address, or with activity that aggravates traffic or noise levels in the neighborhood. You can appeal an unfavorable zoning ruling or seek a variance, but it is difficult to prevail once the system has been challenged. The most practical solution in the face of a serious challenge is to rent an inexpensive office in a commercial area, some time-share space, or a small area within another business person's facilities. Use the commercial space as your official place of business, and work at home as much as you like. As long as you don't disrupt the neighborhood, it is unlikely that further complaints about quiet administrative activity inside your home would be pursued.

Why you need to know it Zoning problems for home businesses are vestiges of old laws intended to keep people from starting objectionable enterprises in residential neighborhoods. They are seldom enforced without complaints and are undergoing change to accommodate the realities of modern home offices. Your best strategy is to operate quietly and not give your neighbors any reason to challenge you. Support rational modernization of zoning laws to address the needs of desirable home businesses.

Where to learn more

▶ Look in the local government listings of your telephone directory for the zoning office.

▶ CPA Bernard Kamoroff's *Small-Time Operator: How to Start Your Own Small Business, Keep Your Books, Pay Your Taxes, and Stay Out of Trouble* is available from Bell Springs Publishing, Laytonville, CA 95454; 707-984-6746.

▶ David R. Eyler's *Starting and Operating a Home-Based Business* (John Wiley & Sons) and Paul and Sarah Edwards' *Working from Home* (Tarcher) discuss the zoning issue.

◗ *Home Office Computing*'s November 1993 issue included a special report on "The 10 Best Cities for Home-Based Businesses." Consider one of them if you plan to relocate; use their example to influence your local zoning authorities. Check your library or contact: Reprint Manager, *Home Office Computing*, 730 Broadway, New York, NY 10003; 212-505-3580.

Related topics

Advertising

Attorney

Business address and location

Business use of home

Concerns about working from home

Equipment and furniture

Legal/illegal business operation

License

Negotiating

Noise

Promoting your business

Public relations

Separating business and personal

Start-up

Time-share offices

Appendix

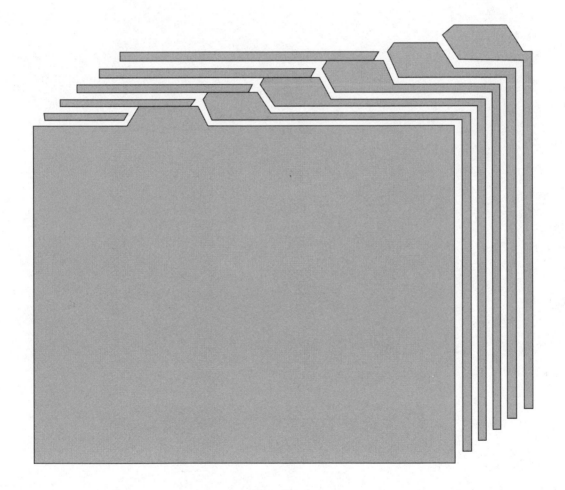

APPENDIX A

Computer-Based Business Forms

If anyone ever needed the paperless office, it is the home-based business person. With limited space and probably no clerical support, you can benefit tremendously from not having to inventory blank forms or to address, mail, and file them. A revolution has taken place in office forms design, production, and management. Computer software, electronic mail, and laser printers now make it possible to design your own forms or adapt masters provided by the software companies, and transmit or print them as needed. Take additional steps and you can benefit tremendously from computerized forms software. Here are some of the useful things you can do with it:

- Complete forms while they are still on your computer;
- Use data you already have in other files to complete forms;
- Use spreadsheet-like math calculators to compute entries on forms;
- Check the spelling of both forms and entries before distributing them;
- Use electronic mail to send forms to those who need to complete them, and let them respond the same way;
- While the recipient is on-line completing the form, prompt him or her with clarifications that encourage more accurate responses;
- Use the response data to drive databases and other files linked to your electronic forms;
- Get instant authorized "signatures" via security-coded responses;
- Prevent alterations by electronically protecting information on the forms;
- Generate reports from data on the electronic forms;
- File forms electronically, never turning them into hard copy unless you find that step to be necessary.

Although their features vary (call the manufacturers for detailed information), the following software products produce and use forms in the electronic format:

- *Perform Pro Plus for Windows* and a more sophisticated program called *Form-Flow*—available from Delrina (800-268-6082);
- *WordPerfect® InForms for Windows* (800-451-5151).

WordPerfect is developing a Macintosh version of *InForms*. Delrina's forms products are for PCs, but they have file exchange protocols that let them interact with Macintosh systems and software. Both PC and Macintosh users will find other forms-generating software in the catalogs and trade publications catering to their operating system. (See Appendix C.)

Most programs contain 100 or so predesigned business forms for purchasers to customize and use. The following list and the samples given on subsequent pages represent the forms contained in *WordPerfect InForms for Windows:*

1. Bid Sheet (p. 237)
2. Income Statement (p. 238)
3. Balance Sheet (p. 239)
4. Application for Employment (p. 240)
5. Telephone and Address Directory (p. 243)
6. Telephone Conversation Record (p. 244)
7. Daily Planner (p. 245)
8. Monthly Planner (p. 246)
9. To-Do List (p. 247)
10. Memo (p. 248)
11. Invitation (p. 249)
12. FAX Cover Sheet (p. 250)
13. Return Authorization (p. 251)
14. Packing List (p. 252)
15. Straight Bill of Lading (p. 253)
16. Travel Itinerary Form (p. 254)
17. Travel Expense Report (p. 255)
18. Service Report (p. 256)
19. Sales Call Report (p. 257)
20. Cash Disbursements (p. 258)
21. Debit Memo (p. 259)
22. Credit Memo (p. 260)
23. Aged Listing—Accounts Receivable (p. 261)
24. Aged Listing—Accounts Payable (p. 262)
25. Accounts Receivable (p. 263)
26. Accounts Payable (p. 264)
27. Invoice (p. 265)
28. Purchase Order (p. 266)
29. Cash Receipt (p. 267)
30. Payment Past Due Notice (p. 268)

BID SHEET

Date: _____

☐ Pre Bid	Item Num: _____ Close Date: _____

Item Num: _____

Req Type: _____

Req Number: _____

Quantity: _____

Destination: _____

Close Date: _____

Reviewed Close Date: _____

Date Required: _____

Mailing Date: _____

Buyer's Name: _____

☐ Pre Bid

☐ Phone Bids

☐ Send Sample

Vendor Code	Vendor Name	Bid Price 1	Bid Price 2

Cancel Bid: Reason close date Revised:

Recommended bypass bid or accepted other than low bid for following reason:

_____

_____

_____

_____

_____

_____

New Vendor Address:

Recommended By _____   Approved By _____

This form was created using WordPerfect InForms 1.0 by WordPerfect Corporation

Income Statement

Company Name _____ _____ _____ , 19 ____ and 19 ____
                                         Month   Day   Current   Prior

		(Current)	(Prior)
REVENUES		19	19
CURRENT ASSETS			
Sales		_____	_____
Returns and Allowances		_____	_____
COSTS AND EXPENSES	**NET SALES**	_____	_____
Costs of Goods Sold		_____	_____
Depreciation		_____	_____
Selling, general and administrative		_____	_____
Interest		_____	_____
Other		_____	_____
_____		_____	_____
_____		_____	_____
	INCOME FROM OPERATIONS	_____	_____
OTHER INCOME			
_____		_____	_____
_____		_____	_____
	OTHER INCOME	_____	_____
	INCOME BEFORE INCOME TAXES	_____	_____
INCOME TAXES			
Current		_____	_____
Deferred		_____	_____
		_____	_____
	NET INCOME	_____	_____
BEGINNING RETAINED EARNINGS			
Dividends		_____	_____
	ENDING RETAINED EARNINGS	_____	_____

This form was created using WordPerfect InForms 1.0 from WordPerfect Corporation

Balance Sheet

Company Name _____ _____ _____ , 19____ and 19____

	Month	Day	Current	Prior

ASSETS

	(Current) 19	(Prior) 19
CURRENT ASSETS		
Cash	$ _____	$ _____
Marketable Securities **	_____	_____
Accounts Receivable **	_____	_____
Inventories *	_____	_____
Prepaid Expenses	_____	_____
_____	_____	_____
_____	_____	_____
TOTAL CURRENT ASSETS	_____	_____
_____	_____	_____
TOTAL ASSETS	$ _____	$ _____

LIABILITIES AND STOCKHOLDERS EQUITY

	(Current) 19	(Prior) 19
CURRENT LIABILITIES		
Short-Term Notes	$ _____	$ _____
Current portion of long-term debt	_____	_____
Accounts Payable	_____	_____
Accrued Liabilities	_____	_____
Income Taxes Payable	_____	_____
_____	_____	_____
TOTAL CURRENT LIABILITIES	_____	_____
LONG-TERM DEBT, less current portion	_____	_____
DEFERRED INCOME TAXES	_____	_____
STOCKHOLDER'S EQUITY		
Common Stock **	_____	_____
Additional paid-in capital	_____	_____
Retained Earnings	_____	_____
	8,787.00	_____
TOTAL LIABILITIES	$ 8,787.00	$ _____

_____

* Recommend rounding to nearest dollar.
** Present additional detail, if necessary, in notes.

This form was created using WordPerfect InForms 1.0 from WordPerfect Corporation

WORLDWIDE
BUSINESS SYSTEMS

(Please Print)

Name _____
          Last   First   Middle

Address _____
          Street Number   City   State   Zip

Telephone _____   **Social Security Number** [_____]
          Area Code

Driver's License Number _____   **State** _____   **Expiration Date** _____

If you are not a U.S. citizen, what is the basis of your eligibility for employment? _____

APPLICATION FOR EMPLOYMENT

POSITION(S) APPLIED FOR: _____

Have you filed an application here before? ☐ Yes   ☐ No   If Yes, give date: _____

Have you been employed here before? ☐ Yes   ☐ No   If Yes, give date: _____

Are you employed now? ☐ Yes   ☐ No   On what date would you be available to work? _____

Are you available to work ☐ Full Time   ☐ Part Time   ☐ Morning   ☐ Afternoon   ☐ Graveyard

Are any of your educational or employment records under another name(s)? If so, please list below.

_____

Have you been convicted of a crime, or are you currently charged with a crime other than moving traffic violations? If so, please explain:

_____
_____
_____

Are you fluent in any foreign languages? List: _____

SUMMARIZE SPECIAL SKILLS AND QUALIFICATIONS:

_____
_____
_____
_____

FOR OFFICE USE ONLY:

This form was created using WordPerfect InForms 1.0 from WordPerfect Corporation

Education	High School	College/University	Graduate/Professional
School Name			
Diploma/Degree			
Honors Received			
Describe Course of Study			

EMPLOYMENT EXPERIENCE:

List all of your work experience including military and voluntary service assignments. Begin with your present or last position. Attach additional sheet if necessary.

1.

Employer	Telephone	Date Employed From To	Work Performed
Address			
Job Title	Supervisor	Hourly Rate/Salary Starting Final	
Reason for Leaving			

2.

Employer	Telephone	Date Employed From To	Work Performed
Address			
Job Title	Supervisor	Hourly Rate/Salary Starting Final	
Reason for Leaving			

3.

Employer	Telephone	Date Employed From To	Work Performed
Address			
Job Title	Supervisor	Hourly Rate/Salary Starting Final	
Reason for Leaving			

PROFESSIONAL/WORK REFERENCES:

Give name and telephone number of two professional/work references.

Name	Relationship	Home Phone	Daytime Phone

Name	Relationship	Home Phone	Daytime Phone

This form was created using WordPerfect InForms 1.0 from WordPerfect Corporation

ACKNOWLEDGEMENT:

All applicants are considered for positions without regard to race, color, religion, sex, national origin, age, marital or veteran status, or the presence of a non-job-related medical condition or handicap. Verification of eligibility to work in the U.S. will be required if an employment offer is made.

I acknowledge that consideration for employment is contingent on the results of a reference and background check. Therefore, I hereby authorize this Company to (1) investigate the truthfulness of all statements made on this application; (2) contact my former employers and other listed references or any other persons who can verify information; (3) discuss the results of any investigation with other employees of this Company involved in the hiring process; (4) check my driving record if applicable for the target job; and (5) check my criminal record. In addition, I give my consent for all contacted persons including former employers to provide the information concerning this application, and I release each such person from liability for providing information to this Company.

I certify that the information contained in this application is correct to the best of my knowledge, and understand that falsification of this application in any detail is grounds for disqualification from further consideration or dismissal from employment in accordance with company policy.

_____   _____
Signature   Date

AFFIRMATIVE ACTION INFORMATION:

Completion of this information is voluntary. The information supplied will be kept confidential. Refusal to provide this information will not subject the applicant to any adverse treatment and it will be used only in accordance with the Act and regulations cited below.

Executive Order 11246, as amended by Executive Order 11385 and Section 402 of the Vietnam Era Veterans Readjustment Assistance Act of 1974, requires all government contractors and subcontractors with 50 or more employees and contracts from the federal government to recruit, hire, promote, and otherwise guarantee equal employment opportunity for qualified minorities, men, women, handicapped individuals and veterans in all job groups and at all levels of the work force In order for this company to comply with this order and record this data, we ask that you complete the following.

Full Name _____   **Position Applied For** _____

Sex: ☐ Male   ☐ Female   **Handicapped** ☐ Yes   ☐ No   **Disabled Veteran** ☐ Yes   ☐ No

Veteran who served on active duty for more than 180 days during the Vietnam era: ☐ Yes   ☐ No

Race:	☐ Caucasian	☐ Black	☐ Hispanic	☐ Asian or Pacific Islander
	☐ American Indian or Alaskan Native	☐ Other National Origin		_____

Referral Source	☐ Friend	☐ Relative	☐ Walk-In	☐ Job Hotline
	☐ Employment Agency		☐ Other	_____

This form was created using WordPerfect InForms 1.0 from WordPerfect Corporation

TELEPHONE AND
ADDRESS DIRECTORY

1.Name / Firm		**WK Phone:**	
Mailing Address:		**HM Phone:**	
2. Name / Firm		**WK Phone:**	
Mailing Address:		**HM Phone:**	
3. Name / Firm		**WK Phone:**	
Mailing Address:		**HM Phone:**	
4. Name / Firm		**WK Phone:**	
Mailing Address:		**HM Phone:**	
5. Name / Firm		**WK Phone:**	
Mailing Address:		**HM Phone:**	
6. Name / Firm		**WK Phone:**	
Mailing Address:		**HM Phone:**	
7. Name / Firm		**WK Phone:**	
Mailing Address:		**HM Phone:**	

This form was created using WordPerfect InForms 1.0 from WordPerfect Corporation

TELEPHONE CONVERSATION
RECORD

Telephone Conversation	
Spoke with:	Date:
Company:	Time:
Subject:	

○   I Called   ○   Party Called

Message:

Telephone Reply	

o

Reply:

Follow-Up:

Signature:	Approval:

This form was created using WordPerfect InForms 1.0 from WordPerfect Corporation

DAILY PLANNER

Day of the Week: _____   **Date:** _____

Time	To Do	Comments
8:00 - 9:00		
9:00 - 10:00		
10:00 - 11:00		
11:00 - 12:00		
12:00 - 1:00		
1:00 - 2:00		
2:00 - 3:00		
3:00 - 4:00		
4:00 - 5:00		
5:00 - 6:00		
6:00 - 7:00		
7:00 - 8:00		
8:00 - 9:00		
9:00 - 10:00		
10:00 - 11:00		
11:00 - 12:00		

This form was created using WordPerfect InForms 1.0 from WordPerfect Corporation

MONTHLY PLANNER

MONTH : _____

YEAR: _____

NAME: _____

SUNDAY	MONDAY	TUESDAY	WEDNESDAY	THURSDAY	FRIDAY	SATURDAY

This form was created using WordPerfect InForms 1.0 from WordPerfect Corporation

To Do List

Name:

Date:

Priorities

☐
☐
☐
☐
☐

1.

2.

3.

4.

5.

Other

☐
☐
☐
☐
☐
☐
☐

6.

7.

8.

9.

10.

11.

12.

To Do List

Name:

Date:

Priorities

☐
☐
☐
☐
☐

1.

2.

3.

4.

5.

Other

☐
☐
☐
☐
☐
☐
☐

6.

7.

8.

9.

10.

11.

12.

This form was created using WordPerfect InForms 1.0 from WordPerfect Corporation

MEMO

FROM:	DATE:
TO:	TIME:

REGARDING:

MESSAGE:

REPLY   ◯ No   ◯ ASAP   ◯ Today   ◯ Soon   ◯ 1 Day

This form was created using WordPerfect InForms 1.0 from WordPerfect Corporation

YOU ARE

CORDIALLY INVITED

A Personal Invitation

EVENT

Date:	Time:

Location

Direction:

RSVP REQUIRED	By What Date:
◯ YES ◯ NO	

This form was created using WordPerfect InForms 1.0 from WordPerfect Corporation

FAX
Cover Sheet

TO Name		Fax #	
Company		Phone #	
FROM Name		Fax #	
Company		Phone #	

DESCRIPTION

No. of pages (including cover)

Date:	Time:

| If there are any problems receiving this transmission call: | Name: |
| | Phone: |

This form was created using WordPerfect InForms 1.0 from WordPerfect Corporation

RETURN AUTHORIZATION

SOLD
TO:

RETURN
TO:

CUSTOMER NUMBER	AUTHORIZATION NUMBER	P.O. NUMBER	DATE

ITEM	QUANTITY	DESCRIPTION	UNIT PRICE	AMOUNT
			TOTAL	

COMMENTS:

APPROVED BY

This form was created using WordPerfect InForms 1.0 from WordPerfect Corporation

Packing List

List Number

Ship To:		Sold To:			
Address 1:		Address 1:			
Address 2:		Address 2:			
City, ST Zip:		City, ST Zip:			
Date:	Customer Order No.	Our No.	Ship Via	Payment	
				[ ] Prepaid [ ] Collect	

Qty Ordered	Qty Shipped	Qty Back Ordered	Description

No. Cartons	Total Weight	Carton No.	[ ] Order Complete [ ] Balance To Follow	Packed By	Checked By

INSTRUCTIONS: To show "Ship To:" address on carton, turn page face down, fold twice (bottom to top, right to left)

This form was created using WordPerfect InForms 1.0 from WordPerfect Corporation

STRAIGHT BILL OF LADING - SHORT FORM - Original - Not Negotiable.   ☐ By Truck   ☐ By Freight

Received subject to the classification and tariffs in effect on the date of the issue of this Bill of Lading, the property described below, in apparent good order, except as noted (contents and condition of packages unknown), marked, consigned and destined as indicated below, which said carrier (the word carrier being understood throughout this contract as meaning any person or corporation in possession of the property under the contract) agrees to carry to its usual place of delivery at said destination, if on its route, otherwise to deliver to another carrier on the route to said destination. It is mutually agreed as to each carrier of all or any of said property over all or any portion of said route to destination, and as to each party at any time interested in all or any of said property, that every service to be performed hereunder shall be subject to all the terms and conditions of the Uniform Domestic Straight Bill of Lading set forth (1) in Uniform Freight Classification in effect on the date hereof, if this is a rail or a rail-water shipment, (2) in the application motor carrier classification or tariff if this is a motor carrier shipment.
  Shipper certifies that he is familar with all the terms and conditions of the said bill of lading, including those on the back thereof, set forth in the classification or tariff which governs the transportation of this shipment, and the said terms and conditions are hereby agreed to by the shipper and accepted for himself and his assigns.

From

Consigned To and Destination

Date: 8/4/1993
Shippers No.
Carrier
Carrier No.
Delivering Carrier
Route
Car or Vehicle Initials   No.

No Package	*HM	Kind of Package, Description of Articels, Special Marks and Exceptions		**Weight (Sub to Cor)	Class or Rate	✓

Subject to Section 7 of Conditions of applicable bill of lading, if this shipment is to be delivered to the consignee without recourse on the consignor, the consignor shall sign the following statement:
The carrier shall not make delivery of this shipment without payment of freight and all other lawful charges.

(Signature of Consignor)

If charges are to be prepaid, write or stamp here, "To Be Prepaid"

Amount recieved to apply in prepayment of the charges on the property described hereon.

Agent or Cashier

(The signature here acknowledges only the amount prepaid)

Charges Advanced:

* Mark to designate HAZARDOUS MATERIAL as defined in title 49 of federal regulations.
** If the shipment moves between two ports by a carrier by water, the law requires that the bill of lading shall state whether it is "carrier's or shippers weight."
NOTE - Where the rate is dependent on value, shippers are required to state in writing the agreed or declared value of the property.

The agreed or declared value of the property is hereby specifically stated by the shipper to be not exceeding

_____ per _____

Permanent post-office address of shipper:

World Wide Business Sysytems
Manhatten, NY 10004

Shipper per _____   Agent per _____

This form was created using WordPerfect InForms 1.0 from WordPerfect Corporation

Travel Itinerary Form

FOR: _____   Date: _____

Name: _____

Address: _____
_____

Record #: _____

City: _____ ST: ___ ZIP: _____   Agent: _____

Home Phone: _____   Work Phone: _____

Date: _____   Travel Mode: _____   Meal: _____
DEPART Destination: _____ Time: _____ Carrier: _____
ARRIVE Destination: _____ Time: _____ Route No: _____

Date: _____   Travel Mode: _____   Meal: _____
DEPART Destination: _____ Time: _____ Carrier: _____
ARRIVE Destination: _____ Time: _____ Route No: _____

Date: _____   Travel Mode: _____   Meal: _____
DEPART Destination: _____ Time: _____ Carrier: _____
ARRIVE Destination: _____ Time: _____ Route No: _____

Date: _____   Travel Mode: _____   Meal: _____
DEPART Destination: _____ Time: _____ Carrier: _____
ARRIVE Destination: _____ Time: _____ Route No: _____

Date: _____   Travel Mode: _____   Meal: _____
DEPART Destination: _____ Time: _____ Carrier: _____
ARRIVE Destination: _____ Time: _____ Route No: _____

Date: _____   Travel Mode: _____   Meal: _____
DEPART Destination: _____ Time: _____ Carrier: _____
ARRIVE Destination: _____ Time: _____ Route No: _____

This form was created using WordPerfect InForms 1.0 by WordPerfect Corporation

TRAVEL EXPENSE REPORT

Purpose of Expense Report:

Name: _____ First _____ Last

Date:

Dates of Travel	Destination			Meals				Lodging	Airfare	Taxi/Limo Etc.	Auto Rental	Auto Mileage (x .22)	Total Meals/Travel
	From	To	Breakfast	Lunch	Dinner	Total Meals							
TOTALS													

ENTERTAINMENT EXPENSES

Date	Person/Group Entertained	Explanation	Amount
TOTAL			

MISCELLANEOUS EXPENSES

Date	Item	Amount
TOTAL		

Grand Total

Total of ALL Travel, Entertainment, and Miscellaneous Expenses

Subtract Advance	
Balance Due Employee	
Balance Due Company	

Signature of Person Submitting Report

Approved By

This form was created using WordPerfect InForms 1.0 from WordPerfect Corporation

257

Service Report

Customer and Service Information

Customer:		Job#:	
Address:		Date Of Report:	
Contact:		Date Of Call:	
Service Called By:		Date Completed:	

Service Call Record

Purpose of Call:	
Description of Equipment:	

Conditions at Job Site

Visual Inspection:	
Trial Operation:	

Service Call Results

Adjustments, Repairs, Alterations:	
Equipment & Parts Needed:	
Comments & Recommendations:	

Action to be Taken

1.	
2.	
3.	
4.	

Service Rep:	Approval:

This form was created using WordPerfect InForms 1.0 from WordPerfect Corporation

SALES CALL REPORT

Date: _____

Prospect	Address	City, St Zip

Sales Call Type	Call was:	Mail status
☐ In-Person ☐ By Phone	☐ Cold Call ☐ Follow Up ☐ Lead From ☐ Add to Mail List	☐ Drop from Mail List ☐ Send Literature

Customer is:

☐ Regular Customer	☐ Previous Customer	☐ Inactive Customer

COMMENTS

Prospect	Address	City, St Zip

Sales Call Type	Call was:	Mail status
☐ In-Person ☐ By Phone	☐ Cold Call ☐ Follow Up ☐ Lead From ☐ Add to Mail List	☐ Drop from Mail List ☐ Send Literature

Customer is:

☐ Regular Customer	☐ Previous Customer	☐ Inactive Customer

COMMENTS

Prospect	Address	City, St Zip

Sales Call Type	Call was:	Mail status
☐ In-Person ☐ By Phone	☐ Cold Call ☐ Follow Up ☐ Lead From ☐ Add to Mail List	☐ Drop from Mail List ☐ Send Literature

Customer is:

☐ Regular Customer	☐ Previous Customer	☐ Inactive Customer

COMMENTS

Prospect	Address	City, St Zip

Sales Call Type	Call was:	Mail status
☐ In-Person ☐ By Phone	☐ Cold Call ☐ Follow Up ☐ Lead From ☐ Add to Mail List	☐ Drop from Mail List ☐ Send Literature

Customer is:

☐ Regular Customer	☐ Previous Customer	☐ Inactive Customer

COMMENTS

This form was created using WordPerfect InForms 1.0 from WordPerfect Corporation

Cash Disbursements

Period From: _____   To: _____

Date	Paid to	Reason	Account	Amount

TOTAL [_____]

Signature _____   **Approved** _____

Date _____   **Date** _____

This form was created using WordPerfect InForms 1.0 from WordPerfect Corporation

_____ DEBIT MEMO _____

| TO: | SHIPPED TO: | Number: |
| | | Date: |

Your order No. _____

Our Invoice NO. _____

Date of your order: _____

Terms: _____

Shipped From: _____

VIA: _____

REASON FOR CREDIT:

Quantity	Description	Unit Price	Amount
		TOTAL	

Authorized by: _____

Authorization Date: _____

This form was created using WordPerfect InForms 1.0 from WordPerfect Corporation

———— CREDIT MEMO ————

SHIPPED TO:	SHIPPED FROM:	
		Date:
		Number:

Your order No. _____   Our Invoice No. _____

Date of your order: _____   Terms: _____

Date Received _____   Salesperson: _____

REASON FOR CREDIT:

Quantity	Description	Unit Price	Amount
		TOTAL	

Authorized by: _____   Authorization Date: _____

This form was created using WordPerfect InForms 1.0 from WordPerfect Corporation.

Aged Listing - Accounts Receivable

Date _____

Date	Invoice #	Account #	Account Name	30 Days	60 Days	90 + Days	TOTAL
			TOTALS				

This form was created using WordPerfect InForms 1.0 from WordPerfect Corporation

Aged Listing - Accounts Payable

Date: _____

ACCOUNT	AMOUNT	CURRENT	30-60 DAYS	60-90 DAYS	90 + DAYS	COMMENTS

TOTALS | | | | | |

GRAND TOTAL

This form was created using WordPerfect InForms 1.0 from WordPerfect Corporation

Accounts Receivable

Period Ending: _____

Inv Date	Invoice #	Account #	Account Name	30 Days	60 Days	90 + Days	TOTAL

Totals: _____ _____ _____ _____

Grand Total Due: _____

This form was created using WordPerfect InForms 1.0 by WordPerfect Corporation

Accounts Payable

Period Ending: _____

Inv Date	Invoice #	Account #	Account Name	30 Days	60 Days	90 + Days	Total

Totals: _____ _____ _____ _____

Grand Total Due: _____

This form was created in WordPerfect InForms 1.0 by WordPerfect Corporation

INVOICE

SOLD TO:

INVOICE DATE	INVOICE NUMBER
P.O. NUMBER	SALESPERSON
SHIP TO:	

Merchandise Ordered

ORDER NO.	DATE SHIPPED	SHIPPED VIA	F.O.B. POINT	TERMS

QTY ORDERED	B/O	QTY SHIPPED	DESCRIPTION	UNIT PRICE	TOTAL

Comments

Sub Total	
Sales Tax	
TOTAL	

This form was created using WordPerfect InForms 1.0 from WordPerfect Corporation

Purchase Order

Vendor:

Bill To:

Ship To:

Purchase Order Number and Vendor Part
Number (if specified) Must Appear on the
Packing Slip and Invoice.

P.O. NUMBER	P.O. DATE	BUYER	VENDOR NO.	TERMS	SHIP VIA

ITEM NUMBER	DESCRIPTION	QUANTITY	UNIT COST	EXTENDED COST
			TOTAL	

Notes

Authorized Signature

This form was created using WordPerfect InForms 1.0 from WordPerfect Corporation

Cash Receipt

Date: _____

Received From: _____

For the Sum of: _____ Dollars

For:

Method of Payment

☐   **Cash**

☐   **Check**

☐   **Money Order**

Received By: _____

Thank You

This form was created using WordPerfect InForms 1.0 from WordPerfect Corporation

Payment Past Due Notice   Date _____

To

Your account, listed below, is past due. As we have had no reply to previous correspondence, we must ask you to send the amount owing immediately. If you have a question or problem with the billing, please call us immediately

_____   _____   _____
Invoice Date   Invoice Number   Amount Due

Your Response

☐ We enclose payment of   _____   **Comments**

☐ Payment was made on   _____

Check Number   _____

This form was created using WordPerfect InForms 1.0 from WordPerfect Corporation

APPENDIX B

Information Resources

American Institute of Certified Public Accountants, 1211 Avenue of the Americas, New York, NY 10036; 212-575-3655. The national trade association of CPAs.

American Women's Economic Development Corporation, 60 East 42nd Street, New York, NY 10165, 212-692-9100. Fee-based advisory service. Call 800-222-2933 or 800-442-2933 for Alaska, Hawaii, and New York.

Apple Computer local users' groups can be reached via a referral number: 800-538-9696, ext. 500. Nonprofit organizations made up of Apple Computer enthusiasts are located all over the country. They are a source of free advice on computers and software, and they offer personal help in making your system work at its full capability.

Business Radio Network, 888 Garden of the Gods Road, Colorado Springs, CO 80907; 719-528-7040 or 800-321-2468. Information on nationally syndicated business radio shows.

Copyright information: 202-707-0700 (Library of Congress). Information specialists are available on weekdays from 8:30 A.M. to 5:00 P.M.; recorded information can be accessed 24 hours a day. If you know what forms or circulars you want, call the Forms Hotline at 202-707-9100 (24-hour answering service).

Council of Better Business Bureaus, Inc., National Headquarters, 4200 Wilson Boulevard, Suite 800, Arlington, VA 22203; 703-276-0100.

Environmental Protection Agency, Washington, DC; 202-260-7751.

Federal Communication Commission, information line for the Telephone Consumer Protection Act: 202-632-7554.

Federal Information Center: 301-722-9098. This Maryland number can provide you with information numbers within the federal government, many of them regional and toll-free.

Federal Trade Commission, Washington, DC; 202-326-2222.

Insurance Information Institute, 110 William Street, New York, NY 10038; 212-669-9200. Business and Consumer Hotline: 800-331-9146; National Consumer's Helpline: 800-942-4242. Advice, consultation, and publications funded by insurance companies.

Internal Revenue Service Taxpayer Hotline, Taxpayer Information and Education Branch, Taxpayer Service Division, Department of the Treasury, 1111 Constitution Avenue, NW, Washington, DC 20274; 800-829-1040 (information and assistance), 800-829-FORM (forms and other publications).

International Franchise Association, 1350 New York Avenue, NW, Suite 900, Washington, DC 20005; 202-628-8000. An organization of over 800 franchisors.

National Association for the Cottage Industry, P.O. Box 14850, Chicago, IL 60614; 314-939-6490 or 312-871-4900. Membership fee: $45. Telephone advice, publications, meetings, and workshops for the home business owner.

National Association of Credit Management, 8815 Centre Park Drive, Suite 200, Columbia, MD 21045; 301-740-5560. Credit information for small businesses.

National Association for the Self-Employed, 2121 Precinct Line Road, Hurst, TX 76054; 800-827-9990. Membership fee: $48. Newsletter, travel service, credit union, product discounts, and group auto, medical, and property insurance plans for the self-employed.

National Business Incubation Association, One President Street, Athens, OH 45701; 614-593-4331. An association representing the interests of the incubator industry, centers that help small businesses begin and survive the start-up phase.

National Federation of Independent Businesses, 600 Maryland Avenue, SW, Suite 700, Washington, DC 20024; 202-554-9000. Or: 150 West 20th Avenue, San Mateo, CA 94403; 415-341-7441. Annual donation of $75 to $1,000. A 570,000-member independent business advocacy group that lobbies for free-enterprise interests.

National Foundation of Consumer Credit, 8701 Georgia Avenue, Silver Spring, MD 20910; 301-589-5600. Referral hotline: 800-388-2227. An association representing 500 consumer credit counseling services nationally.

National Small Business United, 1155 15th Street, NW, Washington, DC 20005; 202-293-8830. Membership fee starts at $75. A 50,000-member advocacy group for small business interests. Newsletter, seminars, conferences, and group insurance.

National Venture Capital Association, 1655 North Fort Myer Drive, Suite 700, Arlington, VA 22209; 202-528-4370. The national trade association for venture capital firms.

Patent, trademark, and service mark information: 703-557-4636 (Department of Commerce recording).

Service Corps of Retired Executives (SCORE), 1030 15th Street, NW, Washington, DC 20005; 800-827-5722 or 202-653-6958/6279. SBA-sponsored retired executives offer free counseling.

Small Business Administration *Directory of Business Development Publications* is available from: SBA Publications, P.O. Box 1000, Fort Worth, TX 76119.

Small Business Administration, Office of Small Business Loans, 1441 L Street, NW, Washington, DC 20416; 202-653-6570.

Software Publishers Association, 1730 M Street, NW, Washington, DC 20036; 202-452-1600. Guidance on the legal use of software products.

APPENDIX C

Supplies and Software, Books and Other Printed Materials

Business Envelope Manufacturers, Inc., 900 Grand Boulevard, Deer Park, NY 11729; 800-275-4400 or 516-667-8500; Fax 516-586-5988. Sells envelopes, labels, and stationery inexpensively.

Byte, P. O. Box 555, Hightstown, NJ 08520; 800-257-9402. A computer user magazine for all the major operating platforms.

Consultant's National Resource Center, P. O. Box 430, Clear Spring, MD 21722; 301-791-9332. Books, periodicals, software, and other information for consultants and small business owners.

Entrepreneur, 2392 Morse Avenue, Irvine, CA 92714; 800-421-2300. Business plans for a wide range of business ideas are available at a nominal cost.

EZ Legal Books, 384 South Military Trail, Deerfield Beach, FL 33442; 305-480-8933/Fax 305-480-8906. A series of perforated forms books: *Records Organizer, Personnel Director, Credit Manager, Corporate Secretary,* and *301 Legal Forms and Agreements.*

Gale Research, Inc., 835 Penobscot Building, Detroit, MI 48226-4094; 800-223-4253 or 313-961-2242. Publishes a line of extensive and expensive (several hundred dollars) directories to virtually everything (associations, other directories, information industry, and so on).

Home Office Computing: Building Better Businesses With Technology, Scholastic, Inc., 555 Broadway, New York, NY 10012. Subscription information: 800-288-7812. The monthly magazine of the home office movement and the preeminent ongoing source of useful information about working at home. Its BizFAX service (800-227-5638) provides immediate reprints by fax for a fee. For reprints, Reprint Manager, Home Office Computing, 411 Lafayette St., New York, NY 10003; 612-633-0578; Fax 612-633-1862.

Information USA, an exhaustive guide to finding the information you need within the federal government. Written by Matthew Lesko and published by Viking-Penguin, New York. Check your library or bookstore.

Jeffrey Lant's Sure-Fire Business Success Catalog, P. O. Box 382767, Cambridge, MA 02238; 617-547-6372; Fax 617-547-0061. A comprehensive collection of how-to publications and tapes on every subject imaginable, each with a 30-day money-back guarantee.

MacConnection, 14 Mill Street, Marlow, NH 03456; 800-800-2222. A direct supplier of computer software and peripherals for the Macintosh.

MacUser, P. O. Box 52461, Boulder, CO 80321-2461; 800-627-2247. A user magazine for the Apple Macintosh family of computers.

Macworld, Subscription Department, P. O. Box 51666, Boulder, CO 80321-1666, 800-234-1038. A user magazine for the Apple Macintosh family of computers.

Paper Direct, 205 Chubb Avenue, Lyndhurst, NJ 07071; 800-A-PAPERS. A direct supplier of specialty papers for printing letterhead, business cards, brochures, presentation products, and so on, on your laser printer.

PC Computing, P. O. Box 50253, Boulder, CO 80321-0253. A computer user magazine for the IBM and compatible platforms—less technical than *PC Magazine.*

PC Connection, 6 Mill Street, Marlow, NH 03456; 800-800-5555. A direct supplier of computers, software, and peripherals for PCs and clones.

PC Magazine, P. O. Box 51524, Boulder, CO 80321-1524; 800-289-0429. A computer user magazine for the IBM and compatible platforms.

PC World, Subscription Department, P. O. Box 51833, Boulder, CO 80321-1833. A computer user magazine for the IBM and compatible platforms.

Power Up! P. O. Box 7600, San Mateo, CA 94403-7600; 800-851-2917. A direct supplier of software and specialty papers for printing letterhead, business cards, brochures, presentation products, and so on, on your laser printer.

Quill, 100 Schelter Road, Lincolnshire, IL 60069-3621; 909-988-3200 far west; 708-634-4800 midwest and midsouth; 404-479-6100 southeast; 717-272-6100 northeast. A direct supplier of office supplies, equipment, and printed materials for the office.

Reliable Home Office, P. O. Box 1501, Ottawa, IL 61350-9916; 800-869-6000. A direct supplier of quality home office furnishings and equipment.

The Drawing Board, P. O. Box 2944, Hartford, CT 06104-2944; 800-527-9530. A direct supplier of printed materials for the home office.

Windows Magazine, P. O. Box 58647, Boulder, CO 80321-8647. A computer user magazine for the IBM and compatible Windows operating environment.

APPENDIX D

Computer and Software Companies' User-Assistance Telephone Numbers

Abaton Technology	415-683-2226	Digital Research	408-646-6464
Adaptec, Inc.	408-945-2550	Dow Jones News Retrieval	609-452-1511
Adobe Systems, Inc.	415-961-0911	Electronic Arts	415-572-2787
Aldus Corporation	206-622-5500	Enable	800-766-7079
Amdex	408-435-2832	Epson America	213-782-0770
American Small Business	918-825-4844	Forth, Inc.	310-372-8493
AST Research	714-727-9630	Funk Software, Inc.	617-497-6339
Aston-Tate	408-438-5300	Genesis Microsystems	707-542-5000
Atari	408-745-2098	Hayes	404-441-1617
Autodesk, Inc.	800-445-5415	Hercules Computer	
Black Box Corporation	412-746-5565	Technologies	510-540-0749
Bloc Development	305-567-9931	Hewlett-Packard	800-752-0900
Boca Research, Inc.	407-997-6227	Hitachi Sales Corporation	800-447-2882
Borland International	408-438-5300	IBM	800-772-2227
Broderbund Software	415-382-4700	IBM Software Support	800-237-5511
Canon USA, Inc.	800-828-4040	Infocom, Inc.	415-329-7699
Central Point Software	503-690-8080	Intel Corporation	800-538-3373
Central Point Software		Intuit	415-322-0440
(Macintosh)	503-690-9440	Iomega Corporation	801-778-3000
Claris	408-727-9054	Irwin Magnetic Systems	800-348-6242
CMS Enhancements	714-222-6000	Javelin Software Corporation	617-890-8080
Commodore	215-431-9100	Lotus Development	800-223-1662
CompuServe	614-457-8650	Microrim	206-649-9500
Computer Associates	408-432-1764	Microsoft	206-635-7200
Corel Corporation (DRAW)	613-728-1990	Okidata	800-654-3282
Corel Corporation (SCSI)	613-728-1010	Paradise	800-832-4778
Cosmos	206-643-9898	Plus	900-740-4433
Cumulus Corporation	216-464-2211	Quadram Products Group	404-564-5699
DAC Software	214-248-0305	QVS	800-622-9606
Data Transformations	303-832-1501	Reality Technologies, Inc.	215-277-7600
Delrina	416-441-3086	Software Publishing	415-962-8910
	FormFlow;	Toshiba	800-631-3811
	416-441-0921	Western Digital	800-832-4778
	WinFaxPro	WordPerfect	800-321-5906
Digital Communications	800-631-4171		

APPENDIX E

Business Use of Your Home, IRS Publication 587

Publication 587
Cat. No. 15154T

Department
of the
Treasury

**Internal
Revenue
Service**

Business Use
of Your Home

For use in preparing
1993 Returns

Contents

Important Reminder

Form 8829. If you file Schedule C, *Profit or Loss From Business,* with your Form 1040, you must use Form 8829, *Expenses for Business Use of Your Home,* to determine your deduction for business use of your home.

Introduction

You must meet specific tests to take a deduction for the business use of your home. Even if you meet these tests, your deduction may be limited. This publication explains the requirements for taking the deduction and how to figure the limit. A worksheet at the end of this publication will help you figure the limit on the amount you can deduct.

The term *home* includes a house, apartment, condominium, mobile home, or boat. It also includes structures on the property, such as an unattached garage, studio, barn, or greenhouse. However, it does not include any part of your property used exclusively as a hotel or inn.

The publication is written for those who prepare their own returns. It does not discuss renting out your home, part of your home, or vacation property. For information about renting out your property, see Publication 527, *Residential Rental Property.*

The rules in this publication apply to individuals, trusts, estates, partnerships, and S corporations. They do not apply to corporations, other than S corporations. There are no special rules for the business use of a home by a partner or S corporation shareholder.

Useful Items
You may want to see:

☐ **523** Selling Your Home
☐ **534** Depreciation
☐ **551** Basis of Assets
☐ **583** Taxpayers Starting a Business
☐ **946** How to Begin Depreciating Your Property

Form (and Instructions)
☐ **2106** Employee Business Expenses

☐ **4562** Depreciation and Amortization

☐ **8829** Expenses for Business Use of Your Home

Ordering publications and forms.

To order free publications and forms, call our toll-free telephone number 1–800–TAX–FORM (1–800–829–3676). You can also write to the IRS Forms Distribution Center nearest you. Check your income tax package for the address.

Use Tests

Whether you are an employee or self-employed, you generally cannot deduct expenses for the business use of your home. But you can take a limited deduction for its business use if you use part of your home *exclusively* and *regularly:*

1) As the principal place of business for any trade or business in which you engage,

2) As a place to meet or deal with patients, clients, or customers in the normal course of your trade or business, or

3) In connection with your trade or business, if you are using a separate structure that is not attached to your house or residence.

Employee use. Even if you meet the exclusive and regular use tests, you *cannot* take any deduction for the business use of your home if you are an employee and either of the following situations apply to you.

1) The business use of your home is not for the convenience of your employer. Whether your home's business use is for your employer's convenience depends on all the facts and circumstances. However, business use is not considered for your employer's convenience merely because it is appropriate and helpful.

2) You rent all or part of your home to your employer and use the rented portion to perform services as an employee.

Trade or business use. You must use your home in connection with a trade or business to take a deduction for its business use. If you use your home for a profit-seeking activity that is not a trade or business, you cannot take a deduction for its business use.

Example. You use part of your home exclusively and regularly to read financial periodicals and reports, clip bond coupons, and do similar activities for your own investments. You do not make investments as a broker or dealer. Therefore, your activities are not a trade or business and you cannot take a deduction for the business use of your home.

Exclusive Use

"Exclusive use" means only for business. If you use part of your home as your business office and also use it for personal purposes, you do not meet the exclusive use test.

Example. You are an attorney. You use a den in your home to write legal briefs and prepare client tax returns. You also use the den for personal purposes. Therefore, you cannot claim a business deduction for using it.

Exceptions to Exclusive Use

There are two exceptions to the exclusive use test:

The use of part of your home for the storage of inventory, and

The use of part of your home as a day-care facility, discussed later under *Day-Care Facility.*

Storage of Inventory. You can deduct expenses that relate to the use of part of your home for the storage of inventory, if you meet all of the following five tests.

1) You must keep the inventory for use in your trade or business.

2) Your trade or business must be the wholesale or retail selling of products.

3) Your home must be the only fixed location of your trade or business.

4) You must use the storage space on a regular basis.

5) The space you use must be a separately identifiable space suitable for storage.

Example. Your home is the sole fixed location of your business of selling mechanics' tools at retail. You regularly use half of your basement for inventory storage and sometimes use it for personal purposes. The expenses for the storage space are deductible even though you do not use this part of your basement exclusively for business.

Regular Use

"Regular use" means on a continuing basis. Occasional or incidental business use of part of your home does not meet the regular use test even if that part is used for no other purpose.

Principal Place of Business

You can have a principal place of business for each trade or business in which you engage. For example, a teacher's principal place of business is the school. If the teacher also engages in retail selling and uses a part of the home as the principal place for retail selling, expenses for this business use of the home may be deductible.

You can have more than one business location, including your home, for a single trade or business. To deduct expenses for the business use of your home, you must determine that it is your principal place of business for that trade or business based on all the facts

and circumstances. The two primary factors are:

1) The relative importance of the activities performed at each business location; and

2) The amount of time spent at each location.

A comparison of the relative importance of the activities performed at each business location depends on the characteristics of each business. If the nature of your business requires that you meet or confer with clients or patients, or requires that you deliver goods or services to a customer, the place where that contact occurs must be given great weight in determining where the most important activities are performed. Performance of necessary or essential activities in your home office (such as planning for services or the delivery of goods, or the accounting or billing for those activities or goods) is not controlling.

In addition to comparing the relative importance of the activities performed at each business location, you should also compare the amount of time spent on business at your home office with the amount of time spent on business at other locations. The time consideration is particularly significant when a comparison of the importance of the activities performed at each business location yields no clear answer to the location of your principal place of business. This may happen when you perform income-generating activities at both your home office and some other location.

Example 1. Jane Williams is an anesthesiologist. Her only office is a room in her home used regularly and exclusively to contact patients, surgeons, and hospitals by telephone; to maintain billing records and patient logs; to prepare for treatments and presentations; to satisfy continuing medical education requirements; and to read medical journals and books.

Jane spends approximately 10 to 15 hours a week doing work in her home office. She spends 30 to 35 hours per week administering anesthesia and postoperative care in three hospitals, none of which provided her with an office.

The essence of Jane's business as an anesthesiologist requires her to treat patients in hospitals. The home office activities are less important to Jane's business than the services she performs in the hospitals. In addition, a comparison of the 10 to 15 hours per week spent in the home office to the 30 to 35 hours per week spent at the hospitals further supports the conclusion that Jane's home office is not her principal place of business. Therefore, she cannot deduct expenses for the business use of her home.

Example 2. Joe Smith is a salesperson. His only office is a room in his house used regularly and exclusively to set up appointments, store product samples, and write up orders and other reports for the companies whose products he sells.

Joe's business is selling products to customers at various locations within the metropolitan area where he lives. To make these sales, he regularly visits the customers to explain the available products and to take orders. Joe makes only a few sales from his home office. Joe spends an average of 30 hours a week visiting customers and 12 hours a week working at his home office.

The essence of Joe's business as a salesperson requires him to meet with customers primarily at the customer's place of business. The home office activities are less important to Joe's business than the sales activities he performs when visiting customers. In addition, a comparison of the 12 hours per week spent in the home office to the 30 hours per week spent visiting customers further supports the conclusion that Joe's home office is not his principal place of business. Therefore, he cannot deduct expenses for the business use of his home.

Example 3. Fred Jones, a salesperson, performs the same activities in his home office as Joe Smith in Example 2, except that Fred makes most of his sales to customers by telephone or mail from his home office. Fred spends an average of 30 hours a week working at his home office and 12 hours a week visiting prospective customers to deliver products and occasionally take orders.

The essence of Fred's business as a salesperson requires him to make telephone or mail contact with customers primarily from his office, which is in his home. Actually visiting customers is less important to Fred's business than the sales activities he performs from his home office. In addition, a comparison of the 30 hours per week spent selling to customers from the home office with the 12 hours per week spent visiting customers further supports the conclusion that Fred's home office is his principal place of business. Therefore, he can deduct expenses for the business use of his home.

Place To Meet Patients, Clients, or Customers

If you meet or deal with patients, clients, or customers in your home in the normal course of your business, even though you also carry on business at another location, you can deduct your expenses for the part of your home used exclusively and regularly for business. This applies only to an office visited by your clients. It does not apply to a room where you make or receive phone calls, but do not meet with clients.

Doctors, dentists, attorneys, and other professionals who maintain offices in their homes will generally meet this requirement.

The part of your home you use exclusively and regularly to meet patients, clients, or customers does not have to be your principal place of business.

Example. June Quill, an attorney, works 3 days a week in her city office. She works 2 days a week in her home office used only for business. She regularly meets clients there. Her home office qualifies for a business deduction because she meets clients there in the normal course of her business.

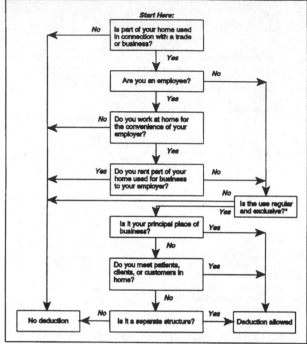

Figure A. Can You Deduct Business Use of the Home Expenses?

* Daycare and inventory storage are exceptions to the exclusive use test.

Separate Structures

You can deduct expenses for a separate free-standing structure, such as a studio, garage, or barn, if you use the structure exclusively and regularly for your business. The structure does not have to be your principal place of business or a place where you meet patients, clients, or customers.

Example. John Berry operates a floral shop in town. He grows the plants for his shop in a greenhouse behind his home. Since he uses the greenhouse exclusively and regularly in his business, he can deduct the expenses for its use subject to the deduction limit, explained later.

Business Part of Home Expenses

If you use part of your home for business and meet the requirements discussed earlier, you must divide the expenses of operating your home between personal and business use. This section explains how to divide each expense.

Some expenses you pay to maintain your home are directly related to its business use. Some are indirectly related, and some are unrelated. You can deduct all of your direct expenses and part of your indirect expenses, both subject to the limit discussed later. You may find it convenient to use the worksheet at the back of this publication to help figure your deductible expenses.

If you use the cash method of accounting, you can deduct only the expenses you pay during the tax year. You use the cash method of accounting if you deduct expenses when they are actually paid. However, a special rule for insurance is explained later under *Insurance.*

The total expenses you can deduct for business use of your home are limited to the gross income from the business use of your home, as discussed later under *Deduction Limit.*

Unrelated expenses benefit only the parts of your home that you do not use for business. These include repairs to personal areas of your home, lawn care, and landscaping. You cannot deduct unrelated expenses.

Direct Expenses

Direct expenses benefit only the business part of your home. They include painting or repairs made to the specific area or room used for business. You can deduct direct expenses in full.

Indirect Expenses

Indirect expenses are for keeping up and running your entire home. They benefit both the business and personal parts of your home. Examples of indirect expenses include:

Real estate taxes,

Deductible mortgage interest,

Casualty losses,

Rent,

Utilities and services,

Insurance,

Repairs,

Security systems, and

Depreciation.

You can deduct the business percentage of your indirect expenses.

Figuring the business percentage. To figure deductions for the business use of your home, find the business percentage. You can do this by dividing the area used for business by the total area of your home. You may measure the area in square feet. To figure the percentage of your home used for business, divide the number of square feet of space used for business by the total number of square feet of space in your home. If the rooms in your home are about the same size, figure the business percentage by dividing the number of rooms used for business by the number of rooms in the home. You can also use any other reasonable method to determine the business percentage.

Example 1. Your home measures 1,200 square feet. You use one room that measures 240 square feet for business. Therefore, you use one-fifth (240 ÷ 1,200), or 20%, of the total area for business.

Example 2. If the rooms in your home are about the same size, and you use one room in a five-room house for business, you use one-fifth, or 20%, of the total area for business.

Real Estate Taxes

If you own your home, you can deduct part of the real estate taxes on your home as a business expense. To figure the business part of your real estate taxes, multiply the real estate taxes paid by the percentage of your home used for business.

For more information on amounts allowable as a deduction for taxes, see Publication 530, *Tax Information for First–Time Homeowners.*

Deductible Mortgage Interest

If you pay deductible mortgage interest, you can generally deduct part of it as a business expense. To figure the business part of your deductible mortgage interest, multiply this interest by the percentage of your home used in business. You can include interest on a second mortgage in this computation. For more information on what interest is deductible, see Publication 936, *Home Mortgage Interest Deduction.*

Casualty Losses

If you have a casualty loss on your home or other property you use in business, you can deduct the business part of the loss as a business expense. Treat a casualty loss as an unrelated expense, a direct expense, or an indirect expense depending on the property affected.

If the loss is on property you do not use in your business, no business deduction is allowed for it (an unrelated expense).

If the loss is on property you use only in your business, the entire loss is a business deduction (a direct expense).

If the loss is on property you use for both business and personal purposes, only the business part is a business deduction (an indirect expense).

If your business property is completely destroyed (becomes totally worthless), your deductible loss is the adjusted basis of the property, minus any salvage value and any insurance or other reimbursement you receive or expect to receive. Figure the loss without taking into account any decrease in fair market value.

In a partial destruction, the deductible loss is the decrease in fair market value of the property or the adjusted basis of the property, whichever is less. You must reduce this amount by any insurance or other reimbursement you receive or expect to receive.

You must figure separately each individual identifiable property damaged or destroyed.

Casualty losses to nonbusiness use property are only deductible if you itemize deductions and the loss exceeds $100 plus 10% of your adjusted gross income. For a loss on property which you use both for business and nonbusiness purposes, these limits will apply only to the nonbusiness part.

If your business property is stolen, your deductible loss is your adjusted basis in the property, reduced by any insurance or other reimbursement you receive or expect to receive.

For information on a casualty loss to nonbusiness property, see Publication 547, *Nonbusiness Disasters, Casualties, and Thefts.*

Rent

If you rent, rather than own, a home and meet the requirements for business use of the home, you can deduct part of the rent you pay. To figure your deduction, multiply your rent payments by the percentage of your home used for business.

If you own your home, see *Depreciation,* later. You cannot deduct the fair rental value of your home.

Utilities and Services

Expenses for utilities and services, such as electricity, gas, trash removal, and cleaning services, are primarily personal expenses. However, if you use part of your home for business, you can deduct the business part of these expenses. Generally, the business percentage for utilities is the same as the percentage of your home used for business, but it may be different.

Example. Your electric bill is $400 for lighting, cooking, laundry, and television. Only the lighting is used for business. If $250 of your electric bill is for lighting and you use 10% of your home for business, then $25 is deductible as a business expense.

Telephone. The basic local telephone service charge, including taxes, for the first telephone line into your home is a nondeductible personal expense. However, charges for business long-distance phone calls on that line, as well as the cost of a second line into your home used exclusively for business, are deductible business expenses. You may deduct these expenses even if you do not qualify to deduct expenses for the business use of your home. Deduct these charges separately on the appropriate schedule. Do not include them in your home office deduction.

Insurance

You can deduct the cost of insurance that covers the business part of your home. However, if your insurance premium gives you coverage for a period that extends past the end of your tax year, you can deduct only the business percentage of the part of the premium that gives you coverage for your tax year. You can deduct the business percentage of the part that applies to the following year in that year.

Repairs

The cost of repairs and supplies that relate to your business, including labor (other than your own labor), is a deductible expense. For example, a furnace repair benefits the entire home. If you use 10% of your home for business, you can deduct 10% of the cost of the furnace repair.

Repairs keep your home in good working order over its useful life. Examples of common repairs are patching walls and floors, painting, wallpapering, repairing roofs and gutters, and mending leaks. However, repairs are sometimes treated as a permanent improvement. See *Permanent improvements,* later.

Security System

If you install a security system that protects all the doors and windows in your home, you can deduct the business part of the expenses you incur to maintain and monitor the system. You can also take a depreciation deduction for the part of the cost of the security system relating to the business use of your home.

Depreciation

The cost of property that can be used for more than 1 year, such as a building, a permanent improvement, or furniture, is a capital expenditure. You generally cannot deduct its entire cost in 1 year. Nor can you deduct the principal payments you make on your home mortgage or on improvements to your property because these payments are capital expenditures. However, you may be able to recover this cost by taking annual deductions for depreciation.

Land is not depreciable property. You generally cannot recover the cost of land until you dispose of it.

Permanent improvements. A permanent improvement increases the value of property, adds to its life, or gives it a new or different use. Examples of improvements are replacement of electric wiring or plumbing, a new roof, an addition, paneling, remodeling, or major modifications.

If you make repairs as part of an extensive remodeling or restoration of your home, the entire job is an improvement. You must carefully distinguish between repairs and improvements. You must also keep accurate records of these expenditures. These records will help you decide whether an expenditure is a deductible expense or a capital expenditure.

Example. You buy an older home and fix up two rooms as a hairdressing shop. You patch the plaster on the ceilings and walls, paint, repair the floor, put in an outside door, and install new wiring, plumbing, and other equipment. The plaster patching, painting, and floor work are repairs. However, since this work is done as part of a general plan to alter your home for business use, the amount you pay for this work is a capital expenditure. You cannot deduct it as a repair expense.

Basis adjustment. You must decrease the basis of your property by the amount of depreciation you could have deducted on your tax returns under the method of depreciation you selected. If you took less depreciation than you could have under the method you selected, you must decrease the basis by the amount you could have taken under that method.

If you deducted more depreciation than you should have, you must decrease your basis by the amount you should have deducted, plus the part of the excess deducted that actually decreased your tax liability for any year.

For more information, see Publication 551.

Depreciating your home. If you began to use part of your home for business before 1993, continue to use the same depreciation method you used in past tax years. See Publication 534 for complete information on depreciation.

If you began to use part of your home for business in 1993, depreciate that part as nonresidential real property under the modified accelerated cost recovery system (MACRS). Under MACRS, nonresidential real property is depreciated using the straight line method over 31.5 years, if you placed it in service

before May 13, 1993. Property placed in service on or after that date is depreciated using the straight line method over 39 years. However, if you had a binding contract to buy or construct the property before that date, the 31.5 year period may apply under a transitional rule. See Publication 946 for more information.

To figure depreciation on the business part of your home, you need to know:

1) The business-use percentage of your home,

2) The first month in your tax year for which you can deduct business use of your home expenses, and

3) The adjusted basis and fair market value of your home at the time you qualify for a deduction.

Adjusted basis of home. The adjusted basis of your home is generally its cost plus the cost of any permanent improvements that you made to it minus any casualty losses deducted in earlier tax years. For a discussion of adjusted basis, see Publication 551.

When you change part of your home from personal to business use, your basis for depreciation is the business use percentage times the lesser of:

1) The adjusted basis of your home (excluding land) on the date of change, or

2) The fair market value of your home (excluding land) on the date of change.

Depreciation table. If 1993 was the first year you used your home for business, you may figure your 1993 depreciation for the business part of your home by using the appropriate percentage from the following table.

Month of Tax Year First Used for Business	Percentages
1	3.042%
2	2.778%
3	2.513%
4	2.249%
5 (May 1-12)	1.984%
5 (May 13-31)	1.605%
6	1.391%
7	1.177%
8	0.963%
9	0.749%
10	0.535%
11	0.321%
12	0.107%

Note: If you began using the property for business on or after May 13, but had a binding contract to buy or construct the property before that date, you may be able to take a larger deduction. See Publication 946 for more information.

Multiply the depreciable basis of the business part of your home by the percentage from the table for the first month in your tax year that you use your home for business. See Tables A–7 and A–7a in Appendix A in Publication 534 for the percentages for all tax years of the recovery period.

Example. In April 1993, George Miller began to use one room in his home exclusively and regularly to meet clients. This room is 8% of the square footage of his home. He bought the home in 1980 for $100,000. He determined from his property tax records that his adjusted basis in the house (exclusive of land) is $90,000. The house had a fair market value of $165,000 in April. He multiplies his adjusted basis (which is less than fair market value) by 8%. The result is $7,200, his depreciable basis for the business part of the house.

George files his return based on the calendar year. April is the 4th month of his tax year. He multiplies his depreciable basis of $7,200 by 2.249% (.02249), the percentage from the table for the 4th month. The result is $161.93, his depreciation deduction for 1993.

Recordkeeping

You do not have to use a particular method of recordkeeping, but you must keep records that provide the information needed to figure your deductions for the business use of your home. You should keep canceled checks, receipts, and other evidence of expenses you paid.

Your records must show:

1) The part of your home you use for business,

2) That you use this part of your home exclusively and regularly for business as either your principal place of business or as the place where you meet or deal with clients or customers in the normal course of your business (however, see the earlier discussion, Exceptions to Exclusive Use), and

3) The depreciation and expenses for the business part of your home.

You must keep your records for as long as they are important for any Internal Revenue law. This is usually 3 years from the date the return was due or filed, or 2 years from the date the tax was paid, whichever is later.

Keep records that support your basis in your home for as long as they are needed to figure the correct basis of your original or replacement home. This includes records of any improvements to your home and any depreciation you are allowed because you maintained an office in your home. You may keep copies of Forms 8829 or the Publication 587 worksheets as records of depreciation.

For more information on recordkeeping, see Publication 583.

Deduction Limit

If your gross income from the business use of your home equals or exceeds your total business expenses (including depreciation), you can deduct all of your expenses for the business use of your home. But if your gross income from that use is less than your total business expenses, your deduction for certain expenses for the business use of your home is limited. The total of your deductions for otherwise nondeductible expenses, such as utilities, insurance, and depreciation (with depreciation taken last) cannot be more than your gross income from the business use of your home minus the sum of:

1) The business percentage of the otherwise deductible mortgage interest, real estate taxes, and casualty and theft losses (these three items are discussed more fully under *Indirect Expenses,* earlier), and

2) The business expenses that are not attributable to the business use of your home (for example, salaries or supplies).

If you are self-employed, do not include in (2) above your deduction for half of your self-employment tax.

You can carry forward to your next tax year deductions over the current year's limit. These deductions are subject to the gross income limit from the business use of your home for the next tax year. The amount carried forward will be allowable only up to your gross income in the next tax year from the business in which the deduction arose, whether or not you live in the home during that year.

If your total mortgage debt is more than $1,000,000 or your home equity debt is more than $100,000, your deduction may be limited. See Publication 936 to compute your deductible home mortgage interest.

For more information on nonbusiness casualty losses, see Publication 547. For information on business casualty losses, see *Casualty losses,* earlier.

Figuring deduction limit and carryover. If you are an employee or file Schedule F, *Profit or Loss From Farming,* use the worksheet at the back of this publication to figure your deduction limit. If you file Schedule C, figure your deduction limit on Form 8829.

Example. You are employed as an outside salesman. You meet the requirements for deducting expenses for the business use of your home. You use 20% of your home for this business. In 1993, your gross income, business expenses, and computation of expenses for the business use of your home are as follows:

Gross income from business	$ 6,000
Less: Deductible mortgage interest and real estate taxes (20% allowable as business part)	3,000
Balance	$ 3,000
Less: Business expenses other than for use of home (business phone and depreciation on office equipment)	2,000
Gross income limit	$ 1,000
Less: Other expenses allocable to business use of home:	
1) Maintenance, insurance, and utilities (20%)	800
Limit on further deduction	$ 200
2) Depreciation (20%)	1,600
Depreciation carried over to 1994 subject to income limit in 1994	$ 1,400

You can deduct all of the business part of your deductible mortgage interest and real estate taxes. You can also deduct all of the business part of your expenses for maintenance, insurance, and utilities, because the total is not more than the $1,000 gross income limit. But your deduction for depreciation for the business use of your home is limited to $200 for 1993 because of the gross income limit. The $1,400 balance can be carried forward and added to your depreciation for 1994, subject to your 1994 gross income limit.

More than one place of business. If part of the gross income from your trade or business is from the business use of part of your home and part is from a place other than your home, you must determine the part of your gross income from the business use of your home before you figure the deduction limit. In making this determination, consider the amount of time you spend at each location, the business investment in each location, and any other relevant facts and circumstances.

Where To Deduct

Deduct expenses for the business use of your home on Form 1040. Where you deduct these expenses on Form 1040 depends on whether you are:

1) An employee, or

2) A self-employed person.

Employees

As an employee, you must itemize deductions on Schedule A (Form 1040) to claim expenses for the business use of your home and any other employee business expenses. This applies to all employees, including outside salespersons.

If you have employee expenses for which you were not reimbursed, report them on line 19 of Schedule A. You must also fill out Form 2106, if:

1) You claim any travel, transportation, meal, or entertainment expenses, or

2) Your employer paid you for any of your job expenses reportable on line 19.

When your employer pays for your expenses, the payments generally should not be on your Form W-2 if you:

1) Account to your employer for the expenses, and

2) Are required to return, and do return, any payments not spent for business expenses.

If you account to your employer and your business expenses equal your reimbursement, do not report the reimbursement as income and do not deduct the expenses.

Accounting to employer. You account to your employer when you give your employer documentary evidence and an account book, diary, or similar statement to verify the amount, time, place, and business purpose of

each expense. You are also treated as accounting to your employer if your employer gives you a fixed allowance that is similar in form to an allowance specified by the federal government and you verify the time, place, and business purpose of each expense. See the Instructions for Form 2106 and Publication 463, *Travel, Entertainment, and Gift Expenses,* for more information.

Deductible mortgage interest. Although you generally can deduct expenses for the business use of your home on line 19 of Schedule A, do not include any deductible home mortgage interest on that line. Instead, deduct both the business and nonbusiness parts of this interest on line 9a or 9b of Schedule A.

If the home mortgage interest you can deduct on line 9a or 9b is limited by the home mortgage interest rules, you cannot deduct the excess as an employee business expense on line 19 of Schedule A, even though you use part of your home for business. To determine if the limits on home mortgage interest apply to you, see the instructions for Schedule A or Publication 936.

Real estate taxes. Deduct both the business and nonbusiness parts of your real estate taxes on line 6 of Schedule A. For more information on amounts allowable as a deduction for taxes, see Publication 530.

Casualty losses. Compute the deductible business portion of casualty losses in Section B of Form 4684, *Casualties and Thefts.*

Other expenses. If you file Form 2106, report the business part of your other expenses (utilities, maintenance, insurance, depreciation, etc.) that do not exceed the limit on line 4 of Form 2106. Add these to your other employee business expenses. Enter the total on line 11. This line instructs you to enter the total amount on line 19 of Schedule A, where it is subject to the 2% of adjusted gross income limit. If you do not file Form 2106, enter your total expenses directly on line 19 of Schedule A.

Business expenses not attributable to use of your home. If you have any employee business expenses not attributable to the use of your home, such as advertising, and you were not reimbursed for them, and you are not claiming travel, transportation, meal, or entertainment expenses, do not fill out Form 2106. Enter these expenses directly on line 19 of Schedule A, where they are subject to the 2% of adjusted gross income limit.

Example. You are an employee who works at home for the convenience of your employer. Your business use meets the requirements for deduction for business use of your home. Your employer does not reimburse you for any of your business expenses, and you are not otherwise required to file Form 2106.

As an employee, you do not have gross receipts, cost of goods sold, etc. You begin with gross income from the business use of your home, which you determine to be $6,000. Your total employee business expenses not attributable to the use of your home, such as advertising, supplies, and telephone use, total $3,000. Subtract this amount from your gross income from the business use of your home. Your balance is $3,000.

The percentage of expenses attributable to the business use of your home is 20%. Your allowable mortgage interest and real estate taxes are $2,000. Deduct this amount on the lines of your Schedule A for interest and taxes. Subtract this $2,000 from your balance of $3,000. Your gross income limit is $1,000. Your other expenses for the business use of your home cannot be more than $1,000.

The business part of your maintenance, insurance, and utilities for your home is $800. The business part of your depreciation is $1,600. Add $1,000 ($800 plus $200 of the depreciation expense) to the $3,000 for your other business expenses, and deduct the $4,000 total as a miscellaneous deduction on line 19, Schedule A. It is then subject to the 2% of adjusted gross income limit. Carry over the $1,400 of your depreciation expense that exceeds the deduction limit to the next tax year, subject to the deduction limit for that year.

Self-Employed Persons

If you are self-employed and file Schedule C, attach Form 8829 to your return. If you file Schedule F, report your entire deduction for business use of the home, up to the limit discussed earlier (line 32 if you used the worksheet) on line 34 of Schedule F. Write "Business Use of Home" on the line beside the entry.

Deductible mortgage interest. If you file Schedule C, enter all your deductible mortgage interest on line 10 of Form 8829. After you have figured the business part of the mortgage interest on Form 8829, subtract that amount from the total mortgage interest on line 10. The remainder is deductible on Schedule A, lines 9a and 9b. Do not deduct any of the business part on Schedule A. If the amount of interest you deduct on Schedule A for your home mortgage is limited, enter the excess on line 16 of Form 8829.

If you file Schedule F, include the business part of your deductible home mortgage interest with your total business use of the home expenses on line 34. You can use the worksheet at the back of this publication to figure the deductible part of mortgage interest.

To determine if the limits on qualified home mortgage interest apply to you, see the instructions for Schedule A or Publication 936.

Real estate taxes. If you file Schedule C, enter all your deductible real estate taxes on line 11 of Form 8829. After you have figured the business part of your taxes on Form 8829, subtract that amount from your total real estate taxes on line 11. The remainder is deductible on Schedule A, line 6. Do not deduct any of the business part of real estate taxes on Schedule A.

If you file Schedule F, include the business part of real estate taxes with your total business use of the home expenses on line 34. Enter the nonbusiness part of your real estate taxes on line 6 of Schedule A.

Casualty losses. To figure the amount of casualty loss that is not subject to the deduction limit, first reduce the loss by $100. Then reduce it by 10% of your adjusted gross income, figured without your gross income from the business use of your home and deductions attributable to that income. If you file Schedule F, carry the business part of casualty losses (line 31 if you use the worksheet) to Section B of Form 4684. If you are using Form 8829, refer to the specific instructions for lines 9 and 27, and carry the amount from line 33 to Section B of Form 4684.

Other expenses. Report the other home expenses that would not be allowable if you did not use your home for business (insurance, maintenance, utilities, depreciation, etc.), on the appropriate lines of your Form 8829. If you rent rather than own your home, include the rent you paid on line 20. If any of these expenses exceed the deduction limit, carry them over to next year. They will be subject to the gross income limit from the business use of your home next year.

If you file Schedule F, include your other home expenses that would not be allowable if you did not use your home for business (insurance, maintenance, utilities, depreciation, etc.), with your total business use of the home expenses on line 34 of Schedule F. If any of these expenses exceed the deduction limit, carry them over to the next year. They will be subject to the gross income limit from the business use of your home next year.

Business expenses not for the use of your home. Deduct in full your business expenses that are not for the use of your home (dues, salaries, supplies, certain telephone expenses, etc.) on the appropriate lines of Schedule C or Schedule F. Because these expenses are not for the use of your home, they are not subject to the deduction limit for business use of the home expenses.

Day-Care Facility

You can deduct expenses for using part of your home on a *regular* basis to provide day-care services if you meet the following requirements.

1) You must be in the trade or business of providing day care for children, for persons 65 or older, or for persons who are physically or mentally unable to care for themselves.

2) You must have applied for, been granted, or be exempt from having a license, certification, registration, or approval as a day-care center or as a family or group day-care home under applicable state law. You do not meet this requirement if your

application was rejected or your license or other authorization was revoked.

If you regularly use part of your home for day care, figure what part of your home is used for it, as explained earlier under *Business Part of Home Expenses*. If you use that part exclusively for day care, deduct all the allocable expenses, subject to the deduction limit.

If the use of part of your home as a day-care facility is regular, but *not* exclusive, you must figure what part of available time you actually use it for business. A room that is available for use throughout each business day and that you regularly use in your business is considered to be used for day care throughout each business day. You do not have to keep records to show the specific hours the area was used for business. You may use the area occasionally for personal reasons. However, a room you use only occasionally for business does not qualify for the deduction.

To find what part of the available time you actually use your home for business, compare the total business-use time to the total time that part of your home can be used for all purposes. You may compare the hours of business use in a week with the number of hours in a week (168). Or you may compare the hours of business use for the tax year with the number of hours in your tax year (8,760 in 1993).

Example 1. In 1993, Mary Lake uses her basement to operate a day-care business for children. Her home totals 3,200 square feet, and the basement includes 800 square or 25% of the total area of the home (800 ÷ 3,200). She uses the basement for day care an average of 12 hours a day, 5 days a week, for 50 weeks. During the other 12 hours, the family can use the basement. During the year, the basement is used for day care for a total of 3,000 hours (250 days × 12 hours). The basement can be used 8,760 hours (24 hours × 365 days) during the year. Only 34.25% (3,000 ÷ 8,760) of the expenses of her basement are business expenses. Mary may deduct 34.25% of any *direct* expenses for the basement. However, only 34.25% of the basement part of her *indirect* expenses are business expenses. Because the basement is 25% of the total area of her home, she can deduct 8.56% (34.25% of 25%) of her indirect expenses.

Mary completes Part I of Form 8829 as shown in Figure B.

Example 2. Assume the same facts as in Example 1 except that Mary also has another room that is available each business day for children to take naps in. Although she did not keep a record of the number of hours the room was actually used for naps, it was used for part of each business day. Since the room was available during regular operating hours each business day and was used regularly in the business, it is considered to be used for day care throughout each business day. Therefore, in figuring her expenses, 34.25% of any direct expenses of the basement and room are deductible. In addition, 34.25% of the indirect expenses of the basement and room are business expenses. Because the basement and room are 35% of the total area of her

7

Figure B.

Form **8829**	**Expenses for Business Use of Your Home**	OMB No. 1545-1266	

Form **8829**

Department of the Treasury
Internal Revenue Service   (T)

Expenses for Business Use of Your Home

▶ File only with Schedule C (Form 1040). Use a separate Form 8829 for each home you used for business during the year.
▶ See separate instructions.

OMB No. 1545-1266

19 93

Attachment
Sequence No. **66**

Name(s) of proprietor(s)

MARY LAKE

Your social security number

412 00 1234

Part I	Part of Your Home Used for Business

1	Area used regularly and exclusively for business, regularly for day care, or for inventory storage. See instructions	1	**800**
2	Total area of home	2	**3,200**
3	Divide line 1 by line 2. Enter the result as a percentage	3	**25** %

• For day-care facilities not used exclusively for business, also complete lines 4–6.
• All others, skip lines 4–6 and enter the amount from line 3 on line 7.

4	Multiply days used for day care during year by hours used per day .	4	**3,000** hr.
5	Total hours available for use during the year (365 days × 24 hours). See instructions	5	8,760 hr.
6	Divide line 4 by line 5. Enter the result as a decimal amount . . .	6	**.3425**
7	Business percentage. For day-care facilities not used exclusively for business, multiply line 6 by line 3 (enter the result as a percentage). All others, enter the amount from line 3 . . . . ▶	7	**8.56** %

home, Mary can deduct 11.99% (34.25% of 35%) of her indirect expenses.

Meals. If you provide food for your day-care business, do not include the expense as a cost of using your home for business. Claim it as a separate deduction on your Schedule C. You can deduct 100% of the cost of food consumed by your day-care recipients and 80% of the cost of food consumed by your employees as a business expense. But you can never deduct the cost of food consumed by you or your family.

If you deduct the cost of food for your day-care business, keep a separate record (with receipts) of your family's food costs.

Do not deduct the cost of meals for which you were reimbursed under the Child and Adult Care Food Program administered by the Department of Agriculture. The reimbursements are not included in your income to the extent you used them to provide food for eligible children.

Sale or Exchange of Your Home

If you sell your home and within 2 years buy one that costs more than the sale price of your old home, you must generally postpone recognizing any gain on the sale. But if in the year of sale you were able to deduct expenses for the business use of a part of your home, postpone recognizing gain only on the nonbusiness part. You must recognize any gain on the business part. Similarly, if you have a loss on the sale of your home, you can deduct the loss only on the business part. You cannot deduct any loss on the nonbusiness part.

To figure whether the cost of your new home is more than the sale price of your old

home for postponing recognition of gain, compare the nonbusiness part of your old home's sale price with the nonbusiness part of your new home's cost.

If your business use does not meet the requirements for the allowance of a business deduction for the year of sale, do not divide the gain on the sale between the business and nonbusiness parts. Under these circumstances, all your gain can be postponed if your purchase of another home meets all the other requirements for this treatment.

For more information on the sale or exchange of a home used partly for business, see Publication 523.

Depreciation. If you used any part of your home for business, you must adjust the basis of your home for any depreciation you were allowed for its business use, even if you did not claim it. If you took less depreciation than you could have under the method you selected, you must decrease the basis by the amount you could have taken under that method. For more information, see Publication 551.

If you used ACRS, MACRS, or some other accelerated method to figure your depreciation, some of the gain on the sale of the business part of your home may be treated as ordinary income.

Business Furniture and Equipment

Even if you do not qualify for a business use of the home deduction, you may be allowed to take a depreciation deduction or elect a section 179 deduction for furniture and equipment you use in your home for business or work as an employee.

There are different rules, explained later, for property you bought to use for business and property you previously used for personal purposes.

If you placed furniture or equipment in service in your business before 1993, you continue to claim depreciation deductions over its recovery period. See Publication 534 for more information.

Listed Property

If you use certain types of property, called *listed property,* in your home, special rules apply to the depreciation deductions you are allowed to take. Listed property includes any property of a type generally used for entertainment, recreation, and amusement (including photographic, phonographic, communication, and video recording equipment). Listed property also includes computers and related equipment unless they are used in a qualifying office in your home. If you use your computer in a qualifying office in your home, see *Property Bought for Business Use,* later. For a complete discussion of listed property, see Chapter 4 in Publication 534.

More-than-50% test. If you bought and placed in service listed property in 1993, special rules apply. More than 50% of your use of the property must be for business (including work as an employee) during the tax year for you to claim a section 179 or an accelerated depreciation deduction. If your business use is 50% or less, you cannot take a section 179 deduction. You must figure the depreciation for it using the Alternate Depreciation System (ADS) method (straight line), as explained under *ADS System,* in Publication 534.

If you use listed property more than 50% in a business in the tax year the property is placed in service but not in a later year of the recovery period, determine your depreciation for property placed in service before 1987 using Table C–16 in Appendix C of Publication 534. For property placed in service after 1986, you must use the ADS method. You determine your depreciation for the tax year and any subsequent tax years as if that listed property were not used more than 50% for business in the year it was placed in service.

In the tax year for which the use is 50% or less you may have to include in income (recapture) part of the depreciation claimed in earlier tax years. For more information on recapturing depreciation, see Publication 534.

Employee. If you use listed property, such as a home computer, in your work as an employee, it will not be treated as used for business for the more-than-50% test unless:

1) The use is for the convenience of your employer, and

2) The use is required as a condition of your employment.

"As a condition of your employment" means that the use of the property is necessary for you to properly perform your work. Whether the use of the property is required for this purpose depends on all the facts and circumstances. Your employer does not have to tell you specifically to have a computer in your home. Nor is a statement by your employer to that effect sufficient.

Investment time. The time you use the computer for investments does not count as business-use time for the more-than-50% test. However, if you meet the more-than-50% test, you can take into account the combined business and investment time to figure your depreciation deduction under MACRS. If you do not meet the test, you can use the combined time to figure the depreciation deduction under the straight line method.

If you use your computer to produce income from investments, see Publication 529, *Miscellaneous Deductions.*

Reporting and substantiation requirements. If you use listed property in your business, you must file Form 4562 to claim a depreciation or section 179 deduction. Begin with Part V, Section A of that form.

You must keep adequate records to prove your business use of any listed property.

Property Bought for Business Use

If you bought certain property to use in your business, you can elect to deduct all or part of its cost as a *section 179 deduction.* You can generally claim the section 179 deduction on depreciable tangible personal property bought for use in the active conduct of your business. You cannot take a section 179 deduction for the basis of the business part of your home.

The total cost you can deduct in 1993 cannot exceed $17,500. But there are certain provisions that can reduce this maximum.

The total cost that you can deduct each tax year is limited to your taxable income from the active conduct of your business during the tax year. Figure taxable income for this purpose in the usual way but without a deduction for the cost of the section 179 property or a deduction for half of the self-employment tax. See *How to Figure the Deduction,* in Chapter 2 of Publication 534, for more information.

You choose how much (subject to the limit) of the cost you want to deduct under section 179 and how much you want to depreciate. You do not have to deduct the full cost of the property. You can deduct part of its cost under section 179 and depreciate the rest over its recovery period. You can spread the section 179 deduction over several items of property in any way you choose as long as the total does not exceed the maximum allowable.

You elect to take the section 179 deduction by completing Part I of Form 4562.

In Part II of Form 4562 you depreciate, under MACRS, the cost of depreciable property bought in 1993 that is not deducted under section 179. Most business property in a home office is either 5–year or 7–year property under MACRS.

> *5–year property* includes computers and peripheral equipment, typewriters, calculators, adding machines, and copiers.

> *7–year property* includes office furniture and equipment such as desks, files, and safes.

Under MACRS, you get half a year of depreciation (which is referred to as the half-year convention) for the first year you use the property in your business unless you must use the mid-quarter convention. You use the mid-quarter if more than 40% of your depreciable basis is placed in service during the last 3 months of your tax year. Figure your depreciation by applying the appropriate percentage from the following table (which has been adjusted for the half-year convention) to each property's cost minus any section 179 deduction taken on the property.

	Percentages	
Recovery year	5–year property	7–year property
1	20%	14.29%
2	32%	24.49%
3	19.2%	17.49%
4	11.52%	12.49%
5	11.52%	8.93%
6	5.76%	8.92%
7		8.93%
8		4.46%

See Publication 534 for a discussion of the mid-quarter convention and for complete percentage tables.

Example 1. On September 16, 1993, Donald Kent bought a desk for $1,500 and three chairs for $475 to use in his office. His total bill was $1,975. For 1993, his taxable business income was $3,000 without any deduction for the office furniture. He can elect to take a section 179 deduction for all or any part of the cost of the furniture.

Example 2. Assume the same facts as in Example 1. However, Donald elects not to take a section 179 deduction for the furniture. The furniture is 7–year property. He multiplies $1,975, his cost, by 14.29% (.1429) to get his depreciation of $282.23.

Property Changed From Personal Use

If you began to use property in your home office that was used previously for personal purposes, you cannot take a section 179 deduction. You must determine the depreciation method that applies to the property.

If you began to use the property for personal purposes before 1981 and change it to business use in 1993, depreciate the property by the straight line or declining balance method based on salvage value and useful life.

If you began to use the property for personal purposes after 1981 and before 1987 and change it to business use in 1993, you generally depreciate the property under the accelerated cost recovery system (ACRS). However, if the depreciation under ACRS is greater than the depreciation under MACRS, you must depreciate it under MACRS.

If you began to use the property for personal purposes after 1986 and change it to business use in 1993, depreciate the property under MACRS.

For a discussion of ACRS, see Chapter 6 in Publication 534. For a discussion of the other depreciation methods, see Chapter 7 of Publication 534.

The basis for depreciation of property changed from personal to business use is the lesser of:

1) The adjusted basis of the property on the date of change, or

2) The fair market value of the property on the date of change.

Example 1. James Roe bought a desk for $1,000 on November 1, 1986. He began to use it in his home office on February 5, 1993, when it had a fair market value of $600. The depreciable basis of the desk is the fair market value of $600, which is less than its cost. Under ACRS, a desk is 5–year property. Under MACRS, it is 7–year property. Under ACRS, its depreciation is $90 (15%, the first year ACRS percentage for 5–year property, of $600). Under MACRS, its depreciation is $85.74 (14.29%, the first year percentage for 7–year property, of $600). Since the depreciation is greater using ACRS, James must use MACRS to depreciate his desk.

Example 2. Assume the same facts as in Example 1. However, the property is a computer. Under both ACRS and MACRS, a computer is 5–year property. Under ACRS, its depreciation is $90. Under MACRS, its depreciation is $120 (20%, the first year percentage for 5–year property, of $600). Since its depreciation is greater using MACRS, James must use ACRS to depreciate his computer.

Schedule C Example

The filled-in forms for Dan Stephens that follow show how to report deductions for the business use of your home if you file Schedule C. The first page of Schedule C, Form 8829, and Form 4562 are shown later. Only the expenses and information that relate to the business use of the home are discussed.

Schedule C. The following bold line references apply to Schedule C.

Line 13. Dan enters his deduction for depreciation of assets used in his home office on Form 4562, shown later, and on line 13.

When Dan began using part of the home for business in 1985, the furniture in it was 5–year property under ACRS. Tax year 1989 was the last year of the recovery period for that property. He has recovered his total depreciable basis in that property. He cannot deduct any depreciation for that property in 1993.

In March 1993 he bought a file cabinet for $600 and a copier for $2,500 to use in his business. He did not elect to take a section 179 deduction for either item. The file cabinet is 7–year property. The percentage from the table under *Property bought for business use,* earlier, for the first year for 7–year property is 14.29%. He multiplies $600 by .1429 to get $86 ($85.74 rounded to the nearest dollar). The copier is 5–year property. The percentage for the first year is 20%. He multiplies $2,500 by .20 to get $500.

Dan enters the $500 depreciation for the copier on Form 4562, line 14(b), because it is 5–year property. He enters the $86 depreciation for the file cabinet on line 14(c) because it is 7–year property. He enters the $586 total on line 13 of Schedule C.

Line 16b. This amount is the interest on installment payments for the business assets Dan uses in his home office.

Line 25. Because Dan had a separate telephone line in his home office that he used only for business, he can deduct the $347 expense for it.

Lines 28-30. On line 28, Dan totals all of his expenses other than those for the business use of his home, and then he subtracts that total from his gross income. He uses the result, on line 29, to figure the deduction limit on his expenses for the business use of his home. He enters that amount on line 8 of Form 8829, and then completes the form. He enters the amount of his home office deduction from line 34, Form 8829, on line 30 of Schedule C.

Form 8829, Part I. Dan began to use one room of his home exclusively and regularly to meet clients in August 1985. In Part I of Form 8829 he shows that, based on the square footage, the room is 10% of his home.

Form 8829, Part II. Dan uses Part II of Form 8829 to figure his allowable home office deduction.

Step 1. First, Dan figures the business part of expenses that would be deductible even if he did not use part of his home for business. Because these expenses ($4,500 deductible mortgage interest and $1,000 real estate taxes) relate to his entire home, he enters them in column (b) of lines 10 and 11. He then subtracts the $550 business part of these expenses (line 14) from his tentative business profit (line 8). The result, $28,295 on line 15, is the maximum amount he can deduct for his other home office expenses.

Step 2. Next, Dan figures his deduction for operating expenses. He paid $300 to have his office repainted. He enters this amount on line

18, column (a) because it is a direct expense. All of his other expenses ($400 homeowner's insurance, $1,400 roof repairs, and $1,800 heating and lighting) relate to his entire home. Therefore, he enters them in column (b) on the appropriate lines. He adds the $300 direct expenses (line 21) to the $360 total for indirect expenses (line 22) and enters the total, $660, on line 24. Because this amount is less than his deduction limit, he can deduct it in full. The $27,635 balance of his deduction limit (line 26) is the maximum amount he can deduct for depreciation.

Step 3. Next, Dan figures his allowable depreciation deduction for the business use of his home. In Part III of Form 8829, he determines that the basis of his home office (line 38) is $6,000. Because he began using the office in August 1985, it is 19–year real property under ACRS. 1993 is the ninth year of the recovery period and, because Dan files his return based on the calendar year, August is the eighth month of his tax year. Using Table C–6 in Appendix C of Publication 534, Dan finds that the depreciation percentage for the ninth year of the recovery period, for assets placed in service in the eighth month, is 4.5%. Therefore, his depreciation for 1993 (line 40) is $270. He enters that amount in Part II on lines 28 and 30. Because it is less than the available balance of his deduction limit (line 26), he can deduct the full amount of depreciation.

Step 4. Finally, Dan figures his total deduction for his home office by adding together his otherwise deductible expenses (line 14), his operating expenses (line 25), and depreciation (line 31). He enters the result, $1,480, on lines 32 and 34, and on Schedule C, line 30.

10

SCHEDULE C
(Form 1040)

Department of the Treasury
Internal Revenue Service   (T)

Profit or Loss From Business
(Sole Proprietorship)

▶ Partnerships, joint ventures, etc., must file Form 1065.

▶ Attach to Form 1040 or Form 1041.   ▶ See Instructions for Schedule C (Form 1040).

OMB No. 1545-0074

1993

Attachment
Sequence No. **09**

Name of proprietor	Social security number (SSN)
DAN STEPHENS	465 00 0001

A	Principal business or profession, including product or service (see page C-1)	B Enter principal business code
	TAX PREPARATION	(see page C-6) ▶ 7 6 3 3

C	Business name. If no separate business name, leave blank.	D Employer ID number (EIN), if any
	STEPHENS TAX SERVICE	

E	Business address (including suite or room no.) ▶ 821 UNION STREET
	City, town or post office, state, and ZIP code HOMETOWN IA 52761

F   Accounting method: (1) ☒ Cash   (2) ☐ Accrual   (3) ☐ Other (specify) ▶ ....

G   Method(s) used to value closing inventory: (1) ☐ Cost   (2) ☐ Lower of cost or market   (3) ☐ Other (attach explanation)   (4) ☒ Does not apply (if checked, skip line H)   Yes | No

H   Was there any change in determining quantities, costs, or valuations between opening and closing inventory? If "Yes," attach explanation . . . .

I   Did you "materially participate" in the operation of this business during 1993? If "No," see page C-2 for limit on losses. . .   ☒

J   If you started or acquired this business during 1993, check here . . . . ▶ ☐

Part I   Income

1	Gross receipts or sales. **Caution:** *If this income was reported to you on Form W-2 and the "Statutory employee" box on that form was checked, see page C-2 and check here* . . . . . . ▶ ☐	1	34,280
2	Returns and allowances	2	0
3	Subtract line 2 from line 1	3	34,280
4	Cost of goods sold (from line 40 on page 2)	4	0
5	**Gross profit.** Subtract line 4 from line 3	5	34,280
6	Other income, including Federal and state gasoline or fuel tax credit or refund (see page C-2) .	6	0
7	**Gross income.** Add lines 5 and 6 . . . . ▶	7	34,280

Part II   Expenses. Caution: *Do not enter expenses for business use of your home on lines 8–27. Instead, see line 30.*

8	Advertising	8	250	19	Pension and profit-sharing plans	19	
9	Bad debts from sales or services (see page C-3) . .	9		20	Rent or lease (see page C-4):		
				a	Vehicles, machinery, and equipment .	20a	
10	Car and truck expenses (see page C-3) . . .	10	1,266	b	Other business property . .	20b	
11	Commissions and fees . .	11		21	Repairs and maintenance . .	21	
12	Depletion	12		22	Supplies (not included in Part III) .	22	253
13	Depreciation and section 179 expense deduction (not included in Part III) (see page C-3) . .	13	586	23	Taxes and licenses	23	
				24	Travel, meals, and entertainment:		
14	Employee benefit programs (other than on line 19) . . .	14		a	Travel	24a	310
15	Insurance (other than health) .	15	750	b	Meals and entertainment . 320		
16	Interest:			c	Enter 20% of line 24b subject to limitations (see page C-4) . 64		
a	Mortgage (paid to banks, etc.) .	16a					
b	Other	16b	200	d	Subtract line 24c from line 24b .	24d	256
				25	Utilities	25	347
17	Legal and professional services	17	350	26	Wages (less jobs credit) . .	26	
18	Office expense	18	600	27	Other expenses (from line 46 on page 2)	27	267

28	**Total expenses** before expenses for business use of home. Add lines 8 through 27 in columns. . ▶	28	5,435
29	Tentative profit (loss). Subtract line 28 from line 7	29	28,845
30	Expenses for business use of your home. Attach **Form 8829**	30	1,480
31	**Net profit or (loss).** Subtract line 30 from line 29.		
	● If a profit, enter on **Form 1040, line 12,** and ALSO on **Schedule SE, line 2** (statutory employees, see page C-5). Fiduciaries, enter on Form 1041, line 3.	31	27,365
	● If a loss, you MUST go on to line 32.		

32   If you have a loss, check the box that describes your investment in this activity (see page C-5).
   ● If you checked 32a, enter the loss on **Form 1040, line 12,** and ALSO on **Schedule SE, line 2** (statutory employees, see page C-5). Fiduciaries, enter on Form 1041, line 3.
   ● If you checked 32b, you MUST attach **Form 6198.**

32a ☐ All investment is at risk.
32b ☐ Some investment is not at risk.

For Paperwork Reduction Act Notice, see Form 1040 instructions.   Cat. No. 11334P   **Schedule C (Form 1040) 1993**

11

Form **8829**	**Expenses for Business Use of Your Home**	OMB No. 1545-1266
Department of the Treasury Internal Revenue Service (T)	▶ File only with Schedule C (Form 1040). Use a separate Form 8829 for each home you used for business during the year. ▶ See separate instructions.	19**93** Attachment Sequence No. **66**

Name(s) of proprietor(s) *DAN STEPHENS*	Your social security number 465 00 0001

Part I   Part of Your Home Used for Business

1	Area used regularly and exclusively for business, regularly for day care, or for inventory storage. See instructions	1	*200*
2	Total area of home	2	*2,000*
3	Divide line 1 by line 2. Enter the result as a percentage	3	*10* %

- **For day-care facilities not used exclusively for business, also complete lines 4–6.**
- **All others, skip lines 4–6 and enter the amount from line 3 on line 7.**

4	Multiply days used for day care during year by hours used per day .	4	hr.
5	Total hours available for use during the year (365 days × 24 hours). See instructions	5	8,760 hr.
6	Divide line 4 by line 5. Enter the result as a decimal amount . . .	6	.
7	Business percentage. For day-care facilities not used exclusively for business, multiply line 6 by line 3 (enter the result as a percentage). All others, enter the amount from line 3 . . . . ▶	7	*10* %

Part II   Figure Your Allowable Deduction

		(a) Direct expenses	(b) Indirect expenses		
8	Enter the amount from Schedule C, line 29, **plus** any net gain or (loss) derived from the business use of your home and shown on Schedule D or Form 4797. If more than one place of business, see instructions			8	*28,845*
	See instructions for columns (a) and (b) before completing lines 9–20.				
9	Casualty losses. See instructions	9			
10	Deductible mortgage interest. See instructions .	10		*4,500*	
11	Real estate taxes. See instructions	11		*1,000*	
12	Add lines 9, 10, and 11	12		*5,500*	
13	Multiply line 12, column (b) by line 7	13	*550*		
14	Add line 12, column (a) and line 13			14	*550*
15	Subtract line 14 from line 8. If zero or less, enter -0- .			15	*28,295*
16	Excess mortgage interest. See instructions . .	16	.		
17	Insurance	17		*400*	
18	Repairs and maintenance	18	*300*	*1,400*	
19	Utilities	19		*1,800*	
20	Other expenses. See instructions	20		,	
21	Add lines 16 through 20	21	*300*	*3,600*	
22	Multiply line 21, column (b) by line 7	22	*360*		
23	Carryover of operating expenses from 1992 Form 8829, line 41 . .	23			
24	Add line 21 in column (a), line 22, and line 23			24	*660*
25	Allowable operating expenses. Enter the **smaller** of line 15 or line 24			25	*660*
26	Limit on excess casualty losses and depreciation. Subtract line 25 from line 15			26	*27,635*
27	Excess casualty losses. See instructions	27			
28	Depreciation of your home from Part III below	28	*270*		
29	Carryover of excess casualty losses and depreciation from 1992 Form 8829, line 42	29			
30	Add lines 27 through 29			30	*270*
31	Allowable excess casualty losses and depreciation. Enter the **smaller** of line 26 or line 30 .			31	*270*
32	Add lines 14, 25, and 31			32	*1,480*
33	Casualty loss portion, if any, from lines 14 and 31. Carry amount to **Form 4684**, Section B .			33	
34	Allowable expenses for business use of your home. Subtract line 33 from line 32. Enter here and on Schedule C, line 30. If your home was used for more than one business, see instructions ▶			34	*1,480*

Part III   Depreciation of Your Home

35	Enter the **smaller** of your home's adjusted basis or its fair market value. See instructions . .	35	*75,000*
36	Value of land included on line 35	36	*15,000*
37	Basis of building. Subtract line 36 from line 35	37	*60,000*
38	Business basis of building. Multiply line 37 by line 7	38	*6,000*
39	Depreciation percentage. See instructions	39	*4.5* %
40	Depreciation allowable. Multiply line 38 by line 39. Enter here and on line 28 above. See instructions	40	*270*

Part IV   Carryover of Unallowed Expenses to 1994

41	Operating expenses. Subtract line 25 from line 24. If less than zero, enter -0-	41	
42	Excess casualty losses and depreciation. Subtract line 31 from line 30. If less than zero, enter -0- .	42	

For **Paperwork Reduction Act Notice, see page 1 of separate instructions.**   Cat. No. 13232M   Form **8829** (1993)

Form **4562**	**Depreciation and Amortization** **(Including Information on Listed Property)**	OMB No. 1545-0172
Department of the Treasury Internal Revenue Service (T)	► See separate instructions. ► Attach this form to your return.	19**93** Attachment Sequence No. **67**

Name(s) shown on return   DAN STEPHENS

Identifying number   465-00-0001

Business or activity to which this form relates   TAX PREPARATION

Part I Election To Expense Certain Tangible Property (Section 179) (Note: *If you have any "Listed Property," complete Part V before you complete Part I.*)

1	Maximum dollar limitation (If an enterprise zone business, see instructions.)	**1**	$17,500
2	Total cost of section 179 property placed in service during the tax year (see instructions) . .	**2**	
3	Threshold cost of section 179 property before reduction in limitation	**3**	$200,000
4	Reduction in limitation. Subtract line 3 from line 2, but do not enter less than -0-	**4**	
5	Dollar limitation for tax year. Subtract line 4 from line 1, but do not enter less than -0-. (If married filing separately, see instructions.)	**5**	

(a) Description of property	(b) Cost	(c) Elected cost
6		

7	Listed property. Enter amount from line 26.	**7**	
8	Total elected cost of section 179 property. Add amounts in column (c), lines 6 and 7 . . .	**8**	
9	Tentative deduction. Enter the smaller of line 5 or line 8	**9**	
10	Carryover of disallowed deduction from 1992 (see instructions).	**10**	
11	Taxable income limitation. Enter the smaller of taxable income or line 5 (see instructions) . .	**11**	
12	Section 179 expense deduction. Add lines 9 and 10, but do not enter more than line 11 . .	**12**	
13	Carryover of disallowed deduction to 1994. Add lines 9 and 10, less line 12 ▶	**13**	

Note: *Do not use Part II or Part III below for listed property (automobiles, certain other vehicles, cellular telephones, certain computers, or property used for entertainment, recreation, or amusement). Instead, use Part V for listed property.*

Part II MACRS Depreciation For Assets Placed in Service ONLY During Your 1993 Tax Year (Do Not Include Listed Property)

(a) Classification of property	(b) Month and year placed in service	(c) Basis for depreciation (business/investment use only—see instructions)	(d) Recovery period	(e) Convention	(f) Method	(g) Depreciation deduction
14 General Depreciation System (GDS) (see instructions):						
a 3-year property						
b 5-year property		2,500	5	HY	200DB	500
c 7-year property		600	7	HY	200DB	86
d 10-year property						
e 15-year property						
f 20-year property						
g Residential rental property			27.5 yrs.	MM	S/L	
			27.5 yrs.	MM	S/L	
h Nonresidential real property				MM	S/L	
				MM	S/L	
15 Alternative Depreciation System (ADS) (see instructions):						
a Class life					S/L	
b 12-year			12 yrs.		S/L	
c 40-year			40 yrs.	MM	S/L	

Part III Other Depreciation (Do Not Include Listed Property)

16	GDS and ADS deductions for assets placed in service in tax years beginning before 1993 (see instructions)	**16**	
17	Property subject to section 168(f)(1) election (see instructions)	**17**	
18	ACRS and other depreciation (see instructions)	**18**	270

Part IV Summary

19	Listed property. Enter amount from line 25.	**19**	
20	**Total.** Add deductions on line 12, lines 14 and 15 in column (g), and lines 16 through 19. Enter here and on the appropriate lines of your return. (Partnerships and S corporations—see instructions)	**20**	856
21	For assets shown above and placed in service during the current year, enter the portion of the basis attributable to section 263A costs (see instructions)	**21**	

For Paperwork Reduction Act Notice, see page 1 of the separate instructions.   Cat. No. 12906N   Form **4562** (1993)

13

Instructions for the Worksheet

Part 1—Part of Your Home Used for Business

If you are an employee or file Schedule F, use the worksheet on the following page to figure your deduction limits for each type of expense. If you file Schedule C, use Form 8829 to figure the deductions and attach the form to your return. The amounts you enter on the worksheet may differ from your actual deductions for business expenses. Differences will be explained when they occur.

If you use the area-basis method, use lines 1 through 3 to figure the business use percentage. Enter the percentage on line 3. You may use any other reasonable method that accurately reflects your business use percentage. If you operate a day-care facility and you meet the exception to the exclusive use test for part or all of the area you use for business, you must figure the business use percentage for that area as explained under *Day-Care Facility,* earlier.

Part 2—Figure Your Allowable Deduction

If you file Schedule F, enter your total gross income from the business use of your home on line 4. This would generally be the amount on line 11 of Schedule F.

If you are an employee, enter your total wages which were from business use of the home on line 4.

Enter your total expenses paid for deductible mortgage interest, real estate taxes, and casualty losses on lines 5 through 7 of the worksheet. Under column (a), *Direct Expenses,* enter expenses which benefit only the business part of your home. Under column (b), *Indirect Expenses,* enter expenses which benefit the entire home. You generally enter 100% of the expense. However, if the business percentage of an indirect expense is different from the percentage on line 3, enter only the business part of the expense on the appropriate line in column (a), and leave that line in column (b) blank. See *Utilities and Services,* earlier.

Enter only the amounts that would be deductible whether or not you used your home for business. In other words, these amounts would normally be allowable as itemized deductions on Schedule A. Only the part of a casualty loss which exceeds $100 plus 10% of adjusted gross income is included here.

Multiply your total expenses by the business percentage from line 3. Enter the result on line 9. Add this amount to the total Direct Expenses and enter the total on line 10.

On line 11, enter any other business expenses that are not attributable to business use of the home. For employees, examples include travel, supplies and business telephone expenses. Farmers should generally enter their total farm expenses before deducting office in the home expenses. Do not enter the deduction for half the self-employment tax. Add these expenses to the line 10 amount, and enter the total on line 12. Subtract the line 12 amount from line 4, and enter the result on line 13. This is your gross income limit. You use it to determine whether you can deduct any of your other expenses for business use of the home this year. If you cannot, you will carry them over to next year.

If line 13 is zero, deduct your expenses for deductible home mortgage interest, real estate taxes, and casualty losses that would be deductible if you did not use your home for business. Also deduct any business expenses not attributable to use of your home on the appropriate lines of the schedule(s) for Form 1040 as explained earlier under *Where To Deduct.*

On lines 14 through 18, enter the total expenses for the business use of your home that would not be allowable if your home were not used for business. These include utilities, insurance, repairs, and maintenance. If you file Schedule F, they also include any part of your home mortgage interest that is more than the limits given in Publication 936. (If you are an employee, do not enter any excess home mortgage interest). In column (a), enter the expenses that benefit only the business part of your home (Direct Expenses). In column (b), enter the expenses which benefit the entire home (Indirect Expenses). Multiply line 19, column (b) by the business use percentage and enter this amount on line 20.

If you claimed a deduction for business use of your home on your 1992 tax return, subtract line 23 on your 1992 worksheet from line 22 on your 1992 worksheet. Enter this amount on line 21 of your 1993 worksheet. If the amount is less than zero, enter zero.

On lines 24 through 29, figure your limit on deductions for excess casualty losses and depreciation.

On line 25, figure the excess casualty loss by multiplying the business use percentage from line 3 by the part of casualty losses which would not be allowable if you did not use your

home for business ($100 plus 10% of your adjusted gross income).

On line 26, enter the depreciation deduction from Part 3 below.

On lines 27 through 29, figure your allowable excess casualty losses and depreciation.

If you claimed a deduction for business use of your home on your 1992 tax return, subtract line 29 on your 1992 worksheet from line 28 on your 1992 worksheet. Enter this amount on line 27 of your 1993 worksheet. If the amount is less than zero, enter zero.

On line 30 total all allowable business use of the home deductions.

On line 31, add the casualty losses shown on line 10 and line 29. This amount must be carried to *Form 4684.* See the instructions for that form for information on how to report these amounts.

Line 32 is the total amount (other than casualty losses) allowable as a deduction for business use of your home. If you file Schedule F, report this amount as an entry on line 34 of Schedule F and write "Business Use of Home" on the line beside the entry. Do not add the specific expenses into other line totals of Part II.

If you are an employee, see *Where To Deduct,* earlier, for information on how to claim the deduction.

Part 3—Depreciation of Your Home

Figure your depreciation deduction on lines 33 through 38. On line 33, enter the smaller of the adjusted basis or the fair market value of the property at the time you first used it for business. Do not adjust this amount for changes in basis or value after that date. Allocate the basis between the land and the building on lines 34 and 35. You cannot depreciate any part of the land. On line 37, enter the correct percentage for the current year from the tables in Publication 534. Multiply this percentage by the business basis to get the depreciation deduction. Enter this figure on line 38 and line 26. Complete and attach *Form 4562* to your return if this is the first year you used your home or an improvement or addition to your home in business.

Part 4—Carryover of Unallowed Expenses to 1994

Complete these lines to determine the expenses that must be carried forward to next year.

Table 1.   **Worksheet to Figure the Deduction for Business Use of Your Home**

PART 1—Part of Your Home Used for Business:

1) Area of home used for business .... 1)_____

2) Total area of home... 2)_____

3) Percentage of home used for business (divide line 1 by line 2)........................ 3)_____

PART 2—Figure Your Allowable Deduction:

4) Gross income from business (see instructions) .... 4)_____

	(a) Direct Expenses	(b) Indirect Expenses
5) Casualty losses	5)_____	_____
6) Deductible mortgage interest	6)_____	_____
7) Real estate taxes	7)_____	_____
8) Total of lines 5 through 7	8)_____	_____

9) Multiply line 8, column (b), by line 3... 9)_____

10) Add line 8, column (a), and line 9 .... 10)_____

11) Business expenses not from business use of home (see instructions) .... 11)_____

12) Add lines 10 and 11... 12)_____

13) Gross income limit. Subtract line 12 from line 4 .... 13)_____

14) Excess mortgage interest	14)_____	_____
15) Insurance..	15)_____	_____
16) Repairs and maintenance	16)_____	_____
17) Utilities...	17)_____	_____
18) Other expenses...	18)_____	_____
19) Add lines 14 through 18	19)_____	_____

20) Multiply line 19, column (b) by line 3 .... 20)_____

21) Carryover of operating expenses from 1992 (See Instructions) .... 21)_____

22) Add line 19, column (a), line 20, and line 21 .... 22)_____

23) Allowable operating expenses. Enter the **smaller** of line 13 or line 22 .... 23)_____

24) Limit on excess casualty losses and depreciation. Subtract line 23 from line 13 .... 24)_____

25) Excess casualty losses (see instructions) .... 25)_____

26) Depreciation of your home from line 38 below..................................... 26)_____

27) Carryover of excess casualty losses and depreciation from 1992 (See Instructions) .... 27)_____

28) Add lines 25 through 27 .... 28)_____

29) Allowable excess casualty losses and depreciation. Enter the **smaller** of line 24 or line 28 .... 29)_____

30) Add lines 10, 23, and 29 .... 30)_____

31) Casualty losses included on lines 10 and 29 (Carry this amount to **Form 4684**) .... 31)_____

32) Allowable expenses for business use of your home. (Subtract line 31 from line 30). See instructions for where to enter on your return .... 32)_____

PART 3—Depreciation of Your Home

33) Smaller of adjusted basis or fair market value of home (see instructions) .... 33)_____

34) Basis of land .... 34)_____

35) Basis of building (Subtract line 34 from line 33) .... 35)_____

36) Business basis of building (Multiply line 35 by line 3)..................................... 36)_____

37) Depreciation percentage (from applicable table or method) .... 37)_____

38) Depreciation allowable (multiply line 36 by line 37) .... 38)_____

PART 4—Carryover of Unallowed Expenses to 1994

39) Operating expenses. Subtract line 23 from line 22. If less than zero, enter –0–............... 39)_____

40) Excess casualty losses and depreciation. Subtract line 29 from line 28. If less than zero, enter –0–....................... 40)_____

List of Tax Publications for Individuals

General Guides

1 ...... Your Rights as a Taxpayer
17 ..... Your Federal Income Tax
225 .. Farmer's Tax Guide
334 .. Tax Guide for Small Business
509 .. Tax Calendars for 1994
553 .. Highlights of 1993 Tax Changes
595 .. Tax Guide for Commercial
          Fishermen
910 .. Guide to Free Tax Services
          (Includes a list of publications)

Specialized Publications

3 ...... Tax Information for Military
          Personnel (Including Reservists
          Called to Active Duty)
4 ...... Student's Guide to Federal
          Income Tax
54 ..... Tax Guide for U.S. Citizens and
          Resident Aliens Abroad
378 .. Fuel Tax Credits and Refunds
448 .. Federal Estate and Gift Taxes
463 .. Travel, Entertainment, and
          Gift Expenses
501 .. Exemptions, Standard Deduction,
          and Filing Information
502 .. Medical and Dental Expenses
503 .. Child and Dependent Care
          Expenses
504 .. Divorced or Separated Individuals
505 .. Tax Withholding and Estimated Tax
508 .. Educational Expenses
513 .. Tax Information for Visitors to the
          United States
514 .. Foreign Tax Credit for Individuals
516 .. Tax Information for U.S.
          Government Civilian Employees
          Stationed Abroad
517 .. Social Security and Other
          Information for Members of the
          Clergy and Religious Workers
519 .. U.S. Tax Guide for Aliens
520 .. Scholarships and Fellowships
521 .. Moving Expenses
523 .. Selling Your Home
524 .. Credit for the Elderly or the
          Disabled
525 .. Taxable and Nontaxable Income
526 .. Charitable Contributions
527 .. Residential Rental Property

529 .. Miscellaneous Deductions
530 .. Tax Information for First-Time
          Homeowners
531 .. Reporting Tip Income
533 .. Self-Employment Tax
534 .. Depreciation
537 .. Installment Sales
541 .. Tax Information on Partnerships
544 .. Sales and Other Dispositions of
          Assets
547 .. Nonbusiness Disasters, Casualties,
          and Thefts
550 .. Investment Income and Expenses
551 .. Basis of Assets
552 .. Recordkeeping for Individuals
554 .. Tax Information for Older
          Americans
555 .. Federal Tax Information on
          Community Property
556 .. Examination of Returns, Appeal
          Rights, and Claims for Refund
559 .. Survivors, Executors, and
          Administrators
560 .. Retirement Plans for the
          Self-Employed
561 .. Determining the Value of Donated
          Property
564 .. Mutual Fund Distributions
570 .. Tax Guide for Individuals with
          Income from U.S. Possessions
571 .. Tax-Sheltered Annuity Programs for
          Employees of Public Schools and
          Certain Tax-Exempt Organizations
575 .. Pension and Annuity Income
          (Including Simplified General Rule)
584 .. Nonbusiness Disaster, Casualty,
          and Theft Loss Workbook
587 .. Business Use of Your Home
590 .. Individual Retirement
          Arrangements (IRAs)
593 .. Tax Highlights for U.S. Citizens
          and Residents Going Abroad
594 .. Understanding The Collection
          Process
596 .. Earned Income Credit
597 .. Information on the United States-
          Canada Income Tax Treaty
721 .. Tax Guide to U.S. Civil Service
          Retirement Benefits
901 .. U.S. Tax Treaties

907 .. Information for Persons with
          Disabilities
908 .. Bankruptcy and Other Debt
          Cancellation
909 .. Alternative Minimum Tax for
          Individuals
911 .. Tax Information for Direct Sellers
915 .. Social Security Benefits and
          Equivalent Railroad Retirement
          Benefits
917 .. Business Use of a Car
919 .. Is My Withholding Correct for
          1994?
925 .. Passive Activity and At-Risk Rules
926 .. Employment Taxes for Household
          Employers
929 .. Tax Rules for Children and
          Dependents
936 .. Home Mortgage Interest Deduction
938 .. Real Estate Mortgage Investment
          Conduits (REMICs) Reporting
          Information
945 .. Tax Information for Those Affected
          by Operation Desert Storm
946 .. How To Begin Depreciating Your
          Property
947 .. Practice Before the IRS and Power
          of Attorney
1244 .. Employee's Daily Record of Tips
          and Report to Employers
1544 .. Reporting Cash Payments of Over
          $10,000
1546 .. How to use the Problem Resolution
          Program of the IRS

Spanish Language Publications

1SP .. Derechos del Contribuyente
556SP .. Revisión de las Declaraciones de
          Impuesto, Derecho de Apelación y
          Reclamaciones de Reembolsos
579SP .. Cómo Preparar la Declaración de
          Impuesto Federal
594SP .. Comprendiendo el Proceso de
          Cobro
596SP .. Crédito por Ingreso del Trabajo
850 .. English–Spanish Glossary of Words
          and Phrases Used in Publications
          Issued by the Internal Revenue
          Service

Tax forms, publications and instructions listed on the order blank

You can get the following forms, schedules, and instructions at participating banks, post offices, or libraries.

Form 1040
Instructions for Form 1040 & Schedules
Schedule A for itemized deductions
Schedule B for interest and dividend
income if over $400; and for answering the
foreign accounts or foreign trusts questions

Schedule EIC for the earned income credit
Form 1040A
Instructions for Form 1040A & Schedules
Schedule 1 for Form 1040A filers to report
interest and dividend income

Schedule 2 for Form 1040A filers to report
child and dependent care expenses
Form 1040EZ
Instructions for Form 1040EZ

You can photocopy the items listed below (as well as those listed above) at participating libraries or order them from the IRS.

Schedule 3, Credit for the Elderly or the
   Disabled for Form 1040A Filers
Schedule C, Profit or Loss From Business
Schedule C-EZ, Net Profit From Business
Schedule D, Capital Gains and Losses
Schedule E, Supplemental Income and
   Loss
Schedule F, Profit or Loss From Farming
Schedule R, Credit for the Elderly or the
   Disabled
Schedule SE, Self-Employment Tax
Form 1040-ES, Estimated Tax for
   Individuals
Form 1040X, Amended U.S. Individual

   Income Tax Return
Form 2106, Employee Business Expenses
Form 2119, Sale of Your Home
Form 2210, Underpayment of Estimated
   Tax by Individuals and Fiduciaries
Form 2441, Child and Dependent Care
   Expenses
Form 3903, Moving Expenses
Form 4562, Depreciation and Amortization
Form 4868, Application for Automatic
   Extension of Time To File U.S.
   Individual Income Tax Return
Form 5329, Return for Additional Taxes

Attributable to Qualified Retirement
   Plans, Annuities, and Modified
   Endowment Contracts
Form 8283, Noncash Charitable
   Contributions
Form 8582, Passive Activity Loss
   Limitations
Form 8606, Nondeductible IRA
   Contributions, IRA Basis, and
   Nontaxable IRA Distributions
Form 8822, Change of Address
Form 8829, Expenses for Business Use of
   Your Home

Page 16

*U.S. Government Printing Office: 1993 — 301-644/80002

APPENDIX F*

Getting Started and Installing IN THE BLACK

In The Black combines a business accounting system, a financial information system, and a personal finance organizer. It has a familiar Microsoft Windows based interface, and it speaks your language—your choice of either simple English or standard accounting terminology.

The Product Package

Your software package contains everything you need to install, register, learn, and run *In The Black,* including:

- A license agreement, which describes your rights and obligations in using the software.

- A registration card; for information about registering, see "Registering your software," later in this appendix

- One set of 3.5-inch high-density (1.44 MB) program disks and a coupon for ordering 3.5-inch double-density (720 K) or 5.25-inch high-density (1.2-MB) disks

- A business reply card for ordering the User Manual

- Forms catalog

- Customer Support Card

Hardware and Software Requirements

You need the following hardware and software to run *In The Black:*

- A computer with an 80386 or higher microprocessor
- 4 MB of random access memory (RAM)
- A hard disk with 11 MB of free space
- A 3.5-high-density or double-density drive or a 5.25-inch high-density disk drive
- A Microsoft Windows-compatible mouse or pointing device
- A VGA monitor
- MS-DOS version 3.1 or later
- Microsoft Windows 3.1

---

*Note that this Appendix applies to the cloth edition of this book, ISBN#0-471-59578-0, which contains diskettes.

You can improve your computer's performance by using:

- A processor with a speed of 25 MHz or faster
- More than 4 MB of RAM
- A Super VGA color monitor
- MS-DOS version 5.0 or later (recommended)
- Windows in 386 enhanced mode

How to Make a Backup Copy of Your Diskettes

Before you start to use the enclosed diskettes, we strongly recommend that you make backup copies of the originals. Making backup copies of your diskettes allows you to have a clean set of files saved in case you accidentally change a file or delete a file. Remember, however, that a set of backup diskettes is for your own personal use only. Any other use of the backup diskettes violates copyright law. Please take the time now to make the backup copies, using the instructions below:

If Your Computer Has Two Floppy Disk Drives:

1. Insert your DOS disk into drive A of your computer.
2. Insert a blank disk into drive B of your computer.
3. At the **A:>**, type **DISKCOPY A: B:** and press **ENTER**.
   You will be prompted by DOS to place the Source disk into drive A.
4. Place the first disk into Drive A.

Follow the directions on screen to complete the copy. When you are through, remove the disk from drive B and label it immediately. Continue to copy the rest of the diskettes using the same commands. Remove the original from drive A and store it in a safe place.

If Your Computer Has One Floppy Disk Drive:

1. Insert your DOS disk into drive A of your computer.
2. At the **A:\>**, type **DISKCOPY A: A:** and press enter.
   You will be prompted to place the source disk into drive A.
3. Place the first disk into Drive A.
4. When DOS has finished copying the source disk, you will then be prompted to insert the destination disk into Drive A.

Follow the directions on screen to complete the copy. When you are through, remove the disk from drive A and label it immediately. Continue to copy the rest of the diskettes using the same commands. Remove the original from drive A and store it in a safe place.

If Your Computer Has One Floppy Disk Drive and a Hard Disk:

If you have a hard disk computer, you can copy the files from the enclosed diskettes onto your hard disk in lieu of making a backup copy by following the installation instructions.

Installing IN THE BLACK

The Setup program creates the directory ITB on your hard drive and installs the program files there. You cannot simply copy *In The Black* program files directly to your hard drive because the files are compressed on the program disks. The Setup program also lets you create an In The Black program group and icons in Windows.

Note: Before you install the *In The Black,* locate the product serial number, which is on the product registration card. The hard disk drive that contains DOS (Disk Operating System)-typically, your "C" drive-must have at least 500k of free space for the installation program to run.

To Install IN THE BLACK:

Insert Setup Disk #1 in your floppy disk drive.

1. In the Windows Program Manager, choose **File: Run** . . .
2. Type a:\setup in the "Command Line," and click OK.
3. If your floppy disk drive is not a:, type the appropriate drive letter instead. For instance, type b:\setup.
4. Follow the instructions on the screen.
5. When you are prompted to do so, insert Disk #2. Click OK.

    Repeat this step for each of the remaining program disks.
6. Click OK to acknowledge the successful setup.

After you install *In The Black,* read the README.TXT.

The README.TXT will include tips and late breaking informations. **To read the README.TXT:** Double-click the "*In The Black* Readme" icon in the "In The Black" program group in Windows Program Manager.

Registering Your Software

Registering gives you access to Customer Support. Specifically, it lets you:

- Receive notification of *In The Black* product upgrades.
- Give feedback so that Microrim can improve the product for you in the future.

To register your copy of the program, do one of the following:

- Fill in the postage-paid registration card that comes with the product, and mail it to Microrim, Inc., Customer Service, 15395 SE 30th Place, Bellevue, WA 98007. Customer Service is $1.50 per minute for Wiley book purchasers.

- Fill in the postage-paid registration card and fax a copy of it to Microrim Customer Support. The fax number is listed on your registration card.

Getting Information about Your System

In The Black makes getting important system information easy. Without leaving the program, you can get information such as processor type, memory size, amount of free disk space, and system configuration to :

- Help you understand and use your support system resources more efficiently.
- Help Microrim Customer Support resolve problems in running your program.

To Obtain System Information

1. Choose **Help:System Information** . . .
2. Examine the displayed system information.

To view or edit system configuration files, such as CONFIG.SYS, WIN.INI or ITB.INI, click the button for that file. You will be in View Mode, which means you can't edit the file. If you want to change the file, choose **Edit-Mode** from the file window.

Note: Editing your configuration files is not advisable unless you thoroughly understand the effect of the changes. See Figure 1.

3. Click OK when you are done.

Figure 1.

Getting Customer Support

If you have problems using the program, you have several ways to get quick answers:

- Refer to *online help* for context-sensitive information about a command, form, register, or dialog box.
- Use *Quick Help* to answer a question about a particular option, button, or field.
- Refer to README.TXT; it contains program information not in the *User Manual*.

If none of these resources solves your problem, contact Microrim Customer Support.

To get Customer Support:

Be sure your registration number is at hand and that you are at your computer with *In The Black* running. Then call Customer Support at (206) 649-9300 between 7:00 A.M. and 4:00 P.M. (Pacific time) for assistance. You can also find the Customer Support number on the registration card that came with *In The Black,* or by choosing **Help:System Information** . . .

BIBLIOGRAPHY

Note: The Bibliography does not list each information source cited under the 150 individual business topics.

Alvarez, Mark. *The Home Office Book.* Woodbury, CT: Goodwood Press, 1990.

Ammer, Christine, and Dean S. Ammer. *Dictionary of Business and Economics.* New York: The Free Press, 1977.

Arden, Lynnie. *Franchises You Can Run from Home.* New York: John Wiley & Sons, Inc., 1990.

Argenti, Paul A. *The Portable MBA Desk Reference.* New York: John Wiley & Sons, Inc., 1994.

Attard, Janet. *The Home Office and Small Business Answer Book.* New York: Henry Holt, 1993.

Basic Facts about Trademarks. Washington, DC: U.S. Department of Commerce, 1992.

Brabec, Barbara. *Homemade Money.* Whitehall, VA: Betterway Publications, Inc., 1989.

Business Use of a Car. Publication 917. Washington, DC: Internal Revenue Service, 1993. (Revised annually.)

Business Use of Your Home. Publication 587. Washington, DC: Internal Revenue Service, 1993. (Revised annually.)

"Catching Up on Homework." *Home Office Computing,* June 1993, p. 16.

Charland, William A., Jr. *Career Shifting.* Holbrook, MA: Bob Adams, Inc., 1993.

Chatzky, Jean Sherman. "Body Slammed." *Smart Money,* December 1993, pp. 117–123.

——————. "Everything You Ever Needed to Know About Insurance, But Were Too Confused to Ask." *Smart Money,* October 1993, pp. 120–125.

Darsa, Deirdra. "Turnaround Tactics: Remedy for Ill Business." *Washington Business Journal,* August 6–12, 1993, p. 34.

Davidson, Jeff. *Breathing Space.* New York: Mastermedia, Ltd., 1992.

Davidson, Robert L., III. *Contracting Your Services,* New York: John Wiley & Sons, Inc., 1990.

Diamond, Michael R., and Julie L. Williams. *How to Incorporate: A Handbook for Entrepreneurs and Professionals.* New York: John Wiley & Sons, Inc., 1987.

Edwards, Paul, and Sarah Edwards. "Little Loans, Big Benefits." *Home Office Computing,* July 1993, pp. 54–60.

——————. *Working from Home.* Los Angeles: Jeremy P. Tarcher, Inc., 1990.

Eyler, David R. *Starting and Operating a Home-Based Business.* New York: John Wiley & Sons, Inc., 1990.

Gifis, Steven H. *Law Dictionary* (3d ed.). Hauppauge, NY: Barron's Educational Series, Inc., 1991.

Hedtke, John. *Using Computer Bulletin Boards.* New York: MIS Press, 1992.

Holtz, Herman. *The Consultant's Guide to Hidden Profits.* New York: John Wiley & Sons, Inc., 1992.

——————. *The Consultant's Guide to Proposal Writing,* New York: John Wiley & Sons, Inc., 1986.

Kishel, Gregory, and Patricia Kishel. *Start, Run and Profit from Your Own Home-Based Business.* New York: John Wiley & Sons, Inc., 1991.

Kutscher, Ronald E. "New BLS Projections: Findings and Implications." *Outlook* 1990–2005. BLS Bulletin 2402, May 1992, pp. 1–10. Washington, DC: U.S. Department of Labor, Bureau of Labor Statistics.

Lerner, Michele. "Home Office Is Red Flag to IRS." *The Washington Times,* August 12, 1993, p. F4.

Matusky, Gregory. "The Best Home-Based Franchises." *Home Office Computing,* December 1993, pp. 79–83.

Miller, Theodore J. *Kiplinger's Invest Your Way to Wealth,* Washington: Kiplinger Books, 1992.

Morgenstern, Steve. *No-Sweat Desktop Publishing.* New York: American Management Association, 1992.

————. "Preparing Pages for a Print Shop." *Home Office Computing,* September 1992, pp. 50–52.

Pae, Peter. "In Area Homes, Businesses Are Booming." *The Washington Post,* October 24, 1993, pp. B1 and B6.

Reich, Lawrence R., and James P. Duffy. *You Can Go Bankrupt without Going Broke.* New York: Pharos Books, 1992.

Schine, Gary. *How You Can Buy a Business without Overpaying.* New York: Consultant Press, 1991.

————. "How to Buy a Business Without Overpaying." *Home Office Computing,* August 1993, pp. 26–28.

Siegel, Eric S., et al. *The Ernst & Young Business Plan Guide.* New York: John Wiley & Sons, Inc., 1987.

Simon, Julian L. *How to Start and Operate a Mail Order Business.* New York: McGraw-Hill, 1987.

Smith, Wesley J. "Business in a Box." *Home Office Computing,* October 1992, pp. 53–61.

Stern, Linda. "Need $10,000, $50,000, $250,000?" *Home Office Computing,* September 1992, pp. 64–69.

Stewart, James B., and James J. Cramer. "Invest for Retirement." *Smart Money,* November 1993, pp. 89–105.

Tax Guide for Small Business. Publication 334. Washington, DC: Internal Revenue Service, 1993. (Revised annually.)

Taxpayers Starting a Business. Publication 583. Washington, DC: Internal Revenue Service, 1993. (Revised annually.)

Taylor, Stephen. *Telecommunications: The Macintosh Modem Book.* New York: MIS Press, 1992.

Tooly, Jo Ann. "Leaving the Office Nest." *U.S. News & World Report,* December 26, 1988– January 2, 1989, p. 120.

Totfoy, Charles N. "Factors to Consider in Pricing Your Product." *Washington Business Journal,* August 6–12, 1993, p. 51.

Travel, Entertainment, and Gift Expenses. Publication 463. Washington, DC: Internal Revenue Service, 1993. (Revised annually.)

A Special Offer from Microrim, Publishers of

In The Black

We hope you are enjoying the **In The Black** software included with your copy of *The Home Business Bible*. To fully realize the benefits of **In The Black**, we would like to offer you complete user documentation which includes the **In The Black** User Manual, Getting Started Guide, and a catalog of custom forms for your business.

User Documentation

The complete documentation for **In The Black** is only $5.00 plus $2.95 shipping and handling. Order today by calling 800-248-2001. Be sure to mention *The Home Business Bible* when you order. You will be automatically registered to receive information about **In The Black** enhancements and new releases.

Technical Support

Premium Technical Support is also available to you for just $1.50/minute. The Premium Technical Support number is 900-555-2121. **In order to receive technical support, you must be registered.** Register your copy of **In The Black** by calling 800-248-2001. Please mention *The Home Business Bible* when you register.

*Thank you for keeping your business and your home **In The Black**!*